Development and Disasters
2nd edition

Praise for this book

'The second edition of the book re-emphasizes the non-"natural" nature of disasters. With specific theory and practical examples, the book clearly identifies the importance of addressing different types of vulnerability, as well as the dynamic nature of the changes in the vulnerability. A must-read for researchers, practitioners and policy makers.'

Rajib Shaw, Professor, Graduate School of Media and Governance,
Keio University, Japan

'From poverty to aging and depopulation, vulnerabilities in our societies are growing in scale and range. Focusing on preventative action before risks become disasters, and centring on reducing these vulnerabilities, Lewis and Kelman provide essential knowledge for policy makers and practitioners on how to achieve truly sustainable development.'

Mami Mizutori, former Special Representative of the UN Secretary General
for Disaster Risk Reduction

'This book deepens the understanding that disasters stem from human-made vulnerabilities rather than natural events. Through thoughtful writing and rich historical examples, the authors vividly illustrate how development processes often create and perpetuate these vulnerabilities. The book underscores the crucial need to integrate vulnerability reduction into development practices to mitigate the impact of future disasters. Essential reading for policymakers, practitioners, and scholars alike.'

Bruce D Malamud, Director, Institute of Hazard,
Risk and Resilience, Durham University

'In this significantly revised edition of his main opus published 25 years ago, James Lewis, accompanied by Ilan Kelman, crafts a comprehensive picture of the links between what we call development and disasters. More importantly, the authors identify key pathways to address some of the underlying issues that underpin people's vulnerability in facing natural hazards. A must read for scholars, policy makers and practitioners.'

Professor JC Gaillard, The University of Auckland

Development and Disasters

Natural hazards and vulnerability reduction

2nd edition

James Lewis and Ilan Kelman

Practical
ACTION
PUBLISHING

Practical Action Publishing Ltd
25 Albert Street, Rugby,
Warwickshire, CV21 2SD, UK
www.practicalactionpublishing.com

A catalogue record for this book is available from the British Library.
A catalogue record for this book has been requested from the Library of Congress.

ISBN 978-1-78853-394-2 Paperback
ISBN 978-1-78853-396-6 Electronic book

Citation: Lewis, J., and Kelman, I. (2025) *Development and Disasters: Natural hazards
and vulnerability reduction: 2nd edition*, Rugby, UK: Practical Action Publishing
http://doi.org/10.3362/ 9781788533966

Since 1974, Practical Action Publishing has published and disseminated books and
information in support of international development work throughout the world.

Practical Action Publishing is a trading name of Practical Action Publishing Ltd
(Company Reg. No. 1159018), the wholly owned publishing company of Practical
Action. Practical Action Publishing trades only in support of its parent charity
objectives and any profits are covenanted back to Practical Action
(Charity Reg. No. 247257, Group VAT Registration No. 880 9924 76).

Cover photo shows: Development in the Netherlands for their approach to addressing
disasters.
Cover photo credit: Ilan Kelman
Cover design by Katarzyna Markowska, Practical Action Publishing

Typeset by vPrompt eServices, India

The manufacturer's authorised representative in the EU for product safety is
Lightning Source France, 1 Av. Johannes Gutenberg, 78310 Maurepas, France.
compliance@lightningsource.fr

Contents

About the authors

James Lewis has been an architect-on-site sequentially on three continents – in New York State, the United Kingdom, and Hong Kong – where he was frequently confronted by the challenging powers of weather and climate and their associated hazards. His appointment as Leverhulme Senior Research Fellow at the Universities of Bradford and then Bath was followed by creating in 1980 Datum International for consultancies to United Nations organizations, such as UNCTAD, UNEP, UNESCO, UN-Habitat, and WHO, as well as the Commonwealth Secretariat/Commonwealth Fund for Technical Cooperation and the European Commission. In 2005, he was commissioned as author to Transparency International Berlin for the Global Corruption Reports on Corruption in Construction and again in 2011 for Corruption and Climate Change. As a Member of the Royal Institute of British Architects since 1957, his involvement has been in applications, implications, management, and inspection of construction, destruction, or reconstruction, also in Algeria, Bangladesh, Caribbean and Pacific island states, and Maldives.

Ilan Kelman (https://www.ilankelman.org/ and Instagram/Threads/X @ILANKELMAN) is Professor of Disasters and Health at University College London, UK and a Professor II at the University of Agder, Kristiansand, Norway. His overall research interest is in linking disasters and health, integrating climate change into both. Three main areas are: 1) disaster diplomacy and health diplomacy https://www.disasterdiplomacy.org/; 2) island sustainability focusing on safe and healthy living and livelihoods https://www.islandvulnerability.org/; and 3) risk education for health and disasters https://www.riskred.org/

Foreword from the first edition

The division between crisis and disaster response on one hand, and development on the other, has long marred the efficiency of efforts to prevent damage in advance of disasters or to strengthen the impact of post-disaster actions, so that these contribute to reduced vulnerability in the future. Disasters occur in a long-term and local context, and it is unrealistic to assume a separation between 'normal' existence and those, often frequently recurring, periods that are disasters. Vulnerability, as this book shows, is an ongoing state. It needs to be addressed as such.

The over-narrow vision that many agencies and authorities charged with disaster preparedness and response have too often placed on the imminence and immediate aftermath of a disaster is a mistake, despite the argument that the means available and the urgency justify this limitation of scope. This narrow vision overlooks, or at least pays insufficient attention to, the broad-based and evolutive nature of vulnerability in its local context, and does not explore fully the circumstances in which disasters occur. Vulnerability can be addressed only through a co-ordinated and integrated strategy of preparation and response that considers the entire local context and its development, over time.

James Lewis's book makes an important contribution to these issues. First, it states clearly that the development process and the relief process must not be separated. Secondly, it brings an important and long under-valued argument to the fore, that 'a disaster is not a physical happening, it is a social event' (Quarantelli, 1986). This being the case, actions to reduce vulnerability and the subsequent impact of disaster must embrace social, economic, and political contexts, as well as the material and technical concerns and 'solutions' which tend to dominate, often because they are easier to quantify and handle.

The book illustrates through careful and thorough argument and telling case studies that vulnerability to disaster requires a locally developed strategy based on recognition of the full range of factors that contribute to vulnerability. Most interestingly, James Lewis draws attention to the intimate quality of vulnerability and disaster, the fact that disasters, when they strike, are a personal, family, community event, and only then a national or regional event. The suffering is individual and local. In the final resort, the resources – human and material – to reduce vulnerability, must also be local. This is a poignant expression of the reality that those disasters that make the news are not necessarily the most significant. The implication is clearly that one cannot rely on international response to small-scale events of potentially immense local importance.

For many years James Lewis has seemed at times to be a lone voice urging us to consider the broad vision of vulnerability, while others have focused on the more tangible area of disaster response. It is time for his message to be heard.

John Norton, Development Workshop, France, June 1999

Preface from the first edition

This book is one person's contribution to an internationally active and multi-disciplinary subject. The writer is also a researcher, 'individual consultant' and sole practitioner – albeit from time to time a 'team leader'. He is necessarily a generalist – and a generalist is a specialist in his own right. As more and more specialists are spawned, there is greater need for a generalist or two.

Academic roles usually allow or necessitate personal selection of subject area and its specialist pursuit. Consultancy, on the other hand, must largely and necessarily follow a path set by the inquiries, objectives or policies of others – which come to be modified (if at all) after the contribution of consultants. I have never been asked to undertake a task about which I had misgivings or which I felt I could not satisfactorily undertake or which I did not want to do. This says a lot for those who identify consultants – although some may have had their misgivings afterwards! One task, however, has often fortuitously led to another in a most satisfying way. Each subsequent consultancy has drawn upon previous work – each client has unknowingly contributed to the purposes of the next!

Writing for journal publication as a by-product of most assignments undertaken – insofar as contractual obligations allowed – resulted in work which is essentially 'experiential'. Research developed as Leverhulme Senior Research Fellow and co-founder and leader of the Disaster Research Unit at the University of Bradford, and similarly in the Centre for Development Studies at the University of Bath, where participation continues as Visiting Fellow in Development Studies.

Nevertheless, the series of studies forming the central part of this book, although expressing a continuation and progression, are not the product of an established academic programme, nor are they the by-product of an academic occupation.

From these multifarious sources there is a logical progression. The book places the studies together and in an ordered sequence, having introduced their overall subject of vulnerability in Part 1, and draws conclusions from them and other work in Part 3.

Influences upon this continuing work have been many and varied and, as custom has it, 'too many to mention by name'. Those who should not escape are Phil O'Keefe, Ken Westgate, and Sue Jeffery who, already by then established in their respective disciplines, tolerated me at Bradford and Bath; Geoff Wood and colleagues likewise at the Institute for International Policy Analysis, University of Bath (for more years than they care to remember), and the writings of the Natural Hazards Group at the Universities of Colorado and Toronto, references to which appear in the text and which it would be inappropriate to omit here because they indicate something of the long history of the study of 'natural hazards'.

Very belatedly, my gratitude also goes to the Leverhulme Trust, which funded my work at the Universities of Bradford and Bath. This book is a product of those times, as well as of work undertaken since – which would not have been possible were it not for work facilitated by the Trust. Though I am conscious of the time that it has taken to publish more than an occasional paper or two, I otherwise make no apology for references to work of 15 or more years ago – most of the processes and conditions of vulnerability to which this book refers are regrettably as extant now as they were then.

In addition to all of these have been the encounters with the many and various places, situations and experiences, and the many hundreds of people in the meeting rooms, houses and fields, villages and cities, institutions and governments, and on the aeroplanes, Land Rovers, carts, cars, trains, buses, bicycles, and boats, with whom it has been my boundless privilege and pleasure to be all too briefly associated.

My wife Sarah, who follows her own career in which she is also an author, is another who cannot be permitted to escape the briefest mention. It is she and a young family who tolerated and coped with my absences, always, as it turned out, at crucial times. It is she to whom I turn initially with a new idea or to test the sense of something written – and it is she from whom many ideas and thoughts have originated. Above all, it is she who is the crucial source of encouragement when the point of what is being done has sometimes seemed so remote and difficult.

The onus is upon me for what I have done or not done in the light of these many opportunities and influences; I can only hope that I have given them deserved justice and that the small outcome presented here may be of some continued interest and usefulness.

James Lewis, 1999

Preface for the second edition

When James Lewis wrote in the 'Preface to the first edition' that 'This book is a product of those times', he was referring to his time at universities in the UK. An unintentional *double entendre* emerges of this book being a product of those times of academia, policy, practitionership, and the world, when he was at the University of Bradford from 1973 to 1977 and the University of Bath from 1977 to 1980. This time period was two generations ago. This book's first edition highlighted those years, although with plenty of added material to bring it up to date for publication in 1999, a generation ago.

The world has moved on. Or has it?

These days – the 'here and now' for us, but ancient history a few decades hence – academia, policy, practitionership, and the world display remarkable repetition regarding development, disasters, natural hazards, vulnerability, and vulnerability reduction. For now, it all might be framed as disaster risk reduction (DRR) and disaster risk management (DRM), with those acronyms bandied about with ease and with a lack of clarity regarding their similarities and differences. These phrases and acronyms emerged, at latest, in the 1980s, yet at the time of this book's first edition were not as engrained as today. A generation from now, will they be common vernacular or will they have vanished?

This second edition of the allegedly 'ancient history' that is the first edition shows some changes in the world of development, disasters, natural hazards, vulnerability, and vulnerability reduction in tandem. Those changes are not extensive. We have not moved on from failing to develop and progress in a manner that addresses disasters through accepting and redressing their real causes: vulnerabilities.

In particular, we have not learned from many past failures; that is, disasters. This situation represents the value of most of the examples throughout this book: remembering disasters past to contribute to averting disasters future. Most examples here have not been updated and most are not recent, specifically to avoid the usual 'presentism' of emphasizing the most recent disasters and, typically, neglecting the past. They also indicate how much was known at the time, yet neither learned nor applied.

As this Preface was beginning to be written, horrific disasters involving floods were ongoing from Germany to Australia. Sadly, little difference is seen from the floods decades ago discussed in this book, showing that the knowledge was available long ago to stop the disasters unfolding today. And the reporting pattern continues to focus on the water, damage, and evacuations here and now, rather than delving into why the water is leading to damage and evacuations. That is, little effort is made to understand and explain the 'ancient history' of the past generation or past 10 generations that led to – that created – the disasters today.

Conversely, despite this book being based on the premise from the beginning of Lewis's career in this field that disasters are not natural, we see prevalent use of the term 'natural disaster'. Too often, querying or critiquing the term produces a hostile response. Yet 2023's catastrophes narrate the same tales of known and permitted vulnerabilities: earthquakes in Morocco, Syria, and Türkiye; floods in Libya, China, and the UK; heatwaves fuelled by human-caused climate change across Europe and South Asia; the lingering effects of the COVID-19 pandemic and responses to it; the ongoing pandemics of cholera and HIV/AIDS; horrific violent conflicts in Afghanistan, Democratic Republic of the Congo, Iraq, Israel/Palestine, Ukraine, Yemen, and elsewhere; and many more which would require an entire book to list and document. As shown by the previous sentence, we even still identify the disasters by their hazards. Instead, we could have written simply 'Yet 2023 narrates the same catastrophic tale of known and permitted vulnerabilities everywhere'.

Nonetheless, the world has moved on in some ways from this book's first edition, with some examples discussed in Chapter 10. The baselines remain ever-present with so much work to do in order to achieve development in the context of disasters, natural hazards, and vulnerability. And so much work remains impeded by petty battles among egos and those who seek only followers for their leadership, liking power for the sake of power rather than for enacting positive change. When we cannot even get 'experts' in this area to talk to each other and collaborate, how could we blame others for failing to change destructive baselines?

With the baselines of disaster effectively remaining unchanged, so do many of the examples in this second edition. This decision could be rightly criticized. So, too, could the decision to lose this knowledge by being more presentist. The examples are thus generally old and not up to date. These traits do not make them outdated.

Yes, the first edition of this book was 'a product of those times', from 1974 to 1999. It sadly remains a product of today's times, as much as this second edition. Will we all use what we know for development, disasters, natural hazards, and vulnerability reduction in order to show that this second edition can, as it should, become ancient history?

James Lewis and Ilan Kelman, 2024

Acknowledgements

With thanks to University College London's Open Access team for covering the fee required to make this book freely downloadable.

CHAPTER 1
Introduction

Vulnerability pasts

The objective of this book is to demonstrate that good development could and should avert disasters by reducing vulnerability and that vulnerability reduction to avert disasters is good development. The relationship between disasters and development is a recurring issue. On the one hand, development is regarded as deterministic and a major cause of vulnerability and disasters. On the other hand, development is regarded as the necessarily inevitable and appropriate vehicle for vulnerability reduction and averting disasters.

That vulnerability is the root cause of disasters – that disasters are not 'natural' – should no longer be a new issue, although it somehow remains contentious. This book seeks to explore and to expose some of the processes that have led to conditions of vulnerability. In doing so, it becomes evident that disasters are contextual. Prevailing environmental and social conditions, as well as their intertwining, from local to global and from the past to the present, determine the severity of vulnerabilities and their consequences for individuals, populations, and places.

Some of those consequences relate to the title's least-used phrase throughout this book: 'natural hazards'. 'Natural hazards' appears in the title partly for honest framing. This book principally, although never exclusively, focuses on phenomena from nature that can become hazardous. It accepts that other hazards – conflicts, violences, chemicals, vehicles, defamations, and more – are never entirely separate from the consequences of 'natural' hazards. In any case, many 'natural hazards' are influenced or caused by human activity, including floods, droughts, earthquakes, slides, and temperatures. The very act of placing a structure alters wind speeds, water depths, air temperatures, and earthquake peak ground accelerations, among other hazard parameters. Hazards are not always 'natural' or 'environmental'. The word 'hazard' does not even exist in many languages, being variously translated as 'threat', 'danger', 'risk', and many more. 'Natural hazards' and 'unnatural hazards' (Hewitt, 1997) meld and overlap, so this book often uses the term 'hazard(s)' without any modifier.

Another main reason for using the phrase 'natural hazards' in this book's title is reader expectations. Just as people continue to search for and report on 'natural disasters', the word 'hazard' and the phrase 'natural hazards' remain common in English. Search Engine Optimization (SEO) persists as one of our dictators! And so, using the phrases 'natural disaster' and 'natural hazard' in this book should help with SEO despite the preference to avoid them. Even as development and disasters ought to move away from the word and concept of 'hazard', we succumb to this modicum of findability and populism. Which, incidentally, also applies to 'development' and 'disaster', both concepts subject to a profusion of definitions, debates, and apposite criticisms.

And thus we settle on and emphasize vulnerability. Among all the jejune jargon and definitional dancing, the beginning of this book's title 'Development and disasters: Natural hazards' deliberately and explicitly zeroes in on the title's ending (and equivalently contested and deliberated) phrase, 'vulnerability reduction'.

Vulnerability accrues as a result of processes of change, including development, disasters, and natural hazards. It is therefore a potential product of all values, behaviours, activities, and undertakings of society. Vulnerability reduction requires a joint and pervasive responsibility that can comprehend and identify those values, behaviours, activities, and undertakings in order to implement their redirection. Such modifications to processes of change are a necessary component of development.

This means that disasters cannot be regarded as discrete events. By doing so, they become externalized from the actions and processes that create their context. Disasters are more usefully regarded as extensions of a pervasive, usual 'hazardousness' and 'vulnerabilityness'. The reason is that usual hazardousness and vulnerabilityness are a comprehensible part of everyone's everyday contexts. To address apparent 'abnormal' phenomena, we must attend to the everyday, everywhere usualness of hazards and vulnerabilities.

Disasters are not events; disasters are processes. Disasters are not unusual; they are expressions of the everyday, everywhere normal (normality). In this sense, disasters are a 'natural' part of life, with the aim being to ensure that they are not.

Development has often been identified as one of the contributors to processes of vulnerability. This book does so again, in that processes of development contribute to processes of vulnerability leading to processes of disaster. The disaster process comes from the vulnerability process created with and influencing inputs from the development process. Yet all development is not derogatorily regarded as a force for environmental determinism or social determinism. The reverse is accepted, that development initiatives can be moulded to become the most appropriate means for vulnerability reduction.

Part of understanding how to do so requires understanding the meanings of the terms. Given how much has been published on definitions for 'development', 'disaster', 'hazard', and 'vulnerability' along with synonyms, variations, and other relevant words, this book does not seek to retrace this ground. Instead, it hopes that the reader can intuit and contextualize the definitions based on the discussion and the references, many of which provide extensive detail on definitional discussions across languages, cultures, and time periods.

For readers still confused about meanings and interpretations, you join us and many others across these fields! The lack of coherence and agreement in defining basic terminology is a major limitation in terms of communicating for joint action. Jargon has exploded leading to technical descriptions that befuddle long-standing experts and seem to deliberately create silos for specialists. Conversely, not referring to complex glossaries and not generating new terminology is a strength for focusing on the basics and baselines to inform action. We might not agree line-by-line on which words to use or word-by-word on precise descriptions. We can hopefully accept the implicit concepts and ethos of how to implement development that reduces vulnerability. In this way, the lack of coherence and agreement in defining basic terminology becomes a major opportunity in terms of communicating for joint action. We can all act in our own ways on our own terms to achieve the common goal.

One concept and ethos to make explicit is this book's avoidance of the phrase 'natural disaster'. The rationale is well-documented in modern science back to Ball (1975) and in European thought back to Rousseau (1756). Other knowledges and cultures across history might have similar descriptions still not documented in English-language science. The rationale for 'no natural disasters' is precisely what this book describes: vulnerability is the root cause of disasters, exposing hazardousness that could otherwise be dealt with via appropriate development. Disasters do not come from hazardousness, including environmental phenomena, so disasters do not come from nature and are not natural. Humanity has the knowledges, skills, and resources to ensure that development does not lead to disasters, sometimes doing so and sometimes not. Disasters are human constructions, not natural phenomena.

Too much of what followed Rousseau (1756), Ball (1975), and others in 'natural disasters' research ignored or bypassed this foundation. It was inherent in some hazards research that there should be exploration of the interface between hazards and the contexts in which they occur and which they affect. It was inherent in much of disaster response, and disaster response research, that those contexts were self-evident, not requiring much thought or description. Thus, according to this approach, disasters were quite obviously different and separate from the self-evident contexts. They must be discrete, unusual, out-of-context events.

A disaster happens and feels as if it has a clear start and end point. When did the earthquake or the rain start and stop? At what point did water supplies appear low, marking a drought, and at what point did they recover, marking the drought's end? When did the first and last damage occur from a volcanic eruption? All these questions are hazard-focused, presuming that the hazard defines the disaster.

Missing is the truism that disasters not only occur as a part of their development contexts, but also that disasters are caused by their development contexts. Contexts are social, environmental, and the ubiquitous interlacing of social and environmental. By definition, enfolding peoples and places incorporates animals, plants, other biota, ecosystems, biomes, and their abiotic components. Other words describing these contexts together include institutional, organizational, political, cultural, spiritual, physical, and natural.

Disasters being caused by their development contexts produces reactions from the people and institutions of those contexts. The very existence, purpose, and formation of institutions can be questioned in the context of development, disasters, natural hazards, and vulnerabilities (Hewitt, 1983). How these institutions react reflects further on how the problem is managed or, too often, not managed. Drawing on and expanding Hewitt (1983), institutions often react to disasters by explaining them as clear limits to knowledge, power, abilities, and resources, initiated and progressed in a way that is – that must be – uncontrollable by society. Hence, they are acts of a deity or an uncaring nature; what happened was unprecedented, unpredictable, and unstoppable; and no one could do anything about these 'natural disasters'.

It is exactly this framing that proves the benefits of dividing off and blaming natural hazards – rather than blaming leaders who make themselves separate from the populations most adversely affected. It becomes convenient to treat calamity as a special problem. This special problem is constructed as being manageable by narrowing and morphing the permitted evidence, analyses, interpretations, and conclusions regarding why the disaster happened. Every lesson is, of course, learned, ensuring the catastrophe will, definitely, never again occur. Then, another disaster happens and the story is repeated.

Rather than accepting society–environment interconnections as axiomatic, they are separated. Natural hazards are not viewed as integrated into society, nor are hazard characteristics accepted as depending on human–nature interactions. As Hewitt (1983) reinforces, hazards and vulnerabilities, and so disasters, are part of everyday, usual conditions and lived experiences. Vulnerability is the normal, so disasters are always either waiting to happen, are happening, or have just happened. Disasters are not abnormal, unusual, unexpected events.

This book covers 'disaster' as 'normal' / 'normality', often experienced as an intermediate transition between 'normal hazardousness' / 'normal vulnera-bilityness' and major calamity. If vulnerabilities to localized disasters could be reduced by development, then vulnerabilities to wider-scale disasters could be reduced by similar actions. The 'small events' may sometimes be recognized as disasters and sometimes not. The views of those with direct experiences might differ from outside observers and evaluators. In some cases, the 'small disaster' may be recognized only by insiders who may or may not be able to cope, and not by outsiders who, if they know of the circumstances at all, may regard it as insignificant or irrelevant.

Considering the modern foundations of Anglophone-focused disaster research, Haas et al. (1977) observed that prevailing conditions ('long-term trends') before a disaster governed the rate and quality of recovery after a disaster. Later, Golec (1980) expanded by Quarantelli (1985) observed that focusing on the 'causal primary' of disaster impact leads to a misunderstanding of at least some post-disaster problems. It also leads to a failure to recognize that the most efficacious solutions may reside in changes to public policy and in interventions aimed at changing aspects of social structures.

Later, Mitchell et al. (1989) emphasized that, since hazards come from a variety of sources, it is desirable to design policies to account for that variety and of an inevitable interrelatedness among them. Doing so involves those whose work focuses on specific natural hazards and a broad spectrum of organizations and groups that affect, and are affected by, the many contexts of those natural hazards. As is well-accepted now, these studies are saying that hazard-related activities seemingly outside of their academic disciplines and managerial sectors perhaps have the greatest significance on the outcomes and impacts from hazards. This point frequently remains elusive in practice.

Back to the beginnings of contemporary Anglophone understandings, Kates (1970: 450) had much earlier explained that 'many of the real determinants of human behavior related to natural hazard lie outside the interface of the natural and human systems modeled here', referring to human actions outside of hazard-related consequences. One example given was encouraging cash cropping and prohibiting migration by colonial administrations in East Africa, decisions that had probably intensified the disastrous effects of droughts in the 1930s. In other words, it is most likely to be the policies and activities which seemingly are undertaken without reference to natural hazards, that eventually have the greatest bearing upon them. Kates (1970) further noted that such critical circumstances, seen as important with hindsight, are not easily handled by means of 'adjustments to hazards'. Much more is required than a focus on hazards. A similar pattern was documented for the disastrous effects of the Sahel drought from 1968–74 (Glantz, 1976), ongoing at the time that Kates (1970) was writing.

These situations are still not part of an overall understanding, least of all part of an overall strategy, for dealing successfully with natural hazards – or, more to the point, dealing successfully with vulnerabilities. 'Adjustments' by affected individuals, households, communities, and locations presume options and resources with which to implement the adjustments. This statement is valid for countries that are allegedly rich (irrespective of national debt and budget deficits) or in countries that are allegedly poor (irrespective of enormous wealth from tourism or minerals). People, households, and groups who are poor and who lack access to basic facilities and services such as health, education, water, and sanitation have much fewer possibilities for 'adjustments' than those who have access to their own resources, facilities, and services.

Then, development from external initiatives and external funding ambles along, trumpeting their own external agendas and desires, which might or might not align with local interests and needs. This development fails to notice the potential for natural hazards; does not understand or wish to acknowledge vulnerabilities; and erodes local cultural and historical skills, understandings, and contributions. In these contexts, changes to prevailing conditions and the chronic lack of opportunities have been far more significant in natural hazard impacts than 'adjustments' could ever have been.

Although it should seem obvious that development practices should have moulded (adjusted) themselves to the eventual manifestation of natural hazards within them, this has demonstrably not been the case. Then, a disaster manifests and the issue of the relationship of development and disasters fades in the wake of demand for sadly much-needed emergency action, recovery, and reconstruction. The short-term responses save lives immediately while eclipsing the reasons for the need for these short-term responses to save lives.

These reasons disregard the longer term; they do not learn from and apply history. The subject of disasters, even with the misnomer 'natural', has been and is essentially event-driven. No sooner are there indications of consensus about the importance of long-term baseline analyses, accounting for history and culture in order to build a future with less vulnerability/fewer vulnerabilities, then are we pressed to deal with another set of headlines about suffering from one-off 'events'.

This pressure to move on to new circumstances and new issues has exacerbated a failure to retain some basic concepts established in the 1960s and 1970s, if not much earlier. This book recalls, reasserts, and reapplies some of these basic concepts, repeating the original message (from the foundations of contemporary Anglophone disaster science) that development is the prime medium and mode of vulnerability and its reduction. This book wants history to be remembered, not discounting the importance and relevance of recent experience, while also not discounting the importance and relevance of much farther past experience. As noted in the 'Preface for the second edition', examples in this second edition tend not to repeat the most recent headlines. The examples instead reiterate the horror and not-learned (even unlearned) lessons from disasters which would otherwise be forgotten. They might feel like ancient history from another world. They are, but are no less useful in being so.

This approach is adopted deliberately at the expense of much recent work and references, which can merely repeat what is already known without acknowledging what is already known. Too many recent examples generate so much writing and pontificating, from Hurricane Maria in 2017 in Puerto Rico to the 2020–23 COVID-19 pandemic, to the 2023 earthquakes along the Türkiye-Syria border. They all have precedents and they were all known to be strong possibilities long before the hazard was present. Compare, too, the number of publications mentioning each of these three disasters with the number of publications mentioning, respectively, each of gender-based violence in Puerto Rico, respiratory syncytial virus (RSV), and human trafficking across the Türkiye-Syria border – all rightly termed 'disasters' and all stemming from development problems.

This contemporary attitude and behaviour among academics is understandable, given the expectations to publish as much as possible and to be cited as much as possible, coupled with the ever-expanding formats and venues in which to publish. The deficiency of not learning from newer authors, newer framings, newer styles, and some newer ideas is an important limitation of this second edition. This limitation is actively embraced in order to overcome the limitations of newer contributions that fail in expressing the long-standing basic understandings from long-standing basic publications that remain impressively relevant. This limitation is also actively embraced in order to offer historical material to practitioners, doing their best to improve situations today without having the time or skills to delve into why situations today need to be improved. Learning from history is about learning from humanity, avoiding the flavour-of-the-month approach to much current disaster research, policy, and practice.

Where older work is less relevant now and newer contributors have plenty to offer, then successful examples are detailed. As are not-so-successful examples.

All this leads into the overall structure and progression of this second edition. This chapter sets the stage, offering the reasoning behind the book and its key points. Chapters 2, 3, and 4 expand on these basics to feed into Chapter 5, which outlines overarching and baseline problems and concerns: From where, how, from whom, and why do detrimental vulnerability–development interactions arise? This work is mainly conceptual. Chapter 6 is mainly empirical, detailing evidence of the problem and concern through examples from the first edition, while also hinting at possible ways forward in practical terms. Chapters 7 and 8 take these hints, shifting back to a more conceptual tone to expound how the problem and concern ought to be addressed: From where, how, from whom, and why could detrimental vulner-ability–development interactions be addressed and overcome? They feed into Chapter 9, which provides the fundaments of possible resolutions in theory, policy, and practice. Chapter 10 summarizes what this book offers, the reasoning for the offerings, and considerations for continuing and improving the work presented in this book.

Certainly, major improvements are needed. No book could ever be complete, exact, or error-free. It is for readers to identify this book's gaps and limitations in order to do better, so that everyone can learn and improve, most notably this book's authors.

One common thread linking theory and empirics, linking past and future, and linking problem and resolution is that, often, development is still regarded – and yet not identified – as the long-term objective after a disaster. According to some disaster responders, with a bit of modification and long-term thinking, recovery, rehabilitation, and reconstruction could lead as a sequence into development. This thinking surrounding the relationship between development and disasters has been, and still is with many recent authors, about how post-disaster activities can better be made to relate to development. In the meantime, development has been interrupted and impeded (or even negated) by the disaster and by the post-disaster response, but development remains apart from such inconveniences. And never should we examine the manner in which bad development caused the vulnerabilities that caused the disaster.

The disaster-development 'continuum' or 'nexus' has certainly been espoused, theorized, advocated for, stated as being observed, and challenged.

Less frequently articulated and critiqued is development and disaster as different expressions of the same societal values, activities, and undertakings.

Development objectives are not and cannot be an immutable panacea or nirvana, achievable only when all the hurdles have been jumped. Development should be a planned process of positive change. As the creator of prevailing conditions and contexts within which people live and die, development becomes the framework within which all else happens, planned or unplanned, disastrous or advantageous. As the source of prevailing conditions within which natural hazards occur, it follows that one role of development has to be incorporating adjustments to these natural hazards – even preventing them from being hazardous.

Development should affect disasters by lessening or removing adverse consequences; that is, so that disasters do not happen. Development should be the long-term change so that the conditions and contexts for disaster are constructively modified without leading to further problems. Such an objective is not easily identified or accepted, least of all achieved, when popular attention spotlights short-term measures for emergency relief and post-disaster assistance. The immediate saving of lives is a laudable task. Views differ on how much responsive humanitarianism should seek longer-term improvements, why this responsive humanitarianism so often causes longer-term problems, and most importantly why this responsive humanitarianism is needed in the first place (Cuny, 1983; Terry, 2002). The answer, typically, refers back to development, with humanitarianism and development ending up clashing rather than complementing.

It should be accepted, but is often not of interest for discussion, that development for vulnerability reduction is not the last in line of a sequential process that has to wait for a disaster to start it. Invariably in practice across all disaster processes including conflict, necessary immediacy of short-term action takes priority over long-term action. If longer-term policies and actions were already established, then short-term action would have a positive context within which to contribute to development. Implementation of policies and actions for vulnerability reduction within development would be the norm and could continue.

So much attention is garnered by death, damage, and disruption, and understandably so. An equivalent focus is absent on avoiding death, damage, and disruption over the long-term, which is less understandable. After all, if we do not want to see people suffering, then pay attention to how to stop them suffering.

Instead, attention and action are overly influenced by global comparisons of disaster magnitude, by large organizations trying to counter disasters of larger magnitude, and by costly technological infrastructure in response. At times, the comparisons use arbitrary metrics, the large organizations caused the problems to which they are responding, and the technological responses augment vulnerabilities and hazards. No wonder disasters recur and those perpetuating the disasters are insufficiently concerned with local experiences, contexts, and daily survival – as well as being insufficiently engaged with local contributions, knowledges, skills, and abilities.

As extensions of everyday hazardousness and vulnerabilityness, 'small' disasters occur for 'small' numbers of people. News about them rarely reaches the accountants of the global statistics. They occur in places far from international reporting networks and in countries with populations smaller than the number of casualties in some disasters of international repute. These disasters are deemed irrelevant for international attention.

When considering specific numbers, caution is always needed. One of the most widely used disaster databases is EM-DAT (Emergency Events Database), started in 1988 and recording disasters from 1900 until the present that conform to at least one of the following criteria:

- 10 or more people dead.
- 100 or more people affected.
- The declaration of a state of emergency.
- A call for international assistance.

Widely circulated, high-level reports draw conclusions about disaster trends from this database while academic papers run complicated correlations and infer causations. EM-DAT is arguably the most comprehensive and complete disaster database in the world. The question remains open about whether or not it is comprehensive and complete enough to support the analyses conducted with it and the conclusions drawn from it. To give credit to EM-DAT, it has moved away from differentiating 'natural disasters' and 'technological disasters' to reporting 'disasters'. Disasters 'related to natural hazards' and related to technological hazards are separated.

The category of 'people affected' is defined as 'requiring immediate assistance during a period of emergency'. Aside from the technicalities of excluding disasters involving intangible heritage losses or people requiring assistance after the immediate period of emergency, there are other considerations to incorporate into any analyses.

The ability and legal scope to declare a formal emergency and to call for international assistance have changed substantially since 1900, affecting the baseline of what a 'disaster' is. As well, such declarations and formally calling for help might not necessarily be based on actual disaster impacts, since they are mainly political decisions. Leaders can show reluctance, despite palpable need, because they might lose face and look incompetent. Conversely, they may call for help in order to seem decisive or to take credit for incoming aid.

The importance or arbitrariness of the numbers '10' and '100' needs to be considered. Could 11 and 99 respectively, or other numbers, serve just as well? At what point might quantitative thresholds not fully account for some disaster experiences? A village of 90 people lacking the power to declare a state of emergency could lose nine people in a lightning strike and manage with nearby aid. It would not count as a disaster, despite the obvious local calamity. Or the 'nearby aid' might be a neighbour over an international border, suddenly satisfying the criterion 'a call for international assistance'. As this book shows, the overall cumulative effect of 'small', more frequent disasters has the potential to outweigh the impacts of 'big' ones matching EM-DAT's criteria.

Another disaster database, DesInventar, was set up in 1994 to improve understanding of local impacts and disaggregated data. Due to its short time period of coverage compared to EM-DAT, any computations from DesInventar could not fully reflect disaster patterns.

This discussion does not dismiss the importance of large-scale disasters. It is about disasters of all scales being considered together, not disasters of different scales pitted against each other. Perhaps over 50 million died in the 1918–20 H1N1 flu pandemic and over 7 million out of a much larger world population in the 2020–23 COVID-19 pandemic. Although these tolls do not account for deaths related to and prevented by response measures to each pandemic, both diseases devastated the world. The importance of the disaster database critiques is about recognizing the contextuality and localization of disaster experience, irrespective of quantitative scale and metrics.

Disasters occur repeatedly and are a matter of everyday existence, as they always have been. Local attention to 'small' matters in the face of externally perceived massive catastrophe is sensible and effective. Popular concern, including among disaster researchers and practitioners, nonetheless continues mostly with disasters of globally 'impressive' magnitudes.

Development then forgets, precludes, or destroys local strategies and mechanisms. Awe of disaster magnitude and absolute numbers has brought about a separation of disasters and their management from everyday affairs; that is, a separation from development. 'Disaster (risk) management' and reduction have been separated from 'development'. Vulnerability is neglected and consequently exacerbated. This separation needs to be redressed so that appropriate development can attend to vulnerability reduction, a prevailing requirement common to the effects of all natural hazards, before, as, and after they occur.

Conventional development is often framed as economic growth and economic expansion. Neither growth nor expansion is a prerequisite for vulnerability reduction. Achieving vulnerability reduction would in itself be development, whereas short-term economic growth or expansion is frequently achieved by creating and exacerbating vulnerability. Development should be meeting basic needs for vulnerability reduction within local environments, capacities, and aspirations, mirroring many definitions of and approaches to 'sustainable development' (for example, Salas-Zapata and Ortiz-Muñoz, 2019). In fact, disaster recovery and vulnerability reduction should express sustainability, because measures for achieving recovery must themselves be sustainable. This sustainability means precluding the need for future disaster recovery by precluding both disaster and vulnerability.

For sustainability and development, or sustainable development, it matters less what kind of disaster is likely, than ensuring that local contexts can deal with local vulnerability reduction, local disaster impacts, and local disaster aftermaths. Aftermaths will eventually become the context for the next disaster or, preferably through more vulnerability reduction, the lack of a next disaster.

Taking this approach and framing contributes toward redressing the balance of attention devoted to large-scale disasters of global significance. The balance is with contexts and prevailing conditions everywhere, the ever-present vulnerability process producing the ever-present disaster process, rather than 'disaster this or disaster that'. Then, a wider understanding will be achieved and applied for action on the processes of vulnerability accretion and consequently the processes of vulnerability reduction. This wider understanding extends to action on recognizing the overlaps among all disasters. Development devised to avoid disasters involving entirely natural hazards should not neglect, although it equivalently serves the avoidance of, disasters involving human-influenced hazards, human-made hazards, and all forms of conflicts and violences.

None of this denies the real need for emergency response, humanitarian assistance, and disaster relief. It repeats that they attend to symptoms rather than causes. The tagline for health as well as disasters is that 'prevention is better than cure' – and prevention is typically cheaper than cure. Yet cure continues to be a high-profile mega-industry with the popular appeal that many mega-industries seek in order to perpetuate themselves. Development aid continues as its own mega-industry with actions to avoid disaster (reiterating the current lingo of disaster risk reduction (DRR) and disaster risk management (DRM)), unclear and uncertain regarding how exactly to define its budget and its activities – and even why actions to avoid disaster should be defined and budgeted separately from development.

Having equitable education and healthcare for boys/men and girls/women is definitely development. It creates long-term processes that reduce vulnerability, so is it also disaster-related aid? Programmes enhancing local livelihoods and using those livelihoods to diversify food and freshwater sources are development. They support health, constructive human–environment interaction, and people's living options. They also reduce vulnerability. If a storm surge floods fields with saltwater, then fishing boats and wells should have been protected, so that people and livestock can still eat and drink while rehabilitating agriculture. If climate variabilities such as the El Niño Southern Oscillation (ENSO) drive fish farther out to sea, then crops and livestock should have developed to still produce food. Are livelihood programmes therefore disaster-related aid?

Ultimately, the label does not matter. Disaster-related development or development-driven vulnerability reduction are just phrases. The key is the actions which help people to survive and thrive in their contexts, irrespective of natural hazards – and often using the natural 'hazards' for daily life, livelihood, and lifestyle.

PART ONE
A pattern of vulnerability

CHAPTER 2
Meanings of vulnerability

Local-to-global vulnerabilities

Disasters have rightly been adopted as a world problem. The response to this local-to-global problem has in many cases been the application of global, globalized, and generalized 'solutions'.

Disasters inflicting colossal losses have pervaded human history. The 14th-century bubonic plague pandemic across Europe, Western Asia, and North Africa might have killed 50 million people, representing about half these regions' entire population. China's 1556 earthquake probably killed over 800,000 people. The volcanic explosion and eruption of Krakatoa/ Krakatau in 1883, in what is now Indonesia, killed 36,000 people, including from consequent tsunamis. The 1887 and 1931 floods in China each appear to have crossed the mark of 1 million deaths. The earthquake of 1923 in Japan killed over 100,000 people, many in fires that ensued. In 1970, a cyclone in what is now Bangladesh might have killed up to 500,000 people. Throughout, multiple droughts, famines, and wars have been recorded as killing tens of millions of people. Genocides have sought to entirely wipe out nationalities, ethnicities, cultures, and religions.

Without denigrating the importance of these disasters and the need to investigate them, preoccupation with individual disasters of largest magnitudes of death and destruction is misleading. Strategies are required in all places and for hazards of every type and every magnitude, across a wide variety of conditions – namely, strategies to reduce vulnerabilities of every type and every magnitude. If the impact of lesser and often unreported disasters were to be aggregated, the sum could be as great as any single large disaster in terms of people affected, homes and heritage destroyed, or disruption experienced.

Tallying consequences of a particular pandemic is needed. So is totalling up deaths and other consequences from non-pandemic diseases such as malaria and measles – alongside the lives saved by taking action on these diseases, including vaccine development/distribution and stopping transmission. More to the point, how many people die from not having access to quick, affordable healthcare, notably for prevention? In the UK, hours waiting for an ambulance and weeks waiting to start cancer treatment after diagnosis seem ludicrously and appallingly luxurious compared to places in the world without ambulances or cancer diagnosis facilities. Small disasters are still disasters, including dying because an ambulance or cancer treatment was delayed.

In small countries, the total national population can be less than the number of deaths in a disaster in a larger country – and the annual number of preventable post-diagnosis cancer deaths. Many disasters in smaller countries therefore seem insignificant by any metric comparing disasters with these *absolute* impacts, the total of who and where was affected and how they were affected. *Proportional* impacts tend to be far greater upon populations with small numbers and places with small land areas.

The tropical cyclone which swept into the Indian state of Andhra Pradesh in 1974 rendered 2 million people homeless, 4 per cent of the state population and less than 1 per cent of India's national population. When in 1972, 120,000 people were made homeless by Cyclone Bebe in Fiji, they represented 22 per cent of the national population. The 11 million people made homeless in what soon became Bangladesh by the cyclone of 1970 was a horrific and cataclysmic situation, yet, by comparison to Fiji, affected 17 per cent of East Pakistan's population and 9 per cent of the national population.

Three-quarters of the population of Dominica were left homeless by Hurricane David in 1979. Twenty-two per cent of Tonga's housing stock was destroyed and 50 per cent of the national population were made homeless by Cyclone Isaac in 1982 (see also Chapter 6, 'Vulnerability in Tonga'). Thirty-four per cent of Jamaica's population were made homeless by Hurricane Gilbert in 1988. Close to or exactly 100 per cent of Dominica's 72,000 people were badly affected by Hurricane Maria in 2017. The total numbers for these island countries are far smaller than for India and Bangladesh, but the proportional impact is immense.

Comparison of proportional impacts at national levels can be applied sub-nationally between administrative units and localities of a single country. Similar conclusions regarding proportional impacts are reached by analyses of casualties in comparably affected townships and districts of Guatemala's 1976 earthquake, Hurricane David of 1979 in the Dominican Republic, and the Algerian El Asnam earthquake of 1980. The smallest administrative units, which are invariably rural rather than urban, suffered the highest proportional impacts. Similarly, for Sri Lanka's 1978 cyclone, it was not the coastal urban areas bearing the storm's full force, but rural areas inland that suffered the greatest proportional damage and greatest magnitude of damage (see Chapter 6, 'Cyclone in Sri Lanka'). Yet the spectacular, concentrated, and easily accessible damage in Batticaloa, a city on Sri Lanka's east coast, became the focus of national and international assistance. Rural disaster impacts can be greater than urban damage, even though the latter can appear more impressive and can be more accessible.

In comparisons of individual, family, and household impacts, the poorest people can easily lose all they have, making it 100 per cent losses. The comparatively rich may lose quantitatively more, because damage to an individual's expensive house, car, or heirloom can far exceed the total assets of a poorer household. The proportional impact upon the comparatively well-off is therefore much less, because they have more in reserve upon which to survive and thrive – and they might have insurance and other resources with which to cope.

Globalized comparisons of aggregated disaster magnitudes and assumptions of generalized or generic vulnerability then obscure different experiences in the same or comparable hazard due to different vulnerability contexts. Categorizing disasters by absolute magnitude metrics remains an important level of understanding. It nevertheless reflects a remote and privileged comparative view which tends to exclude disasters of a lesser absolute degree, even though these disasters might still represent catastrophic national and local impacts. It also obscures a major part of vulnerability as a local, prevailing condition, with its understanding ensuing from local context, experience, and analysis. Though vulnerability pervades in a global sense, understanding its causes and characteristics is incomplete with generalized 'globalization'.

This statement does not deny transferable and parallel aspects of vulnerability across local and national contexts, especially for considering proportional vulnerability and absolute vulnerability in tandem. Certainly, global policies and actions for vulnerability reduction have their place – particularly when augmented by local and national programmes. It is to some degree about subsidiarity – governance at the smallest jurisdiction feasible. These local and localized programmes are far less dramatic than the disasters they seek to avoid. They are unlikely to create news headlines, as disasters do. In their multiplicity and integration, small-scale programmes reduce vulnerability – proportionally and absolutely – and hence reduce those disasters of greatest local significance and impact. In turn, they contribute to global endeavours of vulnerability reduction and avoiding disasters.

Islands and vulnerability

One often-neglected local context is islands. Debates on what an island is and how different definitions influence analyses are not considered here, as they are covered extensively elsewhere (for example, Baldacchino, 2018; Selwyn, 1980).

An island-focused analysis fully embraces the wide variety of islands described in nissology (island studies) (Baldacchino, 2005; McCall, 1994). In addition to island and archipelago sovereign states such as Barbados, Comoros, Madagascar, New Zealand, and Tuvalu (see Chapter 6, 'Sea-level rise and atolls'), many island and archipelago territories, protectorates, and dependencies exist, some of which are, in effect, often colonies. Examples are Anguilla, Bouvet Island, Christmas Island (Australia's island of that name), New Caledonia, Isle of Man, Kalaallit Nunaat (Greenland), and Rodrigues. Islands and island groups can be subnational jurisdictions or a non-jurisdictional part of island and archipelago sovereign states, as shown by Barbuda, Chatham Islands, Galveston Island, Huvadhu Atoll, Kyushu, Nevis, Praslin, and Roatán. Places with ocean, sea, lake, or waterway coastlines and shorelines often have plenty of islands on which people live, from the cities of Toronto and Paris to the countries of Kenya and Thailand.

Characteristics of place and placeness have a significant bearing on identifying strategies for development and vulnerability reduction anywhere. The place and placeness will have had its influence upon local cultures and vice versa. Local and non-local perceptions and analyses of them are necessary for understanding local and non-local influences upon vulnerability and strategies to counter vulnerability, preferably before a disaster but often after one.

In the shifting interplay of contributing factors to vulnerability and vulnerability reduction, what happens in islands will be much the same as what could happen at local levels anywhere. The difference is that islands are frequently 'local level' immediately, including when the island is a country. Appropriately identified strategies are implementable locally, being manageable and small-scale, even if still national. National and local vulnerabilities conflate. Islands offshore of a much larger country or territory require processes of development and vulnerability reduction designed on their behalf, and with their participation, rather than sharing only in national or subnational programmes. The latter can still see the islands exclusively as part of the larger whole.

Marginalization remains an overriding risk shared by all places, with smallness potentially leading to particular difficulties. Islands offshore of their governing countries or subnational jurisdictions face logistical and political difficulties in fully participating in wider governance, such as in a national, provincial, state, or territorial legislature. Islands and islanders are too easily discounted there and in international participation.

Conversely, islands may be endowed with national and international strategic significance, most commonly defined by those who do not live in the islands. Outside forces are inevitably happy to use islands for military bases, prisons, resource extraction, and transition points on longer journeys. Notorious examples are the forced eviction of Chagossians from Diego Garcia in the Indian Ocean so that the UK could offer the archipelago to the US as a military base; Napoleon spending his final years in Saint Helena in the South Atlantic Ocean; and Nauru wrecking its landscape to mine phosphate, which has now run out, at the behest of external manipulation. More positively nostalgic examples are when Gander, Newfoundland was the main refuelling point for transatlantic flights, even into the 1990s, and when the Azores were a key stop for transoceanic flying boats a century ago.

As always, it is a balance. Islanders display rich and diverse cultures, languages, societies, histories, governance forms, and livelihoods. Island characteristics such as perceived isolation, restricted land area, and limited domestic land-based resources offer challenges, especially for engagement and development beyond the local context. These same sets of characteristics yield opportunities for tackling the challenges effectively. Traits such as tight kinship networks, a strong sense of identity, and direct and accepted intertwining of natural and cultural heritages produce closely knit communities with fulfilling and flexible livelihoods. Remittances from islander diasporas and circulatory migration between islands and other locations are a frequent boon. All these points also apply to many others around the world.

This mesh of advantages and difficulties, of attention and lack thereof, come to the fore for development and disasters. Islas de la Bahía, along the north coast of Honduras, form one of the Honduran government departments and were severely affected by Hurricane Mitch in October 1998. No study found compared the full impacts there or the people's rate of recovery with that of the other severely affected departments, although some work focuses on ecosystems. Meanwhile, Johnston (2015) describes how, for Fiji, more isolated villages had used development to augment their capabilities for dealing with cyclone impacts, precisely because they had not received as much post-cyclone aid as places better connected to the capital city. This isolation helped them to reduce local vulnerability through local action.

Large disasters in large countries and in urban areas have nevertheless become established as a common basis for public and official opinions and action concerning generalized response. These disasters have become both an emotive persuader and a medium for despair with regard to the apparent impossibility of doing anything about disasters through development.

Yet the apparently small disasters – in terms of absolute metrics rather than considering the full scope of impacts – which recur much more frequently than the large ones, and affect similarly large numbers of people in total, escape attention and international action. These disasters in islands – as well as in mountain villages and fishing hamlets – can lack outsider interest and support. They have at least as much impact and require as much attention as apparently larger disasters (Lewis, 1984b; Marulanda et al., 2010). Islanders' experiences could inform action elsewhere, were they given the chance, by balancing this unfortunate global norm – while still never neglecting any form of disaster or opportunity to reduce vulnerability, irrespective of scale by any metric.

Meaningfulness of vulnerabilities

Vulnerability is a process, not a state. Variously interpreted as expressing the potential to be harmed by a hazard, the degree of susceptibility to a hazard, and how a hazard might produce adverse impacts, it should also by definition explain 'why'. Why might a hazard produce adverse impacts, why is there susceptibility to a hazard, and why does potential harm exist? Vulnerability as a process embraces the long journey toward current observations and reasons for the current observations. The vulnerable present cannot be understood without incorporating into it the vulnerable past in order to shift to a less vulnerable future.

The concept of the vulnerability process is not merely a significant contribution to understanding disaster; it is the understanding of disaster across disciplines, decades, and continents (Baird et al., 1975; Bankoff and Hilhorst, 2022; Gaillard, 2022; Hewitt, 1983; Hossain et al., 1992; Maskrey, 1989;

O'Keefe et al., 1976; Winchester, 1992; Wisner et al., 2004). The vulnerability of populations and places is the cause of disasters, irrespective of the input from physical phenomena – natural hazards. Natural hazards are often assigned as the cause of the disaster, although their role is to reveal vulnerabilities.

Natural hazards are natural forces and energies, albeit frequently altered by human activities. Seen afterwards are the results of the impacts of those forces and energies. These results – as in death, damage, and disruption – are conditioned by behaviours, decisions, and actions of society over time. Responsibility – cultural, institutional, organizational, political, and individual – exists for the behaviours, decisions, and actions, underpinned by values supporting or permitting the behaviours, decisions, and actions. This responsibility should be for removing or alleviating the conditions creating and maintaining vulnerabilities. Typically, it is the opposite.

Vulnerability is the product of sets of prevailing conditions within which disasters may occur, often only accepting vulnerability's existence after a disaster has manifested. Vulnerability has to be addressed not only by post-disaster concern and response, but also as a part of day-to-day management of positive change-seeking improvements, whether or not that change is called development. The pervasive conditions of vulnerability cannot be allocated as the responsibility of one desk, one department, one discipline, or one silo. They are the prerogative of all, preferably collaborating, for all activities, policies, and practices. Without these approaches, these activities, policies, and practices may ferment the causative conditions for vulnerability and hence disaster, which so often go unrecognized, unattended, and uncared for until emergency response is necessitated.

Separation of post-disaster responses from pre-disaster contexts inhibits the creation of necessarily wider, deeper, and longer-term strategies. Some activities, policies, and practices contribute inadvertently or deliberately to the causes of disasters by supporting vulnerability. The response and relief sectors of the same governments, institutions, and organizations are then called upon to attend to and to pay for the consequences from the conditions that they created.

Meanwhile, disaster-affected people are rarely the perpetrators of the disaster they are experiencing. More commonly, the disasters affecting one group of people are caused by another group in the same or in a different place, and at the same or at a different time. Then, the perpetrators of one disaster can be impacted by a different disaster caused by others.

Given that disasters result from actions and inactions, it is incorrect to say that disaster-affected people are 'in the wrong place at the wrong time'. Vulnerability is sometimes interpreted as simply a matter of location or place, with some places being more vulnerable than others. The meaning of vulnerability is much more. It is much more than vulnerable conditions viewed through physical recognition and identification as a particular state of being at a particular time. It is much more than physical resistance to natural forces and energies incorporated into construction and planning. The meaning of vulnerability is about the social and societal – cultural, historical, institutional, organizational, political, livelihood, and individual – circumstances, situations, and issues that have evolved through various time scales and across various space and governance scales.

Adopting this approach facilitates a shift of emphasis from the place as a distant, transient, and 'unknown' post-disaster phenomenon, to insider experience, knowledge, and wisdom of the prevailing vulnerable nature of places and peoples, irrespective of natural hazards. Recognizing and identifying locationally or socially vulnerable sectors of populations and places together is itself only an indicator of the processes that have brought about those conditions. They are the visible and tangible manifestation on the surface of made-to-be-invisible and intangible undercurrents.

Part of this meaningfulness is the deliberate switching in this book between 'vulnerability' (singular) and 'vulnerabilities' (plural). They are processes (plural) involving multiple interacting factors (plural) layered in several ways (plural) to intersect across multiple aspects (plural). People and places have vulnerability. This vulnerability is not all the same or manifest in a single way, hence vulnerabilities. Vulnerability and vulnerabilities together.

Historical analysis facilitates evaluation of plural measures, consequences, their interrelationships, and their efficacy or otherwise. Problems exposed, brought about, or resolved can be tracked alongside the swings of concern from one disaster aftermath to another, typically shying away from concerns about the prevalent conditions and processes of vulnerabilities.

Understanding contexts, histories, and narratives affords a backdrop against which both short-term responses and long-term trends can be evaluated as parts of the long-term morphology of hazardousness and vulnerabilityness. A complete picture would enfold those developments misunderstood as not having anything to do with hazards or vulnerabilities. Values and attitudes need to be identified to explain why observed circumstances arose, what could have been done to produce less vulnerable pathways, and what should be done now to follow less vulnerable pathways.

Identified prevailing conditions and trends of vulnerability reflect effects and experiences of hazards over time, across all phenomena. 'The hazardousness of a place' (the title of Hewitt and Burton, 1971) relates not to one phenomenon or to another, but to all hazards affecting the place. As this hazardousness then intersects with 'the vulnerabilityness of a place', within and as a part of local understandings, the social and physical characteristics will direct toward specific strategies. The place takes on board its hazardousness and hazardousness becomes a part of its expression, as with vulnerabilityness.

These analyses of places, as the contexts of the manifestation of hazards, illustrate how contextual vulnerability analysis is applied for disaster avoidance as part of development (Hewitt, 1983). Otherwise, vulnerability is seen as a technocratic snapshot of people in their place. It becomes a mechanistic expression of presumptions foisted on what people are with respect to vulnerability without investigating why they are vulnerable. It cannot change the processes that cause and maintain vulnerability when it does not admit they exist.

Accepting the meaning of vulnerability as a social process that pushes people into situations in which they cannot help themselves deal with hazards then leads to accepting the meaning of disaster as resulting from human actions. In line with foundational thinking (O'Keefe et al., 1976; Hewitt, 1983; Jeffery, 1982; Lewis, 1979a; Torry, 1979), disaster is a social process, not a physical, natural, or environmental event. Development cannot address disasters by focusing on the environment. Development must enfold vulnerability reduction within its policies and programmes to ensure that development and disasters do not end up separate.

These baseline ideas point to the need for a broader framework for disaster analysis and for strategies to reduce vulnerability as an integral part of long-term development. Local studies placed problems apparently caused by natural hazards firmly into the context of everyday shortcomings of policy and practice. Natural hazards exposed these shortcomings that had built up over a long time period. Issues relating to local water and food supplies, planning and construction, health, sanitation, education, and livelihoods illustrated how social, economic, cultural, and political contexts could be moulded positively to reduce, or moulded negatively to increase, the impact of natural hazards of any magnitude and intensity.

From the same time period, research into post-disaster activities supported the ethos that disasters are symptoms of chronic vulnerabilities (Oliver-Smith, 1979; Snarr and Brown, 1979). Those vulnerabilities created the need for humanitarian aid in the first place and humanitarian aid perpetuated the vulnerabilities.

Why are meanings of vulnerability pretended to be more physical and static, supporting surficial and superficial analyses? Because it is easier to envisage a state of affairs in physical, boxed-in terms, especially to explain quickly strong images of physical damage and destruction with people suffering. Not just 'explain', but also 'explain away'. Framing vulnerability as a physical state of being and framing disasters as one-off, natural events absolves the commentator, typically a leader of the affected peoples and places, of blame. Who would retain their position of power for long by admitting that they had the chance to redress vulnerabilities and to avoid a disaster, but chose otherwise? Instead, they focus on programmes and budgets bolstering resistance to the physicalities of natural hazards, visible in the apparent strength and size of infrastructure. It is tangible and appears to be doing something, anything.

Doing so without an understanding of the social contexts, from local to global, as creators of vulnerabilities means that the efforts must eventually fail. It is similar to painting over the hole where water enters to flood a house, or cracks from an earthquake, without attending to the reasons for the water's ingress or the wall cracking.

In infrastructure, the physical aspects of quality of construction, appropriateness of form and material, age, and maintenance are easily identified. That vulnerability is visibly and more obviously related to infrastructure and the damage that it sustains, is one reason why the less obvious aspects of vulnerability may go unattended. These aspects of vulnerability are important, but could never provide the entire picture. The greater value of these and other characteristics is as metaphors for other conditions, those that are less material or non-material. These metaphors are similarly applicable to the social services of, for example, health and education; to livelihoods, such as agriculture and teaching; and to institutional and organizational management across sectors.

Vulnerability is not so much what happens to people and places during a natural hazard, but rather why the lack of ability exists to deal with the natural hazard. Events and processes which may contribute to that inability accrue over time. They are internal and external, being as diverse as livelihood opportunities, national economic decisions, lack of land tenure, a push from subsistence farming to cash cropping, chemical contamination of an ecosystem, ill health and lack of accessible and affordable healthcare, and the death of family members or working animals. All could emerge as disaster consequences as well as adding to the overall effect of disasters. These factors run deeply, covering everyday experiences including sexism, racism, homophobia, ableism, discrimination, bullying, harassment, marginalization, and oppression.

When options and opportunities are removed from people to help themselves, by definition, vulnerability gathers and grows. Vulnerability as a condition of hazard impacts and as a state of being susceptible to hazard impacts are small parts of the overall, pervasive, negative, long-term, and chronic condition and process of vulnerability.

Vulnerability and risk

With vulnerability always present, there is always risk. As with all words and concepts, books have been written and debated for defining, explaining, and analysing risk (Adams, 1999; Aven, 2015; Beck, 2013; Wilde, 2014). At its basis, risk is taken to be the potential for something to happen, ostensibly due to hazard and vulnerability together. It combines the probability of an outcome (ostensibly the parallel for hazard) with the consequences of that outcome (ostensibly the parallel for vulnerability). How that combination is effected varies, from a straightforward multiplication (probability times consequences) to a complicated function (such as mathematical integration over the time period in question of different components as functions of time inputting into probability and consequences). In one simplified manner among many sporting significant imperfections in vocabulary, risk becomes a function of hazard and vulnerability.

In developing various definitions, mnemonics, and equations for risk, other words are added. Climate change discourse has adopted a model in which vulnerability and 'exposure' are separate (IPCC, 2021–2022), leading to detailed discussion on their differences and their overlaps. Other common terms in a risk equation or mnemonic are 'mitigation' and 'capacity' (Wisner et al., 2004), all of which would require definition and discussion.

The key here is the meaning of vulnerability and risk for people and places affected. Assessing and describing risk can focus on 'elements at risk', using the factors quantitatively in order to aim for a quantifiable calculation of that risk. Examples are the numbers and categories (for example, by sex, gender, sexuality, age, and other individual variables) of people injured and killed; numbers and categories of infrastructure damaged and destroyed; the amounts of agricultural assets lost; and economic metrics. Risk assessment in this manner focuses upon snapshots of hazard and vulnerability.

The snapshot of hazard can focus on a phenomenon or process such as drought, tornado, or avalanche as a distinct event affecting distinct elements such as people, infrastructure, and livelihood objects, crops, or animals – which is the snapshot of vulnerability. The snapshot of hazard might also determine elements at risk (the snapshot of vulnerability) to a particular hazard parameter or set of parameters, such as peak ground acceleration of an earthquake, maximum wind gust speed of a hurricane, or maximum flood depth in a river. When quantified, risk assessment highlights the origin of hazard and the effects of that hazard upon elements at risk. Above all, in this manner, risk is concerned with the *product* or *result* of hazard. It does not explain why risk arises.

Vulnerability, on the other hand, looks at the *processes* at work between the sequence of hazard apparently leading to risk. These processes lead to disaster. This approach to vulnerability reverses the conventional approach, and focuses upon the locations and conditions of the elements at risk and reasons for those locations and conditions, notably how and why they came about. By attending to the vulnerability process, the effects of all potential hazards can be accommodated to some degree, so that hazard inputs minimally into risk. Measures to decrease vulnerability, so that hazard has limited effect, are partially integrative with usual, everyday, collective conditions. They would be small-scale and individually less costly, bringing other gains and thus being more achievable.

Focus on fearful risks of large magnitude clouds perception of a reality characterized by the continuous persistence and accumulation of smaller risks. Making risks large and calculative makes it more difficult to realistically conceive, identify, and address risks which are smaller and more frequent – more everyday – but which are nonetheless devastating, such as vehicle crashes, drowning, and assault.

Risk, when accepted as the probable manifestation of a hazard and the impacts of that hazard, might highlight the potential of occurrence without fully accounting for the complete situation within the period of time for which that occurrence is assessed. From the vulnerability process, risk is a prevailing condition or continuous state of affairs, not the damaging event itself. Changes will inevitably occur during the time period, which will affect the degree of susceptibility to hazard and the amount of potential damage or actual damage sustained. The point of development should be to effect such changes so that vulnerability and hence risk decrease, irrespective of hazard. Thus, where and when a hazard occurs, the adverse effects should be different – and preferably less – at the end of the time period than they would be for a similar hazard at the beginning of the time period.

This evolving risk typically has:

- Multiple hazards each with multiple impacts; for example, flood depth, flood speed, floodwater contaminants, and forces from waves, all as functions of time and three-dimensional space).
- Numerous elements experiencing the hazard parameters.
- Numerous changes which take place within the hazards and the elements.
- Different rates of change.

Thus, this evolving risk typically has ever-varying conditions of the slew of words used: susceptibility, exposure, mitigation, capacity, capability, ability, and others.

The overall condition that results is the evolving vulnerability process. Risk highlighting hazard and exposure, especially as being separate from vulner-abilities, moves toward being static and hypothetical, although reassessable over time. Vulnerability is accretive, is morphological, and embodies a reality applicable to any hazard and hazard combination as well as to any suscep-tibility, exposure, mitigation, capacity, capability, ability, and combination thereof. Vulnerabilities do not have to be dependent upon, or applicable to, only specified sources of hazard or a specified time or space snapshot.

If presumed to be only calculable, quantitative, objective, universal, a product, and a value, risk is actuarial, bypassing the reality of vulnerability being actual. Whether or not risk is appropriately assessed and addressed, vulner-ability will change – accruing or diminishing. Failing to accept the processual and contextual nature of vulnerability, declining to notice how vulnerability is accretive and aggregative, makes risk an assumed totality of a single event brought about by forces over which we have no control – or over which we have lost control or decided not to have control. Countermeasures against risk are therefore conceived as separate from usual activities. These measures must preferably be powerful, massive, tangible, and visible, tending toward high cost and high disruption. Forgotten are other complementary measures – small-scale, everyday, and individual, familial, or household – which are obscured when total risk is presented as being an external imposition. This perception of total risk may be so intensive, painful, and fearful, as to inhibit the very measures that might otherwise bring about its mitigation.

Two significant issues emerge from these concepts. First, the condition of risk is taken to be a construct and calculation for which certain static values are necessary. Fluid or changing situations do not necessarily lend themselves to simple mathematical 'certainties' – the usual difficulty of high precision without examining accuracy and the common exclusion of ranges and sensitivity analyses.

Second, risk as a mathematical calculation, often conceived as the product of hazard and vulnerability or the product of probability and consequences, means that hazard and vulnerability must be identified, specific, static, and of a given magnitude. As a component in the equation, vulnerability is made to be secondary to the consequence of the equation, which is risk. Risk is a final number for action, rather than emphasizing the real source of damage or loss, which is vulnerabilities.

External governments, institutions, and organizations may be interested in risk as a value from and for other places. They may not examine or understand vulnerability as a prevailing condition or interrelated set of conditions experienced by people and places. The vulnerability process ends up divorced from their own decisions. Though assessable by 'outsiders', vulnerability as a prevailing condition is inevitably an 'insider' experience. To those undertaking localized activities, vulnerability is the more relevant condition compared to risk, as people perceive vulnerability for themselves (Rahman, 1991).

Meanwhile, experiences of hazards can be considered in three overlapping and fuzzy stages. The first stage relates to descriptions of what might happen. A tornado watch is issued, a cornice near a mountain's top looks ready to become an avalanche, a new pathogen is identified, or an undersea volcano starts erupting suggesting tsunami potential. The second stage is that a hazard's impacts are felt. A tornado, avalanche, microbe, or tsunami has swept through a settlement. The third stage relates to the aftermath and to survivors continuing to survive and thrive in the longer term. Sustained survival requires an effective culture and infrastructure of local assistance, resources, livelihoods, and services.

The outcomes from all three stages rest principally on vulnerability. What abilities and resources do people and places have to think and act? In stage one of the hazard experience, are they ready to monitor and prepare? In stage two, had they acted to lessen damage and disruption? In stage three, were they anticipating how to respond, recover, and reconstruct? All these actions must occur long before the hazard manifests, knowing that hazards must manifest at some point, which is really stage zero – everyday life. All these actions are about reducing vulnerability as a process in order to reduce risk, however calculated, qualified, or defined.

CHAPTER 3
Present vulnerabilities

Observations and identifications of vulnerability

A huge variety of tools, techniques, and technologies exists to help observe the world, as has always been the case. In the realm of modern science, much about disasters was observed and described by outsiders. They looked at the 'others' experiencing disaster or who might experience disaster. Observations through research have also recently been partitioned by discipline. Seismology and meteorology, for instance, divided the study of earthquakes and tropical cyclones between them. Silos are as narrow as those siloizing wish to make them. Volcanological chemists did not always respect volcanological seismologists and vice versa; meteorologists and climatologists had difficulty communicating.

These disciplinary divides – even studying experiences of different natural hazards by the same people in the same place at the same time – cannot convey a semblance of the reality of people's vulnerabilities and, hence, disasters. Various histories of disaster studies offer various points at which a significant shift occurred to examine a cumulative range of hazards over time, aiming to present ideas of vulnerability. These histories are, unsurprisingly, divided by discipline, with anthropology, architecture, development studies, engineering, human geography, medicine, philosophy, political science, psychology, and sociology being among the claimants.

With all these disciplines and more contributing substantially, being stronger together, the trend is toward the study of hazards in a context of humanity and toward the disasters that ensue. This approach diverges from the study of the hazards that were assumed, from afar, to be exogenous and to have caused the disaster as 'an event'. The difference from looking at only a hazard was the incorporation into disaster impacts of peoples, their cultures, their settlements, their societies, their histories, their infrastructures, and their placements within and as part of their environments. Simultaneously, hybrid fields entered the fray, including environmental studies, human ecology, island studies, and political ecology, with hazard studies and disaster studies emerging as distinct fields – interestingly, not including anyone founding vulnerability studies or vulnerability research as a distinct discipline.

These changes brought understandings nearer to the reality of disasters as they are experienced, rather than as they are studied. Instead of discrete events bounded in space and time for mono-disciplinary study, disaster studies is now concerned with the manifestation and exposure of hazardousness in contexts of vulnerabilityness. These viewpoints remained confined to some silos, being published mainly in English, mainly from universities, and mainly in the structure and style expected by contemporary Anglophone science. These characterizations are not exclusive (for example, Copans, 1975; Davis et al., 1980), but dominated.

Not that physical observations of the Earth and interest in the impacts are new. The story of the first known seismograph is that philosopher Chang Heng invented it in China in the year 132 (this expression of the year obviously being culturally biased) and soon after detected an earthquake. Even earlier, the eruption of Mount Vesuvius, now in Italy, in the year 79 was recorded along with its impacts by Pliny the Younger. What inventions, explanations, or analyses regarding impacts and vulnerabilities, centuries ahead of contemporary work, might have emerged from cultures around the world, lost in the collapse of civilizations from the Diné to the Khmer or waiting to be uncovered in archives or soil layers?

Within recent time and in the dominating languages, the early years brought more interest in the hazards than on the impacts on people and places within their social contexts. Scattered exceptions demonstrate the rule:

- Rousseau's (1756) description and analysis of the 1755 Lisbon earthquake and tsunami.
- Rawson's (1868) explanation of the impacts of the 1866 Bahamas hurricane.
- Heilprin's (1903) visits to Martinique after the 1902 Mount Pelée eruptions.
- Prince's (1920) examination of the 1917 explosion in Halifax, Canada.
- Reagan's (1921) detailing of how the flu pandemic affected native Americans in Arizona, although focused mainly on response.
- Angenheister's (1921) discussion of the effects of an earthquake in Tonga (see also Chapter 6, 'Vulnerability in Tonga').

Most studies, though, recorded the environmental phenomena of what inevitably were disasters for the people who experienced them. Detachment from the disastrous impacts of natural hazards has been maintained in many research undertakings today. Magnitudes of distant hazards are recorded and compared – a nonetheless useful and needed endeavour – without balancing investigations into local impacts by considering contexts including land, water, population size, livelihoods, or societal consequences.

Even when disasters are reported, larger disasters predominate. Apparent suddenness, and disasters affecting national and regional capitals, are likely to command attention. Other disasters, of similar impact but in less topical or 'newsworthy' contexts, may receive brief accounts, not commensurate with their magnitude or consequences. By a straight comparison of their coverage, news items are not consistent or logical in the degree of significance, or otherwise, given to disasters (Herman and Chomsky, 2002). Sometimes an individual story grabs attention, overshadowing the rest. A woman gave birth while trapped in a tree during floods in Mozambique in 2000 and then another in 2019 – stories which captivated media attention while hundreds were dying each time.

Inconsistent, or even consistent, reporting of disasters only occasionally succeeds in emotionally conveying what it is like inside the situation. Being inside is much the same, whether the disaster receives headline treatment for 10 days and goes viral, or receives eight lines on only one day with nary a repost. At times, disaster reporting comes straight from the source through citizen journalists, social media, and professionals experiencing direct impacts. This does not mean that the inside view is present.

As Hurricane Maria made landfall on Dominica in 2017, the country's Prime Minister Roosevelt Skerrit was posting live Facebook updates. His house lost its roof and flooded, followed by him being rescued. It is telling that his internet functioned during a strong hurricane while his roof did not. He had the foresight to maintain connectivity, but not to have a flood- and wind-resistant property or to dwell outside the extreme floodplain. During COVID-19's work-from-home stints, journalists reported their own experiences – again framed within connectivity along with the luxury of still having a job and being able to work. All credit to them for telling it as it was for them, informing of their own legitimate lived experiences – unlike the self-appointed epidemiologists raising their own public profiles by undermining solid science and solid journalism – recognizing that people most affected had limited outlet for their stories.

Locals reporting on themselves and local circumstances nonetheless assist a conversion of outsider reporting to insider experience. All stories count, including those told from a privileged perspective such as being Prime Minister or (self-referencing) writing a free-to-download book. The danger is science-for-action by meme, too often adopted even by people with the scientific qualifications and knowledge who deliberately promote only science supporting their preconceived and long-established political viewpoint.

Not that new technology necessarily brings all-new media advantages and limitations. Scanlon and Frizzell (1979) offer numerous lessons about reporting disasters, the pertinence of many having increased, but not being new, due to the advent of social media. As an example (Scanlon and Frizzell, 1979: 316): 'media errors occur mainly when material had no stated source: it was hard to escape the conclusion journalists manufactured many of the inaccuracies. From the journalists [sic] point of view, contrived news may be better than no news at all.' Or 'news' and 'information' are deliberately contrived so as to misinform maliciously, which is hardly a new phenomenon (Herman and Chomsky, 2002; see also McLuhan, 1964). Among disasters, false reporting about war is infamous, whether to mislead the enemy, boost home morale, or manipulate the stock markets (Mathews, 1957).

Even when striving to report accurately and doing so, professional and amateur media have a tendency toward the same, consistent errors or omissions. Proportional impacts are not emphasized as much as absolute impacts. The phrase 'natural disaster' remains common despite a persistent campaign responding to such stories with the hashtags #NoNaturalDisasters and #DisastersAreNotNatural alongside a link to a media pack on why the phrase 'natural disaster' should be avoided.

There would be less reason for concern if inconsistency were admitted within the realms of reportage. News influences public opinion and authorities' responses. Well-read columnists and influencers making a career of it can have a notoriously thin grasp of disaster science and real impacts on people and places. Reporting from all sources can drive the public response in contributions to disaster relief and humanitarian aid. Few comparisons of national impact and limited assessment of the country's own national capacity to respond to its own disaster might be made. Nor are long histories or prevailing conditions made prominent.

One moniker repeatedly assigned to Bangladesh, rightly or wrongly, is being one of the most disaster-prone countries in the world. Some of its disasters rightly receive extensive world attention. What is rarely in the international media headlines or the stories are the regular homelessness from river bank erosion, the chronic landlessness and corruption, and the regular migration from the country seeking better lives. These and other topics reflect the chronic vulnerability conditions and processes that cause disasters, while simultaneously indicating the relationship between context and vulnerability that informs reducing disasters through development.

In the meantime, research reveals evidence of disasters smaller than those of international impact yet of local comparable consequence, alongside local, chronic conditions and issues that a disaster exacerbates or compounds (Rahman et al., 2023; Rayhan, 2010). For external observers coming in for a brief visit or assessment – the FIFO (fly in, fly out) mentality – it can be difficult to distinguish between damage caused by a recent disaster and unrepaired damage caused by earlier disasters or chronic development insufficiencies. Once a specific disaster is placed in its local contexts, including histories, a long-term trajectory emerges of intermittent and recurrent disasters, themselves interrelated and inextricably part of people's continuous living.

Vulnerability as a condition accrues as a variety of processes over long time periods. If analysis of vulnerability does not account for its causative processes, or if it assumes that vulnerability now is a static product of expired processes, then this will perpetuate the chronic development insufficiencies leading to vulnerabilities and disasters.

Identifications and assessments of vulnerability

Vulnerability being an expression of changing conditions, some people and places are made more vulnerable to hazards than others. Comparative vulnerability can change with policies and actions, being created, augmented, and diminished. Vulnerability is neither static nor fixed; vulnerability is dynamic, evolutionary, and accretive.

These processes of vulnerability are most often identified after a disaster's impacts are evident. That is too late for those already affected, so the preference is to identify and assess vulnerability, in order to act on it, before it is exposed in a disaster. If it is desirable and feasible to measure vulnerability as part of the identification and assessment, how much detail is necessary to support development?

At times, indicators of vulnerability per group or per region suffice, even if it artificially homogenizes some aspects of vulnerability and some vulnerability values. For working purposes and to inform development, it may not be necessary to know the vulnerability value per individual, per family, per household, per square metre, or per dwelling. Smaller scales such as families or subsistence farms can share common vulnerabilities, so extrapolation can help for acting more quickly. These indicators may be for individual or family demographic characteristics, locational data, dwelling and livelihood information, and details on services and the places in which people live and work. In some contexts, some data will be at a wider scale rather than individualized, such as transportation and health services.

Accepting somewhat homogenized indicators across a place helps to overcome challenges in seeking detailed, highly localized vulnerability assessment. The latter is time-consuming, requires on-the-ground labour which could have safety concerns, could run into trouble when basic data is inaccurate or unavailable, and might reveal data about people, families, or households which they would prefer to keep confidential.

Remote sensing can assist in collecting high resolution data, provided that resources are available to use satellite data, to hire aircraft, and/or to train and employ operators of uncrewed autonomous vehicles (drones). A drone flying with a 360° camera along streets can rapidly collect significant data needed to assess infrastructure, provided it is not attacked. Then, cleaning, processing, and analysing the data requires time, as would writing programmes to do so automatically. It would be a balance between the noise and errors from automation and the large volumes and data which could be covered. Further care is needed to avoid presuming that one fly-through defines a location. Little information would be available on the inside of infrastructure. People and infrastructure never stop changing, which is why vulnerability is dynamic and processual, meaning that a decision would be needed on how frequently to collect updated data in the same location.

In seeking some level of homogenization, it is dangerously inappropriate to use population numbers or population density as an indicator of vulnerability for the purposes of establishing priorities of need. Small populations and rural populations would indicate low vulnerability, leaving them in a position of low priority for development. Smallness in numbers is not an excuse for smallness in aid. This approach would merely perpetuate the vulnerability process that development is meant to overcome.

Identifying and assessing local vulnerability should also be completed with the people and places whose vulnerabilities are being assessed. An example of what might be called micro-vulnerability assessment resulted from rural village participation in the Philippines (Hall, 1996). With the help of a large three-dimensional village map, made in local materials for the purpose, villagers were asked to indicate the houses they considered to be vulnerable, to which hazards, and for what reasons. Flooding, landslide, and typhoon (tropical cyclone) potential were taken into account by villagers, as were building maintenance, ownership and tenancy, recent settlement and migration, and livestock security. Participatory processes are now much more formalized (Chambers, 2002), as is the method: Participatory Three-Dimensional Modelling/Mapping (P3DM) continues to be applied in the Philippines (Maceda et al., 2009).

Either external or internal observations and perceptions, on their own, tend to be insufficient for identifying and assessing vulnerability. Local perception of hazards and vulnerabilities may not be total. Activities outside of the locality may have created or exacerbated hazards, the effects of which are as yet outside local experience, and vulnerabilities, the effects of which are all too evident, yet their external causes may be difficult to pinpoint locally. Long-standing knowledge cannot account for hazards that have not before manifested in the location or that come from beyond an individual's direct observational power, such as deep inside the Earth or deep into outer space. Meanwhile, any 'community', no matter how small or tight, has its own power games, cliques, and hierarchies. Some individuals are inevitably dismissed in importance or ostracized from inputting into decisions, creating vulnerability for them and, likely, others.

Meanwhile, external observations and perceptions can bring breadth and depth. Huge amounts of freely available, highly credible Earth observations data are available online, with basic laptops and phones offering significant processing and analytical power through freely available software. This work plays important roles in vulnerability assessment, making use of the best that the world can offer online. It remains participatorily poor and culturally impoverished, too easily adopted for expediency. External, remote, desk-based work can supplement such data with remote participatory processes. Online interviews, surveys, community walkthroughs, mapping exercises, PhotoVoice, and participatory art have all been successful, leading to fruitful exchanges where each location helps the other, even being continents apart.

Any approach – in person and online, physical science data and social science data, quantitative and qualitative, and externally driven and locally driven – has advantages and disadvantages for vulnerability identification and assessment. The best successes are achieved by combining them all, using various techniques to fill in remaining gaps and admitting the limitations, uncertainties, and unknowns. Conversely, the more techniques used, the more resource intensive the work becomes. This is especially the case when aiming for a time series to conduct longitudinal analysis and to make the monitoring and analysis of vulnerability as much a process as vulnerability itself.

Hazard, vulnerability, and perceptions thereof are dynamic and shifting. Identification and assessment in a place at a particular time cannot conclusively convey the total picture for that place at that time, nor for any other time in the past or future. Estimates and approximations are inevitable, leading to error bars, uncertainties, and unknowns.

The best, most comprehensive, most accurate, vulnerability identification and assessment would be a fusion of multiple space, time, and governance scales, melding multiscalar vulnerability analyses. How much precision is required and desired would be contextual, as would be the possible need to balance precision and accuracy.

Assessments and analyses of vulnerability

Historical analysis allows the dissection of processes and issues, but history serves a greater usefulness when it interrelates them retrospectively. This is particularly fruitful in examining the historic contexts of disasters. There are many lessons with which to be acquainted, such as the swing away from one method of construction in the aftermath of one disaster, only to increase vulnerability to another hazard. Examples are from timber to masonry after a fire and from masonry to timber after an earthquake. Hence, the value of realizing the full extent of 'the hazardousness of a place' (Hewitt and Burton, 1971) and 'all hazards at a place' (Lewis, 1984b; see also Chapter 6, 'A multi-hazard history of Antigua').

The importance of development not making vulnerability worse emerges from Chiswell in southern England (see Chapter 6, 'Vulnerability in Chiswell, Dorset, UK'). A perception of development for tourism on the one hand and the development of naval facilities on the other, imposed themselves upon local development, obstructing natural drainage of exacerbated sea flooding. Similarly, many islands in the Caribbean and Pacific have struggled with balancing subsistence food crops and cash crops; notably, sugar brings in quick cash at times while at others undermines nutrition and creates vulnerability to hazards and to the whims of world markets. In Tonga, care has to be exercised with producing vanilla, pyrethrum, and passion fruit so as not to displace other food crops, essential in emergencies and helping to avoid dependency upon imported foods (see also Chapter 6, 'Vulnerability in Tonga'). All these examples are social, especially political and cultural, as much as physical and technological. Assessing and analysing vulnerability must account for these interrelationships, between emergency relief and self-reliance as well as between emergency relief and development.

Assessing and analysing vulnerability must further account for interrelation-ships among people and their changing places; that is, population mobilities as part of vulnerability's dynamism in a place and of the people moving. Induced, coerced, forced, desired, planned, and spontaneous population movements increase and decrease vulnerability. People moving removes them from their accustomed livelihood and resource base, creating conditions of dependency (increasing vulnerability) or offering far more opportunity than they had at their origin (decreasing vulnerability). They might move into areas with unfamiliar hazards and not learn about their new environment (increasing vulnerability). They might bring their multi-hazard experience with them and help their new neighbours to be ready for more than before (decreasing vulnerability). They might experience adverse mental health impacts from moving (increasing vulnerability) or have access to much more healthcare, education, and social supports than before (decreasing vulnerability).

These processes may be further compounded, so assessing and analysing vulnerability must account for the complicated interrelationships with various forms of, reasons for, and consequences of population movements. Deprivation or wealth may drive migration, to seek different opportunities, adventure, and/or variety. Migration may cause or alleviate resource overuse, depending on the resource base and consumption rates at the origin and destination. Migration may cause or alleviate overpopulation, underpopulation, a glut of skills, and a lack of skills. Migrants can deplete their origin of professionals such as doctors and engineers, while bringing the local population to levels below which a school or hospital is maintained (all generally increasing vulnerability). At their destination, they might then offer skills that were lacking while boosting the population to a level at which a school or hospital is built (all generally decreasing vulnerability).

Assessment and analysis applying simple population increase or population decrease, or changes in population distribution up or down, as the main factors of vulnerability, will be incomplete and an inadequate expression of vulnerability as a complex and dynamic process. A policy of population reduction or population increase may be one multi-sectoral component for development. If little comprehensive strategy accounts for the full picture of population movements and consequences thereof, then impacts on vulnerability, and especially vulnerability for sub-groups, cannot be fully anticipated.

In parallel, applying simple factors of 'urbanness' or 'ruralness' to assess and analyse vulnerability will mislead. Cities are often assumed to be subject to the greatest disaster impacts. These assumptions result from mono-disciplinary and preconceived judgements. Aside from considering only absolute numbers without equivalent inclusion of proportional impacts and proportional vulnerabilities, post-disaster assessments are often unable or unwilling to reach rural hinterlands. A handful of online posts about the desperation in a hamlet, cut off by landslides and in which all infrastructure has been severely damaged, would be dwarfed by those using a hashtag for the partly impacted capital city or financial centre.

In all settlement densities – rural, urban, suburban, peri-urban, and all those in between – analysing and assessing vulnerabilities means understanding historical decisions, trends, and trajectories to understand the vulnerability process. Infrastructure damage makes manifest many aspects of the hazard's impacts, notably deaths, injuries, and disruption; that is, the disaster. Yet the age, condition, and strength of infrastructure indicates vulnerability without fully defining it, as do materials, planning, design methods, and construction methods. As buildings become less maintained or less upgraded, and more dilapidated, they tend to be occupied and over-occupied by poorer populations or those marginalized for other reasons. This situation was exposed by the 1985 Mexico City earthquake (ECLAC, 1985). Earlier tremors and small earthquakes may have contributed to a weakening deterioration of buildings, which were not monitored, maintained, or repaired.

Physical aspects of infrastructure are merely one set of vulnerability indicators. Traits of people and politics beyond infrastructure are essential and represent significant inputs into the vulnerability process.

Guatemala's capital was moved to its present site after the former capital was destroyed in 1773, after which it was virtually destroyed again by further tremors in 1917 and 1918. The 1976 earthquake killed 22,000 people and destroyed much squatter housing which had been built on the sides of the ravines that surround the city. Buildings in the city centre were relatively undamaged. The majority of casualties and homeless from the 1976 tremor were in rural areas (Olson and Olson, 1977).

Affluence is no guarantee of safety. In Türkiye, many middle-class apartment dwellers perished in the 1999 and 2023 earthquakes when their relatively recent buildings pancaked, crumbled, or toppled. For some, it had been a sign of upward 'social mobility' to move into these high-rises. During the 22 February 2011 earthquake in Christchurch, New Zealand, almost two-thirds of the 185 deaths occurred in a single structure. The Canterbury Television (CTV) building had been weakened during the 4 September 2010 earthquake, but remained open for business in the city's central business district, killing professionals and students when it collapsed (Canterbury Earthquakes Royal Commission – Te Komihana Rūwhenua o Waitaha, 2012).

Catastrophic unpredictability of when earthquakes (and many other natural hazards) will occur can obscure perception of their recurring frequency. The consequently pervasive context of vulnerability can thus come to be disregarded in assessments and analyses, preferring instead deluding and inaccurate labels of 'unprecedented', 'unpredictable', and 'unscheduled'. Historical studies which depict recurrence might do so for only one hazard category and might not fully acknowledge vulnerability. An unrealistic and academic separation of hazards can ensue, divorced from their contexts and unable to portray the interactions of social and environmental realities.

Oliver-Smith (1979) offered a template in referring to the 31 May 1970 earthquake and rock avalanche in Yungay, Peru as the 400-year earthquake. It was not 400 years in terms of the geological return period. It refers to the root causes of vulnerability, as exposed during the shaking, which required centuries to build up. Oliver-Smith (1979) continues with the successes and failures of post-disaster actions, some setting up vulnerability to create the next disaster.

The aftermath of one disaster becomes the vulnerable context for another disaster involving similar or different hazards, as seen in Tonga (Chapter 6,

'Vulnerability in Tonga' and 'Volcano in Tonga') and Antigua (Chapter 6, 'A multi-hazard history of Antigua'). Institutions and infrastructure can be strained or weakened by a hazard, engraining vulnerabilities in the social and physical contexts, meaning that the next hazard cannot be countered. Over-response to one hazard may create vulnerability to another. Decisions for development can be taken with respect to the hazard that just happened, disregarding entire hazardousness. More worryingly, those decisions can emphasize the vulnerability identified after the hazard that just happened, rather than seeking comprehensive vulnerability assessment and analysis. And thus the vulnerability process continues.

Analyses and processes of vulnerability

An overriding issue to emerge from accepting vulnerability as a process is that vulnerable conditions and circumstances are rarely caused by the vulnerable incumbent – neither the people nor the places. Vulnerability is more usually caused by the values, attitudes, behaviours, decisions, policies, actions, and activities of others. Whether linked to poverty, oppression, discrimination, marginalization, inequitable resource distribution, violent conflict, non-violent conflict, or other factors – and most typically a combination – these vulnerability factors are rarely caused by those most vulnerable. Poverty and marginalization, for instance, are not commonly caused by the person who or place which is poor or marginalized. They are more often due to governments, institutions, organizations, corporations, commercial interests, and others who either have or are seeking power over others. It is often ideologically driven, perhaps directed by a deity, by political assumptions, or by desire for power for its own sake.

This means that those who create vulnerability have the potential, power, opportunities, options, and resources to reduce vulnerability. The principal process by which vulnerability reduction can be achieved is development, as framed in this book. Moulding this approach to development to achieve vulnerability reduction, and hence fewer disasters, requires embracing the principles of proportional vulnerability and proportional impact.

These principles entail transferring disaster assessment and action away from remote global comparative accounting, into the place where disaster has been or could be experienced, because vulnerability is experienced as a continuous process. Part of this experience, and part of the expression of this experience, is analysis of the impact that has occurred in relation to what existed before – the proportionality analysis. After the impact, proportionality tallies how many people were killed or injured out of the total population; how many houses were destroyed out of the total that there had been; and how much income has been lost out of the income that was there before. These data can be expressed as percentages. Only then, can realistic comparisons be made, equitably examining absolute and proportional metrics to gain a full picture of the disaster, the vulnerability processes that created it, and the development processes that avoid recurrence.

The scale of development projects follows. If projects are to be designed and programmed so as to be commensurate with jurisdiction size, then local-ization can aid success, tailoring resources and activities to locally expressed needs and circumstances. This approach applies to smaller jurisdictions as much as larger ones. Neither is more important or less important, as they all require development.

The smaller and more tailored development projects are, the more of them will be needed to support everyone. This situation will not sit well with distant administrators who seek economies of scale, whether or not economies of scale are helpful for affected people. It may appear to be more 'efficient' from the provider's viewpoint to go for large projects with minimum duplication of personnel and effort. Appearance of more efficiency does not mean being more effective. From the recipient's viewpoint, it is preferable to achieve local integration through the widespread repetition of small inputs, to recognize that vulnerability is contextual and needs to be dealt with as such.

After all, what is done after one disaster influences the prevailing conditions for the next – or, preferably, the lack of a next disaster because the vulner-ability process was curtailed and reversed. Whatever is done after one disaster should recall its role in reducing vulnerability to each and all subsequent hazards. Present vulnerabilities are ever-present vulnerabilities. Disasters will not be avoided by focusing on hazards, since people experiencing the same hazard can have widely divergent disaster experiences, based on their vulner-abilities. As such, present vulnerabilities are many 'presents' seen through different experiences. These 'presents' are the 'presence' of vulnerability in people's everyday lives, livelihoods, and lifestyles.

CHAPTER 4
Experiences of vulnerabilities

Vulnerabilities inherent and inherited?

Vulnerability as a process is dynamic, changing over time. It is experienced, dependent on actions in the past and at the present.

External assistance and systems not of local origin can help everyone, if used appropriately, and can reduce vulnerability if supporting local practices and improvements. Complete reliance on external assistance and systems, though, typically increases vulnerability. The removal, disappearance, withholding, or failure of the dependency 'prop' results in the need for adjustments and substitutions which might not be immediately forthcoming or feasible. Vulnerability then worsens. The converse of, although preferably complementary to, external dependency and external reliance is self-support, local systems, and cultural norms for the sharing of needs and ways of addressing those needs.

Changes in resource management and improvements in connections with external supply sources have led to growing dependency on external resources; for instance, for food, building materials, markets for local products, and household goods. In Fiji, increasingly heavy cyclone damage highlighted these shifts in dependency (Campbell, 1984). Whereas up to the 1960s, islanders generally handled their own recovery, with advantages and disadvantages, this was no longer possible from the 1970s onwards, with evident disadvantages. Fijians found themselves desperately short of food. Relief supplies were required in large quantities and over a wider range of needs. Johnston (2015) corroborates, noting that, for Fiji, less relief tended to result in more and better self-reliance.

Dependency theory offers a foregrounding for examining the augmentation of vulnerability among people and places. Is vulnerability integral to human nature, inescapable and the removal of which would remove human nature? Is vulnerability inherent to the human condition? Or is vulnerability manufactured when the choice could be to avoid and alleviate it, so that it is not transferred across space to others and not transferred across time to future generations? Is vulnerability then inherited, forced on people who neither need nor expect nor want it?

As always, it is neither one nor the other. Vulnerabilities are both inherent and inherited. By the very nature of human mortality, we are vulnerable; as Handmer (2003) expresses in the title of his paper, 'We are all vulnerable'. This situation does not justify vulnerability created by others and foisted on unsuspecting populations and locations without scope to oppose or reduce it.

Bankoff and Hilhorst (2022) emphasize this in the title of their book, *Why vulnerability still matters*. It matters because it is inherent and inherited. Denying either is to deny people's experiences of vulnerabilities as part of their usual lives – and to deny that vulnerability can and should be reduced through development, so that disasters do not happen because people and places experience less vulnerability to hazards.

Many vulnerabilities

The vulnerabilities of people and places, and the experiences of those vulnerabilities, are usually manifest in groups and locations that are observed, identified, assessed, and analysed as being more vulnerable or less vulnerable than others. These may be integral to members within a location or group, based on characteristics such as age, education level, or health condition. They may be part of distinctly separate groups identifiable or made identifiable by settlement, ethnicity, religion, race, livelihood, or economic status, for example.

Being concerned particularly with measuring vulnerability in conditions of poverty in Andhra Pradesh, India, Winchester (1992) examines in-depth what he terms 'social vulnerability'. He considers it to arise from experiences of sudden 'shocks' – illness, 'accidents', births, deaths, 'natural disasters', and 'civil disturbances' – all impinging upon already unstable conditions accrued over time. To measure this vulnerability, Winchester (1992) distinguishes between poverty and vulnerability which, he explains, are nevertheless inextricably linked. Vulnerability comes not only from being poor, but also from being powerless to do anything about poverty, both resulting from actions and activities of richer and more powerful groups. The controls exercised by richer people over poorer people in their arrangements for share-cropping, water distribution, and money lending are evident examples of this process of vulnerability accretion in this location (Winchester, 1992). Similar examples abound in various forms around the world (Bankoff and Hilhorst, 2022).

Measuring vulnerability in place and in a place at a time is one part of vulnerability, but far from the complete picture. Another is identifying causes over time and how those causes may be rectified. Measurement must be repetitive when what is being measured is so relentless and so pervasive. Documenting the vulnerability process means documenting the vulnerability experiences and any trends to indicate success in vulnerability reduction (or otherwise). As such, it is not as simple as 'social vulnerability' or as simplistic as 'social vulnerability indices' which have proliferated. Vulnerability and vulnerability experiences have many faces and forms interlaced, inherent, and inherited.

Social vulnerability or societal vulnerability, by definition, would simply be vulnerability, since vulnerability is about people and places. Consequently, political vulnerability, organizational vulnerability, institutional vulnerability, and other vulnerabilities are concatenated to focus on authorities, governments, ministries, for-profit entities, and not-for-profits in tandem.

The rise and fall of these organizations are, at times, influenced by their focus on disaster or by their failure to focus on disaster – and, irrespective of their choice, at times being blamed for disaster or managing to escape blame for disaster. Coups, wars, and assassinations are perhaps the most blatant disasters that make and break leaders, their politics, and their institutions. Other disasters amid the disaster of conflict raise questions of how conflict and other disasters are and are not intertwined, although these experiences of vulnerability are not new.

An early documented example of the political consequences of a storm is Stevenson (1892) describing a cyclone's effect in 1889 on German, American, and British ships assembled in Apia Harbour, now the capital of Samoa. The countries were on the brink of war, all but one ship was wrecked in the storm, and, according to Stevenson (1892), the Treaty of Berlin resulted instead. During World War II, a typhoon in 1944 crippled the United States Pacific Fleet in its support of the planned invasion of the Philippines. Three destroyers sank, 28 other ships were damaged, 146 planes were lost, and 790 military personnel died (Brindze, 1973). The November 1970 cyclone, and the subsequent alleged mismanagement of the disaster, was one of many influences that triggered Bangladesh's War of Independence which commenced in March 1971 (Islam, 1992) and which cemented the stature of many politicians. The earthquake that destroyed much of Managua in 1972 accelerated, in its aftermath of blatant government corruption regarding the disaster aid, the armed uprising against, toppling of, and eventual assassination of Nicaragua's President Anastasio Somoza Debayle (Olson and Gawronski, 2003).

Continent-scale power outages can result from solar storms, terrorism including cyberattacks, interdependent systems in cascading failures from an innocuous and local event, and overuse of electricity. These failures impinge immediately upon everyone who has become unavoidably dependent upon reliable electricity. We all experience the vulnerabilities, knowing that we would not be able to complete purchases with credit or debit cards, obtain cash from an automated teller machine (ATM), pump fuel into vehicles or generators, or communicate with anyone remotely. Those few generating their own electricity through household renewable energy, along with a satellite phone and satellite internet, would be slightly better off. In the meantime, ships would be trying to dock, aeroplanes would be trying to land, and emergency medical care would be trying to continue on the basis of emergency back-ups and contingency plans with limited operational timespans.

Consequences of power outage scenarios exemplify what is termed 'economic vulnerability', really just a subset of societal vulnerability, as are all other vulnerabilities, since an economy cannot exist without a society. Many countries prone to tropical cyclones rely on fragile monocrops such as bananas or sugar cane, with little contingency for when a storm or drought wrecks the plants. Quality land once given to food crops for local consumption, supporting local self-sufficiency and local knowledges, have been forced into large-scale production for export. As the world's tastes change, so do the exports, yet maintaining the same vulnerabilities. It remains an open question if the next wave of cash crops will be to grow biofuels to replace fossil fuels.

Aside from these human foibles, ecosystems are vulnerable in themselves and vulnerable ecosystems have implications for the vulnerability of people and places. Populations being made vulnerable impose their own ecosystem damage, on occasion explored through environmental vulnerability indices. Sometimes trees felled by a windstorm or scorched in a vegetation fire contribute to the ecosystem's renewal, reducing its vulnerability. At other times, especially when human actions have changed the species or the hazard, soils are exposed to erosion, so the next rains sluice off mud directly into people's homes. Vegetation and soil loss, with animals then moving elsewhere, may deprive a community of food or livelihoods. Use of firewood demanded by lack of alternatives may exacerbate aridification, desertification, and over-intensive land use to create conditions conducive to soil erosion. People pushed off their own land by large-scale agricultural or mining interests then slash-and-burn forests to eke out a meagre existence and overexploit the soil, compelling them to cut deeper into the jungle.

Ecosystems themselves are never static. The creation by the sea, suddenly or over time, of natural embankments, may create a new coastal ecosystem. In Tuvalu (see also Chapter 6, 'Sea-level rise and atolls'), Cyclone Bebe in 1972 caused a massive upsurge of coral debris to form a 19-kilometre embankment on Funafuti atoll (and others on other atolls) which increased the island land mass by one-fifth (Baines and McLean, 1976b). The long-term behaviour of the embankment in front of Chiswell, UK impacts many vulnerabilities (Chapter 6, 'Vulnerability in Chiswell, Dorset, UK'). Tsunamis have snapped corals in reefs and swept away coastal vegetation. Volcanic ash and pyroclastic density currents (swift, hot clouds of ash and dust) can blanket green in grey. Flash floods, mudflows, and slides dump uprooted upland vegetation and freshwater into the tidal zone. The ecosystems change, experiencing nature's vulnerability as part of nature's processes. Sometimes these hazards and their impacts are shaped by human activities, from cutting a road through an unstable slope or forest through to channelling rivers, and sometimes not.

All these vulnerabilities, with their various names, impinge upon people and places while the people and places impinge upon the vulnerabilities. They are all connected and are often the same, making the experience of many vulnerabilities.

Surviving many vulnerabilities

Without survival, the restoration of wellbeing, and the overcoming of vulner-abilities, post-disaster recovery and improvement are difficult to achieve. Only some aspects of the pervasive condition and process of vulnerability are disaster-specific. Vulnerability to one difficulty or natural hazard is largely vulnerability to another, while basic needs remain the same.

Basic needs for human survival and its continuation and thriving include breathable air, potable water, nutritious food, medical care for physical and mental health and wellbeing, hygiene, sanitation, shelter, warmth or cooling, and preferably livelihood opportunities, cooking facilities, environmental health, social support such as education, communication means, social networks, and information. In addition to the primary impact of disasters and the physical damage sustained, the need that ensues for human survival and thriving requires an availability of, and accessibility to, all these basic resources.

Provision for survival and thriving is much the same as provision for vulnerability reduction. Provision for both purposes is common to all natural hazards, implying common development. Vulnerability is not particularly hazard-specific. Neither are basic needs for and interests in surviving and thriving. Development has the responsibility to ensure the necessary availability and accessibility of basic resources. The means and the system for doing so must be established before disaster, because disaster aftermath is too late – except on behalf of those experiencing the next hazards. Prevailing conditions can be changed to avoid the next hazards becoming the next disasters.

Survival and thriving thus relate directly to development. Provision through appropriate development of basic resources, the need for which is so often exposed by disasters, will improve the quality of life and reduce vulnerabilities before, during, and after disasters – also between disasters, with the expectation that such provision will prevent future disasters. Resource accessibility after a disaster, as an expression of self-reliance, reduces dependency upon post-disaster assistance which may or may not be forthcoming. It facilitates local approaches for response, recovery, rehabilitation, and reconstruction, while limiting the extent and duration of the disaster. As such, it reduces disaster impacts and so is vulnerability reduction through development. In the same way that most post-disaster rescues are carried out by local people right at the site, other local measures should not be abandoned or discouraged in the face of the image of massive catastrophe. These local actions aimed at surviving and thriving reduce the massiveness of catastrophe and support thriving.

The assumption that post-disaster assistance supplies the needs for post-disaster survival and thriving after disaster denies the input necessary from development to improve pervasive vulnerability conditions. Humanitarian aid *assumes* the presence of survivors. In doing so, it sidesteps the need to induce and to facilitate survival and thriving in the first place. Post-disaster stages labelled 'emergency', 'relief', 'rehabilitation', 'reconstruction', and 'recovery' among others suggest a fixed sequence of response, both external and internal, to each disaster. The popular preconception of 'relief' and 'aid' is of goods and materials 'flown in' during an 'emergency'. Recovery, rehabilitation, and reconstruction are necessarily local undertakings, even when they have become dependent upon external inputs (Cuny, 1983; Davis, 1978).

Post-disaster work should be an opportunity to improve, namely reducing vulnerability through development. Physical and metaphorical reconstruction in all sectors is the opportunity to reshape human living, livelihoods, lifestyles, and settlements so that survival in future disasters, and preferably fewer disasters irrespective of hazards, in order to thrive, is more assured. Reconstruction of this kind is development. It embraces both the improvement and the strategies for its achievement, so that the conditions and processes of vulnerability are modified, hopefully for the better.

Often, activities which are the reverse of desired development serve to emphasize the value of development for vulnerability reduction. An indicator of the significance of resources and services for survival and thriving is that in many cases of conflict, military objectives include the destruction of food resources, the killing of livestock, the placement of mines in cropland, the poisoning of water sources, the targeting of relief convoys and distribution centres, sieges of or attacks against market centres, and the murder of aid workers. Attacks upon health centres and their personnel, whether taking hostages in hospitals or killing vaccinators, are similarly indicative of the value of these and other infrastructure and services toward the survival, thriving, and development of the populations they serve.

Basic needs development appropriate to vulnerability reduction for survival and thriving, increases overall quality of life. Where conflict is caused or exacerbated by perceived inequalities or inequities among groups or regions, equitable and equal basic needs development for everyone and all places may start or contribute to a process that renders conflict less likely – at least, conflict based in reasons of inequality and inequity. Conflict can still occur for reasons such as ideology, historical hate, and personalities prone to violence.

Cuny (1983: 219) observed that vulnerability reduction 'will have little impact unless it is conducted in concert with normal development activities'. Cuny's approach was essentially post-disaster and focuses upon how humanitarian actions can either impede or assist development objectives. But it is those development objectives which must fully account for hazards and, more to the point, vulnerabilities. By ignoring hazard potential, or by the assumption that development of any kind will reduce vulnerability, disasters could be made to increase and then survival and thriving impeded.

There are numerous cases where 'development' made matters worse. Development is not a utopian panacea to be subscribed to at every opportunity in any form, least of all by the tuning of 'disaster relief' to support development that may be largely negative. Does importing new foods, reinforced by their provision as post-disaster assistance, weaken motivation for the home production of subsistence food crops, and thus increase vulnerability? Does the desire for the appearance of affluence demand rebuilding fallen timber dwellings in masonry, despite the lack of skills in making structures earth-quake-resistant? Not to mention the tropical climate, with masonry trapping heat while timber and traditional design can help with ventilation while limiting insect ingress.

Then, there is risk transference, in which the hazard is altered leading to behavioural change that increases vulnerability, so risk is transferred into the future (Etkin, 1999). Levees are a prime example (Tobin, 1995). People are told that they are now 'protected' from floods and they see the tangible, solid wall, so they stop reducing their vulnerabilities. Eventually, the levees fail and the resulting disaster is far worse than it would have been without the levees due to the increase in vulnerability. Risk was transferred to the future through higher vulnerability.

Vulnerability of populations and places is inevitably discernible, observable, identifiable, assessable, and analysable before, and regardless of, hazards. Actions must be taken to do so. Development can be made to reduce vulnerability by taking on board the prevailing potential of hazards and their contexts. A hazard becoming disastrous to one place, person, or group, may not be so much of a disaster to another. Drought in Antigua with its disastrous effects on sugar cane production (Chapter 6, 'A multi-hazard history of Antigua') would not have been regarded as drought in Cape Verde, subject and accustomed to a much harsher rainfall regime.

Disasters extend situations which are typical. They manifest and express the normality of vulnerability and thus *seem* extreme while, in reality, are the usual expectation of daily life (Hewitt, 1983). The degree to which, for a particular place, person, or group, a hazard becomes a disaster, is set by these prevailing vulnerability conditions. Development should be changing these conditions for the better.

The role of development planning, programming, projects, and implementation should be continuously to:

- Analyse hazardousness as experienced locally.
- Analyse vulnerability and vulnerabilityness, locally and as experienced locally.
- Identify causes and processes, including multi-hazard contexts, that have created or exacerbated vulnerabilities.
- Devise and implement plans, programmes, and projects for equal and equitable vulnerability reduction.
- Recover from, rehabilitate, and reconstruct damage, forced displacement, and disruption.

These measures have to simultaneously incorporate all vulnerabilities, whether labelled as social, societal, political, institutional, organizational, ecological, environmental, economic, financial, monetary, physical, or otherwise. Physical measures such as shelters, embankments, and infrastructure planning, design, construction, and maintenance must be regarded as components, but not as a programme's entirety. They are enfolded within social measures highlighting access to resources and political power; options and opportunities for self-help without harming others; involving everyone, their skills, and their knowledges; and regular communication and exchange, including for warnings, education, training, practising, testing, and much more.

So much 'development' in response to disasters serves a simplistic objective of rebuilding to the way it was before – returning to 'normal'. The way it was before was a 'normal' kaleidoscope of vulnerabilities. This context of vulnerability caused the disaster. Lives and locations of poverty, destitution, and oppression do not change by rebuilding back to them. In addition to saving lives, livelihoods must also be supported and the quality of life and lifestyles improved. Then, it becomes possible to enable people and places to better survive and to recover without external assistance, so disasters are reduced; that is, thriving.

CHAPTER 5
Making vulnerability
Disaster risk creation

Vulnerability can be created inadvertently and deliberately by development and lack thereof. The specific processes tend to be long-term, complicated, and connected to widespread decisions. Government inspectors for construction are underpaid and subject to arbitrary firings by a minister's friend who is a senior civil servant, so the inspectors support their family by taking bribes to sign off on unpermitted or uninspected buildings. The US Government's desire to avoid what it perceives as enemies taking charge of various countries around North America and South America leads to a brutal dictator forcibly displacing people who then degrade the environment to live. Expectations for men's and women's societal roles are established clearly and inflexibly for boys and girls, so men/boys and women/girls end up in different situations during hazards rather than working together for everyone's survival and thriving.

Vulnerability is thus made and disaster risks are thus created. It is unsurprising that, when a hazard appears, the unpermitted or uninspected buildings collapse, the forcibly displaced people feel the wrath of their degraded environment, and death rates differ between men/boys and women/girls. This is disaster – a disaster created through development processes feeding vulnerabilities.

Comprehensiveness in such analysis is impossible. Instead, specific examples tell the stories, interfolding all the pernicious contributions to the making of the vulnerability process and the creation of disaster risk.

Corruption and siphoning

Corruption is commonly taken to be 'the abuse of entrusted power for private gain' (Transparency International, 2023) with much more theoretical depth evolving (Pozsgai-Alvarez, 2020). It hurts everyone whose life, livelihood, and lifestyle depend on the integrity of people in positions of entrusted authority. The offering of bribes is seen to be as wrong as the taking of bribes. Even though corruption is commonly articulated as something that happens elsewhere and is done by other people, corruption to some degree effectively pervades all authorities, governments, organizations, and institutions. It is so prevalent as to be normalized and expected, usually passed off as, 'Hasn't there always been corruption?', 'Isn't that the usual way of doing things?', or 'Isn't it the oil that makes society work?'

The legacy of corrupt practices is an overall increase in vulnerability, creation of disaster risk, and stymieing of development. The damage it does to everyone and everywhere ought to be recognized, especially in inhibiting so much of development and vulnerability reduction.

One direct and highly visible implication is building construction in seismic zones. Corrupt practice perverts the execution of safe construction. When finance is siphoned off at its source, this further denies the opportunity to build and properly maintain – or reduces the amount and the quality while increasing the cost of – new and retrofitted infrastructure. This construction bad practice, by its very nature, covers up the evidence as finishing touches are put on buildings. It may not be revealed except by an earthquake many years after the developers, builders, and original owners have moved on.

As the maxim goes, earthquakes don't kill people, because collapsing buildings do. Or, preferably, the main cause of casualties in earthquakes is corruption. Beyond the deaths, injuries, and disruption, society pays for the clean-up and reconstruction. Even though construction is recognized as one of the most corrupt industries worldwide, corruption pervades most sectors. Other examples are stealing food and water aid to sell at a market, and backhanders to permit illegal logging which strips people of their livelihoods and strips slopes of vegetation that might lessen flood or slide impacts.

Money and materials siphoned off not only remove resources from the goods and services being offered, but also remove contributions from the tax system which funds public services, such as health, education, and transport. When basic services are not provided and when fewer resources are available to make people safe, the vulnerability process is evident.

Environmental degradation and forced displacement

Algeria, as with most places, has a detailed modern history of population movement. Before the Algerian War of Independence (1954–62), traditional rural economies had been seriously disrupted by the expropriation of fertile land in favour of the French *colons* (colonizers), paralleled by rapid growth in the local population. During the Algerian War of Independence, France instituted a policy of *regroupement* (Sutton, 1969; Sutton and Lawless, 1978). As part of a campaign against guerrilla groups, forced removal of rural populations, upon which the guerrillas relied for support, was initiated. Extensive *zones interdites* (prohibited areas) were created and forbidden to Algerians, who were shot on sight within them. At least 2 million people were 'regrouped' in this way with long-lasting consequences. Many never returned to their former homes, which were often destroyed by French troops. At first, no facilities for rehousing were provided for the expelled people, and serious overcrowding resulted in existing villages outside the zones. When *centres de regroupement* were eventually established, they were inadequate. The Sersou-Ouarsenis border region is described as having been subjected to particularly severe military operations involving *regroupement*.

Forests had been a resource for the rural population in Algeria, but many were destroyed by heavy napalm attack. Replanting was conducted with strict conservation controls. An important component of the traditional rural economy was thus removed or remained inaccessible.

At independence in 1962, traditional economic and social structures, as well as actual settlements, had been seriously eroded. At the same time, 90 per cent of almost 1 million *colons* left for France, and about 200,000 émigrés (emigrants) returned to Algeria from Tunisia and Morocco.

These factors swelled cities. Algeria's urban population grew by nearly 7 per cent between 1954 and 1966. The population of Algiers almost doubled during that time, and lesser towns and cities similarly increased (Descloitres et al., 1973). *Wilaya* is equivalent to a French *departement*, subdivided into *daira*, composed of *communes* incorporating village localities. Reconstruction after the 1954 earthquake ensured the inclusion of El Asnam (now called Chlef) among Algeria's urban population growth, which reached 105,000 in the *daira* by 1966, and increased to 156,000 by 1977, 11 per cent greater than the population increase of the *wilaya* as a whole (ONRS, 1980).

After 1971, there was a programme of 'agrarian revolution' in Algeria (Sutton, 1978), involving the redistribution of land formerly expropriated by the French, and the creation of agricultural co-operatives. Redistributed land was often a considerable distance from the beneficiaries' homes, involving planned movement into new villages. Reflecting its agricultural importance, by 1976 eight of these villages were established in El Asnam *wilaya*, compared to an average per *wilaya* of less than four.

Population relocation and migration caused a fragile social context in which the 1980 El Asnam earthquake brought about further dislocation. In January 1981, on the periphery of the military controlled damage-zone of El Asnam city, large numbers of people had quickly established marketing activities. Expectations of employment in reconstruction served as an attraction to easily unsettled, underemployed rural people. Tented villages for people from the city made homeless by the earthquake were also on the periphery of the city area. Crowded, cold, wet, and muddy living conditions – to some extent serviced with food, water, electricity, and clinics – created conditions in the post-earthquake *villages de toile* (tent or canvas villages) which could have been perceived as better than some 'normal', rural living conditions, and certainly better than had been possible at that time for rural earthquake survivors. In all, the earthquake itself and these post-earthquake conditions, created a pole of attraction at El Asnam, as well as having triggered possibly permanent migration to other urban centres.

Jeffery (1981) examined the long-term history of vulnerability accretion in Martinique and the Dominican Republic. In Martinique, a greater vulnerability to tropical cyclones and storms began for the local population after French colonists defeated the Carib people in 1635 and drove them to the Atlantic side of the island. Mid-17th-century maps show a formal division of the island with a *terre des Français* to the west and a *terre des sauvages* to the east. Later, all Carib people were removed from the island and enslaved people were imported to replace them. Greater vulnerability to storms persists in eastern Martinique for certain low-status groups.

The Dominican Republic occupies the eastern two-thirds of the island of Hispaniola. Haiti occupies the western third. Changes that increased the vulnerability of many rural populations occurred during the era of President Rafael Leónidas Trujillo Molina, who exercised near-complete and personal control over the country from 1930 until his assassination in 1961.

Much of Monte Plata in the Province of San Cristóbal is low-lying and experiences severe flooding in hurricanes. In the aftermath of Hurricane David in 1979, Monte Plata was selected for study because it was *not* the worst-affected locale. Elsewhere, indicators of differential vulnerability may have been obliterated. The causes of Monte Plata's flooding were not a simple matter of topography and rainfall, since deforestation occurred during the decades before Hurricane David to clear land for the mono-cultivation of sugar cane. Although sugar companies had been active in the Dominican Republic throughout much of the 20th century, widespread land clearance did not take place until the 1940s and 1950s during the Trujillo era.

La Caguaza in the Dominican Republic sits in the low-lying flood-prone areas next to the Ozama River. Mainly small-scale cultivators had lived there, with production focused on subsistence crops combined with cocoa, coffee, and bananas, alongside the raising of pigs and cattle. In 1957, Trujillo sent in bulldozers without warning and all existing crops were destroyed, together with extensive woodland. More than half of the 22 households were dispossessed and obliged to leave. No compensation was paid, although the land was said to have belonged to those who farmed it.

This area, and others like it, became treeless and sown mostly with government-owned sugar cane. The river banks, now unreinforced by tree roots, became more prone to recurrent erosion and were consequently much lower than they were before deforestation. As a result, the rivers flooded beyond their banks more frequently and not only as the result of rainfall from hurricanes.

In these circumstances, it is unsurprising that the people are not self-sufficient in food and endure regular flood-related damage. Although some land was returned after Trujillo's death, the best land was retained for sugar cane. Some land used for food crops was prone to flooding, leading to regular harvest losses and therefore was deemed to be unsuitable for sugar cane. Basic food supplies were brought in from outside, so people depended on external sources for food, which can also be unreliable.

This is the marginalization process creating vulnerability. First, the land was taken away from diversified farming; then it was deforested, increasing proneness to erosion; which in turn increased flooding frequency; thereby augmenting damage to food crops grown since the land became available again; and leading to the people depending on outside food sources and so not being self-reliant for food.

Parallel increases in vulnerability were seen among the people who did not return to the land by the riverside. Land prices rose due to interest in sugar cane while food prices rose due to less land to grow local food. Some people settled on previously uncultivated hillsides. To feed themselves, they over-farmed the slopes, leading to erosion and degradation of the soil as well as silting of the river beds. Not returning to their original land after Trujillo's assassination, they responded to the unstable governance by intensifying food production. There was more deforestation, land clearance, and hillside occupation, feeding into the creation of vulnerability. Others moved to urban areas in search of work.

In the country's capital, Santo Domingo, two principal areas of informal settlements expanded. One on low-lying land along the Ozama River downstream from La Caguaza and the other on steep ravines on the northern edge of the city. During storms, these settlements ought to be evacuated to avoid casualties. In 1980, as torrential rains threatened to wash houses into the gullies, one government administration worked with the people for preparedness and evacuation – as per its mandate. There was little under-standing as to why people were living in those places and how their situation might be improved after the waters had receded. Dealing with a hurricane, for the government at the time, was not part of development that might recognize the causes of the growth of migration to these places. Nor did the government administration have the powers and resources to do anything about it by way of relocation, rehousing, and supporting livelihoods that could become self-sufficient.

This vignette mirrors similar informal settlements adjacent to and within cities around the world – on and in ravines, on steep slopes, and in sometimes-dry river beds. All are known to be highly vulnerable. To address this vulnerability, the reasons for their occupation and the lack of other alternatives must be known and understood. These reasons typically relate to poor development. With this understanding, any need for humanitarian assistance could be part of a wider programme of development to prevent the need for future humanitarian assistance.

Forced societal roles and norms

On 26 December 2004, a massive and shallow earthquake off the coast of Indonesia led to a tsunami racing across the Indian Ocean, with deaths ultimately totalling around 250,000. In some settlements, four-fifths of tsunami-related fatalities were women.

In Aceh, Indonesia many women died because they were waiting by the coast for their husbands to return with the morning's fishing catch. The wave had limited impact on the fishing boats at sea, but swept away people and structures when it slammed into the shoreline and tore inland. Few people who bore the brunt of the wave could have survived, irrespective of their demographic characteristics. The high rate of women dying compared to men dying was due to forced societal roles: men as fishers and women helping to bring the catch ashore. The difference in death rates was not due to women and girls being inherently more vulnerable or inherently less capable of dealing with a tsunami than men and boys.

Had the tsunami struck earlier, just when the men were at the coast, about to head out to sea, then perhaps more men than women would have died. Had the tsunami hit later, just when the fish were being offloaded at the coast, then the men–women death rates might have been more equal. These death rates result from differentiated societal roles, reflecting deeper and wider concerns of unresolved disaster vulnerabilities. They say little about the comparative abilities and capabilities of men and women to deal with hazards and vulnerabilities.

Analogously, during inland floods around the USA, the typical pattern is that more men than women perish. One reason is the high proportion of rescuers, trained and untrained, who die in US inland floods while attempting to help others. Men far outnumber women among these would-be rescuers. Following the traditional, sexist adage of 'women and children first' as a ship sinks, men might be driven by societal expectations of sacrificing themselves for women or it might be sheer machoism – or, more likely, a combination with the two reinforcing each other. The actions of firefighters and other trained rescuers, though, can be dominated by doing their job to the best of their ability which, even when properly trained and equipped, means putting their lives at risk for others. The high rate of men dying compared to women is due to forced societal roles and expectations, not due to men and boys being inherently more vulnerable or inherently less capable of dealing with inland floods than women and girls.

What is the contribution of development for vulnerability reduction in the context of the construction of these roles, expectations, and norms? Straightforwardly and generally, the answer is education, equity, and equality. These processes can hone in on specific aspects.

In the USA, many flash flood fatalities occur in vehicles, when people drive through floodwater or are not able to drive away fast enough as the water rises. More data are needed on influencers including drugs, alcohol, drivers being goaded by their passengers to show their prowess by taking on a rising river, and drivers desperate to pick up family members on the other side of the floodwater, notably children at school. The USA has pioneered and promoted the 'Turn around, don't drown' message. Who is not reached by it?

For other hazards, men are expected in many places to stay behind to protect their home or livestock as a vegetation fire or storm surge approaches. Everyone might be fully aware of the hazard and its possible consequences. Development processes have not given adequate opportunities for damage reduction, evacuation, sheltering, and rebuilding. The best option for preserving reputation, livelihood, and possessions is to face the hazard head-on, with society often presuming it to be a man's job.

Development must address such sexism and much more. Where women and girls must have an accompanying man to be out in public; are expected to wear clothes making fast walking or swimming difficult; would be ostracized for removing their clothes; or are the sole carers for young and old family members, then evacuation and sheltering are inhibited. As they are where menstruation is stigmatized; where it is known that places of evacuation lack proper hygiene; and where men want to take on more caring roles, but it is discouraged by societal norms. Anyone might hesitate to evacuate and go to common shelters where they fear assault, violence, or other crimes, including looting of their empty property. Where men and women are agricultural workers, men will usually drink more water than women in heatwaves, so women suffer heat-related consequences more than men. The reason is not that women understand heat less than men, but that it is more accepted for men than for women to urinate outdoors.

Even where individuals know exactly what they should do to survive in a hazard, they are frequently hindered by society, with roots leading back to poor development. Vulnerabilities are made and disaster risk is created.

Conflicts and violences

Another maker of vulnerabilities is conflicts and violences. Damage to infrastructure, from bombs and bullets, makes it less suitable to withstand other hazards. Sporadic communications stop warnings reaching people. Education, health, and social services are disrupted and their buildings may be targeted. Evacuation routes or daily paths to school, fields, and markets may be mined, blocked by checkpoints guarded by drugged-up children with guns, or at the mercy of coherent adult combatants merely expecting a toll or sexual favours. Police, paramilitaries, and uniformed soldiers are not necessarily any better than organized or unorganized guerrillas or mercenaries. All such processes retrogress development and enhance vulnerabilities (Peters, 2022).

As an example, intermittent warfare between Mursi and Bodi in south-western Ethiopia created a context of regular and expected external attacks. Measures taken to ensure the physical survival of people and cattle served to make the economy of the Mursi more vulnerable to climate variabilities (Turton, 1992). Cattle had been a form of insurance against crop failure, since meat could be eaten when there is nothing else. Cattle were the targets of neighbouring Bodi, so cattle raids resulted in the killing of Mursi. The raids were more successful when herds and herders were dispersed as a result of water shortage and grazing due to drought, illustrating the close and intricate relationship of war and vulnerability.

The actual raids and measures to cope with the threat of raids displayed a long-term effect on Mursi wellbeing and consequently increased vulnerability. The withdrawal of cattle from the best grazing, and their concentration into more easily protected herds, brought greater risks of the consequences of water shortage and was more environmentally damaging. The concentration of herds adjacent to settlements created conditions for trampling food crops, while the threat of attack reduced agricultural productivity.

Warfare here was seen as a means of securing the resources of others, of adjusting populations to resource scarcity, and of establishing and maintaining separate political identities of neighbouring groups. Warfare becomes a cause, not a consequence, of political identity. For the Mursi, choice did not exist between physical and political survival. The only way they knew of saving lives was to save their way of life.

It is not just war, declared or undeclared, or chronic modes of immediate physical threat such as terrorism, gangs, and extortion. Violences also take on modes delineating vulnerability, lack of development, and chronic disaster. 'Quiet violence' refers to the incessant imposition of exploitation, poverty, and hunger (Hartmann and Boyce, 1983). In parallel, Watts (1983) evidences 'silent violence' as the social cause of famines, irrespective of environmental inputs into droughts (see also Devereux, 1994; Sen, 1981). The adverse consequences of environmental destruction, including pollution, on people with few options to help themselves and the environment around them is termed 'slow violence' (Nixon, 2011).

Long-term impacts of conflicts and violences are illustrated by the harbour and town of Rabaul on the island of New Britain (epitomizing the prevalence of colonialist names), Papua New Guinea. The harbour sits within a volcanic caldera into which the sea has entered at one side. In this caldera, the town of Rabaul is surrounded by other volcanoes: The Mother, South Daughter, North Daughter, Vulcan, and (adjacent to Rabaul) Matupi. Vulcan was an island formed by a volcanic eruption in 1878. In 1937, Vulcan exploded, reshaping the island as a cone and joining it to the New Britain mainland. Matupi erupted at the same time, smothering Rabaul and its harbour with ash. Around 500 people were killed and the entire town was evacuated.

The Bismarck Archipelago, extending from New Britain, was claimed as a protectorate by Germany in 1884. Rabaul was established in 1910 as the headquarters of the administration of German New Guinea. Taken by an Australian force in 1914 at the start of World War I, it was later administered by Australia under a mandate from the League of Nations as the Mandated Territory of New Guinea. In 1939, as a result of the 1937 eruptions, the administration relocated to Lae on the northern mainland coast. During World War II, Rabaul was captured by Japanese forces in January 1942, after which the town was destroyed by Allied bombardment.

After World War II, Australian administration established the capital at Port Moresby along the southern coast in former Papua. Due to commercial pressure favouring the deep port, the northern administration relocated from Lae back to Rabaul, which has since been entirely redeveloped. Papua New Guinea became self-governing in December 1973 and independent in September 1975.

In 1937, the population of Rabaul was around 5,000; now, it is pushing 40,000. The deep harbour, formed by the tectonic activity which is a source of hazard, was favoured for strategic advantage by both commercial and military interests, bringing prosperity. The historical conflicts shaped the town's waxing and waning fortunes and violence remains layered on natural hazard today.

In 1994, volcanic eruptions destroyed much of Rabaul, but preparedness and evacuation limited the death toll to five people. Rebuilding and living continued under the shadow of active volcanism until another major eruption 20 years later. Ash and sulphur became part of daily life – as is the standard violence around the country. Although Rabaul is currently considered relatively safe compared to the rest of Papua New Guinea, standard warnings apply about armed robbery, unrest, piracy, and unexploded ordnance, making it difficult to pursue successful development including analysing and reducing underlying vulnerabilities. Violence and volcano hazards mingle, slowing development and maintaining vulnerability.

Disasters creating vulnerability

Casualties, damage, and disruption from one disaster can render affected people and places more vulnerable to recurrence of disaster, by the same or different hazards. Response after one kind of disaster can similarly add to, perpetuate, or create vulnerability.

Fire was once the recurrent and prevailing hazard in St. John's, Antigua (Chapter 6, 'A multi-hazard history of Antigua'), where buildings were constructed of timber with shingle roofs. As a result, those who could afford to adopt masonry construction did so for stores, churches, and private dwellings. In the 1843 earthquake, the masonry buildings suffered most, since the flexible timber buildings were more resistant to damage by seismic movement. Moreover, the earthquake particularly affected St. John's' new self-built settlements of recently emancipated enslaved people who had limited resources at emancipation and limited time since then. The colonial government in London provided loans for post-earthquake reconstruction. Only after those loans were repaid, in 1868, could construction start of a reservoir to provide drinking water in times of drought (Lewis, 1984b).

Moreover, the lessons of Cape Verde ought to be heeded. Small dams and water conduits constructed in response to perpetual drought are heavily damaged in earthquakes.

Leaving a disaster-struck location can beget another disaster. Thousands of Haitians currently live without documents in Bahamas, seeking better jobs than they can find at home. This migration is not new, as Haitians have fled the violence and oppression that has marred their country since its 1804 independence. Post-independence violence was exacted by the ex-colonial power France in the name of reparations which Haiti finally paid off in 1947. All this time, and afterwards, the USA imposed its own neo-colonial violences, extracting wealth from Haiti while supporting brutal dictators. No wonder Haitians are desperate to leave for conditions which are slightly better, sometimes fuelled by further disasters in Haiti, such as four major storms in 2008 and the 2010 earthquake.

Informal settlements of Haitians in Bahamas are prone to fire from illegal electricity connections and are perpetually threatened by eviction by the Bahamian Government. They can be among the worst-hit places during other hazards, as happened during Hurricane Dorian in 2019. Not that Haitians would necessarily have been better off at home, through 2016's Hurricane Matthew, 2019's flare-up of political violence, the 2020–23 COVID-19 pandemic, and 2021's earthquake – in parallel with the ever-present gang- and state-based violence.

Development in Haiti to build infrastructure and a society better able to withstand earthquakes, storms, and microbial pathogens, among other hazards, or to institute warning systems and education for these hazards, is merely a small part of what is needed. Relying on these measures can be a dangerously incomplete 'solution' which will suggest a non-existent safety. The interrelationships among all damaging hazards, including between suddenly appearing and chronic hazards, are as significant to the assessment and analysis of vulnerability as the nature and likelihood of each specific hazard. Vulnerability is a morphological, cumulative, and collective process, caused by disasters as much as causing them.

Cyclone Isaac in March 1982 destroyed 22 per cent of housing throughout the Tongan archipelago (see also Chapter 6, 'Vulnerability in Tonga'). In spite of a rehousing programme, months later more than half of those made homeless had not participated, being unable to afford their contribution of a quarter of the cost of a dwelling. Only at this stage was a major long-term housing problem evident, unsolvable by established practice; and only at this stage had the problem become locally recognizable and a significant concern. Accurate information on numbers of houses destroyed and numbers of families accepted for the rehousing programme was only then becoming available, prepared at the request of an external consultant (Lewis, 1983b). The policy of requiring financial participation by the homeless in the reconstruction programme, though perhaps reasonable from certain points of view, caused many who could not afford to participate to be the most vulnerable to subsequent cyclones.

The same post-cyclone work in Tonga (Lewis, 1983b; see also Chapter 6, 'Vulnerability in Tonga') coincided with a period of severe water shortage which affected the entire country, but which was most severe in the islands of the Ha'apai sub-group. Food crops, replanted in the aftermath of Cyclone Isaac, were severely depleted due to drought. Fishing, the traditional standby when other food is in short supply, was impeded because boats and equipment had been destroyed or lost in the cyclone. In June 1983, fishing boats were still urgently needed to help people survive through the drought. Coconut consumption greatly increased for their liquid and nutrients, affecting the economics of copra production. To solve the vulnerability evident across multiple hazards, freshwater supplies, food, housing/shelter, and livelihoods must all factor into development, rather than addressing a subset.

External and internal factors make vulnerability, create disaster risk, form disasters, and then repeat the pattern for the next disaster, in the absence of adequate action, notably on development. These factors emanate from any degree and combination of greed, misuse of power, mismanagement, discrimination, apathy, oppression, marginalization, incompetence, and minoritization, among other behaviours. Tackling disaster risk creation, instead of simply seeking disaster risk reduction and/or disaster risk management, requires detailed investigation into these contemporary and historical realities of the causes and processes of vulnerabilities. Then, informed development would address the wide contexts that foment and perpetuate vulnerability. Disasters inadequately addressed can and do perpetuate the vulnerabilities that set the stage for the next disaster. Many are explored in the detailed examples of Part two.

PART TWO

Vulnerability and development

CHAPTER 6
Detailed examples

With the exception of the section, 'Sea-level rise and atolls', below, which has substantial additions to and edits from the original text, the detailed examples here are presented close to as they were in this book's first edition. The rationale for providing them here with only limited editing is that they represent an important picture of the examples as researched and expressed at the time – as per the first edition's Preface, 'a product of those times'. Population numbers, ministry names, currency values, and some other contemporaneous aspects have been left unchanged. The writing has been copy-edited, some text has been removed, a small amount of restructuring has been completed, measurements have been changed from imperial to metric units, and some limited updates have been inserted regarding recent publications and ideas in order to edit to some extent – but not entirely – the external and colonial gaze conveyed on occasion in the first edition.

As such, many aspects in this chapter remain dated, not least so due to major social and environmental changes since this book's first edition. As examples:

- All of Barbuda was severely affected by Hurricane Irma in 2017 followed by inadequate reconstruction led by Antigua.
- The COVID-19 pandemic from 2020 to 2023 affected all countries.
- Tonga was devastated by a volcanic eruption and tsunami in January 2022.

As important are changes in how we view science and different knowledge types as well as how we conduct research in other locations (RADIX, 2024).

Even if each example had been thoroughly updated, especially accounting for all the material published about each location since this book's first edition, it would not mean that this chapter would be up to date. At the time of finalizing this manuscript, the Caribbean had just started hurricane season, so Antigua and Barbuda could be pummelled by a major storm – or razed by a major earthquake. Anything could happen anywhere between finalizing a book's text and its publication – and after publication.

In any case, 'accounting for all the material published about each location since this book's first edition' is in itself a mammoth, effectively insurmountable, task. Doing so would make each example a book far, far longer than this one! As with any dissemination, from a PhD dissertation to a social media post, material and citations offered are inescapably a small subset of what is available and what could be provided. The examples as presented in the book's first edition and here are no less so.

And that is what this chapter provides: the examples more or less as they were, still forming a subset of the material, understandings, and analyses available at the time. They remain, as with any publication, to be critiqued given their evident limitations. As work continues by readers here and others, the examples in this chapter provide a comparison from history with the time at which new work is completed, lending themselves to powerful, longitudinal analyses. The reader is encouraged to repeat the work detailed in these examples, as closely as possible to the original, in order to further understand the past, present, and future. Changes in the processes of scientific thinking, acting, and publishing must also be accounted for in such work (RADIX, 2024). These comparisons would indicate how much and how little change occurs in development for vulnerability reduction.

Sea-level rise and atolls

Human-caused climate change and its myriad of impacts, including on atolls, are unambiguous (IPCC, 2021–2022). Key, known changes to the oceans are various inputs into rising sea levels, increasingly acidic ocean water (ocean acidification), and augmented sea surface temperatures. These changes affect coastal biology, ecology, geology, chemistry, and physics, leading to drastic changes for the islands including their seas, the people living there, and the infrastructure. A key example is if corals experience significant death rates without recovery, then many atolls currently shielded by hard coral reefs could be exposed to the full force of ocean waves and currents.

Despite the detailed science on all these aspects (IPCC, 2021–2022), as well as a plethora of books published specifically about the impacts on atolls and other islands (for instance, Klöck and Fink, 2019), major uncertainties and unknowns remain. Considering Tuvalu, the latest *in situ* assessment (Kench et al., 2018) evidences increasing land area across the archipelago due to sea-level rise from human-caused climate change. Whether or not this increase will continue in coming years and decades as ocean changes accelerate remain to be seen. Similarly, coral reefs have survived huge environmental changes over tens of millions of years demonstrating their robustness (Stolarski et al., 2011). This situation does not guarantee coral survival over the next decade or next century.

The value of retaining this subsection in this book could thus be questioned, given the extent of new knowledge on the topic since this book's first edition as well as the rapid rate of new knowledge generation. The key, as with the other examples, is how much has been forgotten of the foundations and history of sea-level rise and atolls.

Scientific work on sea-level rise and low-lying islands emerged into prominence in the 1980s (for example, Lewis, 1988; Nunn, 1988) culminating in the Small States Conference on Sea Level Rise held from 14 to 18 November 1989 in Malé, the Maldives. Available documentation from this meeting, including the 'Malé Declaration on Global Warming and Sea Level Rise', is collected on the Island Vulnerability (2024) website.

At that time, Tuvalu particularly stood out with regards to this topic. The material here represents Tuvalu at the time, including population numbers, island characteristics, and political circumstances of that era – with occasional updates.

Tuvalu comprises a chain of nine atolls, all but two of which surround a lagoon. Only one island encloses its lagoon entirely, the majority being made up of various pieces of land (*motu*) surrounding their lagoon and each separate from the other as the atoll rim dips below sea level and reappears, in many places not much wider than single-track width. One island has no lagoon, but a swamp at its centre. Distances across the islands' lagoons are 15–18 kilometres and distances between each island complex are 125–150 kilometres.

The entire atoll chain extends over 700 kilometres of ocean, with a total national land area of 24 square kilometres divided among nine atolls, and subdivided again many times within atolls. The largest single island is 5 square kilometres in area. The country's highest point is listed as 4.6–5.0 metres above mean sea level and most land areas are appreciably lower.

The population of Tuvalu is 8,500, 2,700 of whom live on the principal atoll and capital of Funafuti at a density of 1,150 people per square kilometre. National population density per square kilometre is 354. An economy, of which the dominant export income is from copra (AU$35,000 in 1986), is stabilized by the Tuvalu Trust Fund (Australia, New Zealand, the United Kingdom, Japan, Korea, and Tuvalu), income from the sale of postage stamps (another export), and remittances from Tuvaluans overseas.

Considering the question of whether or not most of Tuvalu will be inundated by the end of the 21st century due to human-caused climate change, uncertainty prevails and will prevail for much of this time period. One point of view suggests that, with a sea already rising and otherwise changing around these islands, continued investment in the development of the country is now doomed, has no usefulness, and will induce people to stay in an increasingly hazardous environment. Another point of view stresses the uncertainty and the decades over which that uncertainty could be prolonged. The realism of evacuating islands, including Pacific precedents (Nunn et al., 2007), proffers situations in which many islanders have preferred defiant and hazardous isolation rather than the unknowns of relocation (Chapter 6, 'Volcano in Tonga'). Tuvaluan experience of the sea and its hazards provides a local knowledge basis upon which to possibly adjust over time, perhaps even toward amphibious living. The imagery of possible ultimate catastrophe should not preclude seemingly minor measures now to improve current conditions, even if complete evacuation ends up being the ultimate, long-term outcome.

The effects of a rising sea level are not new to Tuvalu. Construction of the Funafuti airstrip by American military forces in World War II destroyed the 'lens' of freshwater in the coral rock substrata. Ancient pits filled with vegetal mulch for the growing of root crops (*pulaka*; swamp taro) in otherwise infertile coral sand were the first to show the effects of consequent salination that has been worsening since and which a rise in sea level exacerbates. Efforts to introduce sweet potatoes, grown hydroponically in mounds of sand at ground level, introduce alternative root crops which, for the time being, are less vulnerable to rising sea water and salination.

Sea water flooding is not a new phenomenon for Tuvalu. At the twice-yearly high tides of February and September, parts of densely populated Funafuti atoll are flooded to depths of more than half a metre. Traditional house forms provided a floor level a metre off the ground, as is appropriate for living on land prone to flooding. New house styles from outside of the Pacific introduced concrete floors at ground level and displaced apparently 'outmoded' traditional forms. New building codes have reintroduced floors raised significantly above ground level.

These 'innovations' in food production and house building are thus considering local and locally known hazards. Similarly, construction to prevent coastal erosion was implemented, not on account of a rising sea, but due to a typical ocean. Sea-level rise from climate change, at its beginnings, does not present sets of hitherto unknown conditions, but rather intermittent exacerbation of known hazards. They might be more frequent and more intense, but with periods of typical conditions in between.

Funafuti Atoll was overwhelmed in 1972 by the 15-metre waves of Cyclone Bebe riding on an exceptionally high spring tide and accompanied by winds of up to 277 kilometres per hour (Ball, 1973). Nearly all the 125 village houses were destroyed and government buildings were damaged beyond repair. Five people died and 700 were made homeless. Crops were annihilated and copra production fell by 80 per cent. This storm surge created a coral rubble wall with an average height of 3.5 metres that extended 18–19 kilometres, being larger than some of the pre-storm islands of the atoll (Baines and McLean, 1976a; Maragos et al., 1973).

Vulnerability to hazards of this and lesser kind require people and places able to cope and an infrastructure able to support them in coping. The condition of both people and place before catastrophe is significant as an enabler of actions afterwards. Provision of freshwater for drinking, cooking, and hygiene; the removal of breeding places for mosquitoes and other vectors; and waste disposal and general attention to environmental health are all factors of quality of life that must be continued after any kind of hazard, to lessen the impacts of disaster.

On Funafuti Atoll, the population increased by about three times during reconstruction after the 1972 cyclone and, in following years, in anticipation of national independence in 1978. With a baseline of conditions of overcrowding, environmental degradation, and consequent environmental health hazards, where does vulnerability commence? Is it founded in human choices (internal and external) for a country, in human choices to swiftly alter the planet's climate and other environments, or in both simultaneously?

There might be no complete answer to this and other such questions. Asking these questions and attempting to answer them might be a required process for starting to understand how to focus on vulnerability reduction through development irrespective of natural hazards and their ever-shifting baselines, including from climate change (human-caused and natural). The following sections provide detailed examples on vulnerability and development along these lines.

Vulnerability in Tonga

This example was edited from Lewis (1981a) which was based on the Report of a Technical Assistance Assignment (Lewis, 1978) undertaken on behalf of the UK's Overseas Development Administration in London, for the Government of the Kingdom of Tonga. The Government of Tonga is gratefully acknowledged for the permission granted for the original publication.

The Kingdom of Tonga consists of 172 islands in the South Pacific. The island group extends over an area of about 358,000 square kilometres, with a land area of 747 square kilometres (Figure 6.1). Thirty-six islands of area 647 square kilometres are permanently inhabited, with a total population of approximately 100,000 people, two-thirds of whom live on the principal island of Tongatapu.

Administered from the capital, Nuku'alofa, on the principal island of the Tongatapu group, the Tongan archipelago includes three sub-groups: the three islands of the Niua group in the far north, the Vava'u group, and the Ha'apai group. The overall distance between inhabited islands from north to south is around 690 kilometres. Hazards include tropical cyclones, droughts, earthquakes, tsunamis, and volcanic eruptions. Five islands are active or dormant volcanoes, and two of these are among those permanently inhabited.

The work for the assignment here examined the history, where records permitted, of all hazards and disasters in Tonga. A part of the history, playing its part in moulding the physical and cultural nature of the islands and their populations, has been the more recent recorded history of post-disaster assistance. Some analysis of needs proved helpful in identifying preventive and relief measures to be taken for future disasters. The assignment was undertaken exactly a year after the earthquake of 1977 and within a few months of the end of a serious drought and two severe tropical cyclones, Anne in December 1977 and Ernie in February 1978, all of which provided material to place into longer perspective and comparative analysis.

Across the Tongan archipelago, over the century starting in 1875, 28 tropical cyclones, 22 earthquakes of moderate or greater magnitude, five periods of drought, four volcanic eruptions, and three tsunamis were recorded – a total of 62 recorded events or a national average of one for every one-and-a-half years. Powerful earthquakes occurred in 1917, which raised the floor of the lagoon on the island of Niua Toputapu and caused it to dry out (Angenheister, 1921),

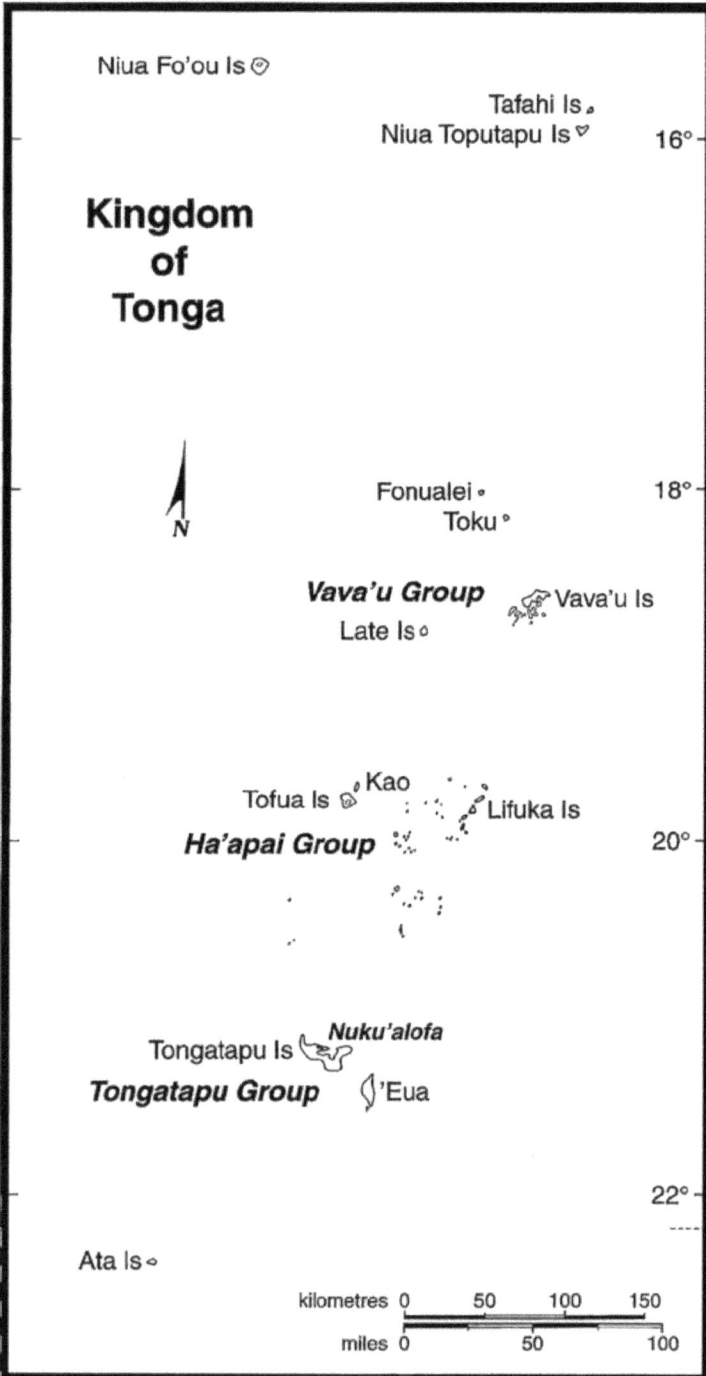

Figure 6.1 Kingdom of Tonga

and in 1919. In addition to the now-underwater island of Fonua Fo'ou (meaning 'New land' and formerly named Falcon Island) which is recorded to have disappeared and reappeared over centuries, there are five active volcanic islands in Tonga, two of which are inhabited. One of these, Niua Fo'ou, remains only partly inhabited after the evacuation of 2,500 people after the eruption of 1946 (see section 'Volcano in Tonga', below).

Tropical cyclones have been the most frequently damaging recorded hazard. Several islands may be seriously affected by one storm, as may be several countries. Cyclone Bebe of October 1972 caused catastrophic damage in Tuvalu (then the Ellice Islands; see also section 'Sea-level rise and atolls', above) and Fiji before striking Tonga and then causing lesser damage in Niue. The scale of impact in these countries is colossal and overwhelming (see Chapter 2, 'Islands and vulnerability'). Ninety-five per cent of all houses in Funafuti, Tuvalu were totally destroyed and a massive section of the reef itself was shifted by the sea (Baines and McLean, 1976b). Twenty-two per cent of the national population of Fiji was rendered homeless.

History in English provides a short record by comparison with Tongan history, as Tongans' ancestors were sailing the ocean for millennia before the arrival of the first Europeans. Descriptively rich Tongan traditions offer information about hazards and responses to them (such as Johnston, 2015; Lavigne et al., 2021). Were environmental hazards simply a fact of life (and death) to be accepted and absorbed in much the same way as night and day? Disaster is expressed as *fakatu'utamaki* but the concept is moulded into the normality of Tongan life. With this perspective, when did the concept of 'disaster relief' first appear, and what were the conditions that made its apparent need so different from traditional responses?

The first found mention of relief in English comes from the Colonial Report of 1909 (Westgate, 1975), a product of the writing of Europeans. After Niua Fo'ou was hit by a cyclone in 1909, 'the Government of Tonga sent in relief but it was not required to any great extent'. Does this brief reference suggest compliance with an external concept by an essentially external administration for which local populations were unprepared? Certainly, in the brief notes taken of the Colonial Reports by Westgate (1975), there is no further reference to 'relief' until the need for emergency shelter for 8,000 people is mentioned after the 1961 cyclone in the Vava'u and Ha'apai island sub-groups.

In the interim, there had been 13 cyclones or severe storms, six periods of drought, two volcanic eruptions, and one 'strong' earthquake, deemed worthy of mention in the Colonial Reports, over the four decades or so during which reports were uninterrupted by World Wars. Twenty-eight other hazard occurrences were recorded in other sources during this time period (Lewis, 1978), making a total of 50. By contrast, in all but four of the hazards in the Colonial Reports, the impact on production, particularly of coconuts or copra, receives significant mention. This was the priority concern of a colonial government.

With the exception of the 1946 evacuation of Niua Fo'ou following the volcanic eruption (see 'Volcano in Tonga', below), and the 'considerable property damage' of the 1961 cyclone, 'disaster' damage to the local population was ignored in the reports. Was this because it was effectively absorbed by the local population, because the colonial administration was insufficiently interested, or a combination?

By common consent among representatives of Tongan central and provincial governments, 1961 represents the point at which significant disaster relief first appeared in response to damage. In that year, 50 per cent of housing in the Vava'u and Ha'apai sub-groups were destroyed or badly damaged, banana crops were wiped out, and coconuts stripped and uprooted. It took two and a half years before the next shipment of copra was despatched (Kerr, 1976). What emergency shelter was provided, if any, was not indicated. Whatever was done was, again by common consent, far less than what has been done since and recently in similarly serious cyclones in other parts of Tonga (Lewis, 1978).

After Tonga became totally self-governing in 1970, Cyclone Juliette in April 1973 led to Tonga's Prime Minister establishing the Hurricane Relief Committee. Across seven islands of the Ha'apai sub-group, 17 villages were seriously affected and 1,250 families required rehousing; that is, 8,000 people, three-quarters of the population of the whole Ha'apai group and 8 per cent of Tonga's national population. Food, water, and planting materials were provided by the Hurricane Relief Committee from central government. Later, a construction programme for the 1,250 families, with financial participation from each household, commenced.

Official reports were not found of the effects of Cyclone Juliette, although the United States Agency for International Development (USAID, c. 1973) provides information from the US Government's perspective. An appeal for assistance was addressed to the New Zealand High Commissioner by the Minister of Works, the Honourable Langi Kavaliku in November (Kavaliku, 1974). There is a significant shift of emphasis by comparison with the Colonial Reports. In a four-page letter, although 'damage to crops' received a passing mention, coconuts and copra production are not referred to at all. The emphasis throughout the Minister's letter, in addition to that of immediate relief, is on necessary improvements to 'normal' infrastructural resources, so that conditions following disasters may be better attended to. The letter did not separate the problems caused by the cyclone from the everyday inadequacies that the cyclone had exacerbated. It also clearly identified the main aspects of concern as being food, shelter (rebuilding), water supply, transport, and communication.

By the time of Cyclone Anne in December 1977, these disaster reports had become well-ordered and highly detailed documents (Central Hurricane Relief Committee, 1978). Using the MV *Kao*, a front-loading, ocean-going barge given by the New Zealand Government as a result of the appeal after Cyclone Juliette, a team of five representatives of the Hurricane Relief

Committee headed by the Minister of Health, visited all 16 islands of the Ha'apai sub-group, a round trip of eight days. Detailed assessments of damage were made in three clearly defined sectors of agricultural food supplies, water sources and supply, and government buildings and private housing. In each sector, the need for improvement of typical conditions, for the purposes of mitigating future disaster damage, is clearly and overtly stated.

The section on water sources and supply estimated damage as T$1,534 but proposed the sum of T$40,836 as being necessary 'for improvements'. The section on government buildings and private housing observed that 'Most of the church buildings and private houses that were damaged or destroyed were very old and should have been pulled down and (or?) repaired long before the hurricane'. The report concludes with recommendations to cabinet which include a national and international appeal for 'hurricane' relief aid, financial concessions to ease the cash burden on households, an allocation of priority for the repair of government and community cisterns, and that three wharfs damaged by the cyclone should be repaired.

In the 12–15 years after the 1961 cyclone, there was a marked change of emphasis, from reductions in copra production to basic local needs. Significant is the change from a situation where not only government ignored the concept of relief, but also, when relief was (first?) offered in 1909, it was not required.

In recognizing the clear relationship between typical conditions and disaster damage, were the ministers of the Hurricane Relief Committee quick to seize upon relief aid, which was readily available for the asking after disaster, to augment their basic needs development programmes? After the earthquake of 1977, relief aid came into Tonga from 15 separate governmental donors and 7 different non-governmental sources. If they were seeking development, then clearly they were not covert in doing so. Their reports are logical, clearly stated, direct, and available. They are nonetheless at the mercy of the international relief, aid, and development machine and industry. By not seizing an opportunity to augment their development budget, they would not be serving their country and people as well as they might. Is this the purpose of relief aid? Should not relief needs be identified more closely so that post-disaster assistance can be more certain of its purpose and of its effectiveness, especially over the long term?

Analysing a number and variety of previous studies and records about disasters in Tonga confirmed that, although there is periodically an apparent emphasis of risk for one island sub-group or another, overall, over longer time periods, no sub-regional allocation of specific risk could safely be made. Recommendations were made for improved methods of climatic and seismic monitoring to be established so that regional locational situations could be reassessed.

Population distribution within the island group is therefore a potential indicator of vulnerability to disaster. With an even spread of hazard occurrence assumed for the time being, which is not a good assumption, where concentrations of population are greatest, vulnerability to loss is also greatest. Movement of population, as well as any natural increase, may therefore lead to changing vulnerability.

At the observatory at Apia, Samoa, Angenheister (1921) wrote:

> The present paper deals with those [earthquakes] whose epicentres are near that part of the ocean known as the Tonga Deep. Fortunately, although these earthquakes are numerous, there are few inhabitants in that part of the Pacific, and consequently, the earthquakes have little destructive effect, more especially as most of them are under the sea.

It is intriguing that the allegedly 'few inhabitants' are seen as unimportant; that is, apparently, larger numbers of people are more worthy of attention. Tonga's population in 1921 was 24,935, about one-quarter of what it is now (Kingdom of Tonga, 1976). The population of the largest island, Tongatapu, on which the capital of Nuku'alofa is situated, has increased sevenfold since 1921. Natural increase and migration (inclusive of the evacuation of 2,500 people from Niua Fo'ou in 1946, 1,800 of whom went on to 'Eua [see 'Volcano in Tonga', below]), thus have a dual effect on vulnerability assessed in this way. Locational vulnerability may be exacerbated by 'vocational vulnerability': activities affecting three basic elements of life support other than oxygen; that is, water, food, and shelter.

Rainfall in 1977 was considerably lower than the annual average for the preceding eight years (Kingdom of Tonga, 1976) and drought prevailed for three months, from October to December. More than half of the year's rainfall fell during the first three months. Most Tongan atolls do not contain freshwater lenses within their porous coral rock formation. Other islands are raised to higher elevations, but have hitherto resisted drilling wells due to their height and the hardness of rock structure. Throughout all islands, drinking water supplies tend to be from roof catchment collection and storage tanks or cisterns on and in the ground. The last major government building programme for constructing cisterns for water storage throughout Tonga was undertaken in 1908–9 (Rutherford, 1977) when the total population was 22,000.

There is piped water supply in the capital and in some principal villages. Elsewhere, population increase has caused more intensive use of storage systems. Rainwater was once collected off several roofs and conveyed by pipe or gutter to communal cisterns. Now in many cases, roofs have disappeared with the buildings themselves, and cisterns are often fed only by the water drained off their own roofs. More recent buildings with large roofs – for example, schools and churches – while collecting water for their own use in private tanks, have ignored communal needs and communal cisterns.

It is not only drought that is exacerbated by inadequate water catchment and storage. Environmental health hazards are more likely to increase in conditions of water shortage and the consequent decrease in standards of personal hygiene. Deprivation will be more widespread where water storage content and capacity are low, following hazards which may have damaged roofs and guttering systems. In July 1978, a concrete cistern capable of holding 68,000 litres held barely 40 millimetres of water to serve an island community of 350 people.

In such conditions, the liquid from young coconuts provides the main source of thirst prevention, while also providing food and nutrients. In times of water shortage and drought, coconut consumption might increase up to four times, with a consequent and corresponding decrease in coconuts available for subsequent copra production. Estimated coconut consumption during the three-month drought of 1977 was equivalent to 11 per cent of the copra production of the Ha'apai island sub-group (Lewis, 1978). Copra is the principal source of cash income for Tonga and Tongans, who cannot afford to have their source of income eroded in this way. Capital expenditure on improved systems of water catchment and storage would be quickly compensated for by maintaining copra production.

Yet over-emphasis on cash cropping, to the exclusion of food crops, increases vulnerability to disasters. Although food crops can be harmed in storms, staple root crops of taro, cassava, yams, and sweet potato remain edible for some time after their foliage has been destroyed. Although damaged, as long as these crops (and others) are present in adequate quantities, there will be food to eat for up to two or three months afterwards. The reduction of food crops in favour of cash crops, such as vanilla, reduces capacity for self-reliance and survival. The availability of cash in lieu serves little purpose when food supplies for market are unavailable as the result of scarcity brought about by cash crops combined with storm damage.

Priority for cash cropping in the most favourable and fertile agricultural sites leads to relocating food crops to marginal ground, which may increase the vulnerability of food crops to damage. The following process occurred in the eastern islands of Fiji (McLean et al., 1977):

> Since the best soils are on the coastal flats and in the lower valley bottoms, increasingly the most favoured areas have been used for coconut plantations ... The gardens have had to extend up-slope and up-valley into areas formerly regarded as too steep, difficult, poor or remote to be cultivated ... These slopes are, however, very exposed to wind and storm damage. In 1975 a larger proportion of the crops was destroyed by the hurricane or subsequently rotted in the ground than was the case in 1948 ... (before the process described had become so well established).

Traditional building construction techniques in Tonga have gradually given way to the adoption of external materials and methods (compare to Reardon, 1992). Corrugated iron sheeting and sawn timber frame construction have been practised in Tonga since colonial times. Sheet roofing has in many instances replaced thatch in traditional Tongan *fale* construction, although the more widespread use of sheet material for roofing makes water catchment more effective and systems for water storage more beneficial. Subsequently, the use of concrete blocks increased, together with the use of reinforced concrete for domestic construction, as well as for government, commercial, and religious buildings.

The estimated cost of damage in the 1977 earthquake, slightly more than NZ$1 m, was for infrastructure damage including wharfs. The buildings most severely damaged were those built of modern materials, reinforced concrete and/or blockwork (Campbell, 1977; Patterson, 1977). Whereas the 1977 earthquake exposed abysmally low standards of construction where modern materials had been used, traditional *fale* buildings were not damaged, nor were the sawn timber buildings, except in some cases by failure of raised masonry foundations or by broken windows. Earthquake damage increases with the unregulated and unmonitored increase in the use of non-traditional building forms and methods. In a future of increased such development, this increase in future earthquake damage will be compounded in the absence of appropriate action, including promulgating, monitoring, and enforcing regulations for planning, design, and construction which account for new building and material types.

Legislation for improved standards of building construction would not be adopted lightly. Construction standards are so low that any general legislation, even if practicable, would impose severe costs on the industry. In the meantime, all available means of instruction should increase awareness of earthquake and other hazards alongside appropriate construction methods for the hazards. Examples are through loan authorities, government labour training programmes, short courses for the commercial sector, leaflets, posters, and schools. Meanwhile, it is understood that those who turned to blockwork and concrete construction following wooden houses being damaged in cyclones, having now suffered most heavily in the earthquake, are rebuilding once more in timber. Opportunity for a governmental lead, in the cycle of destruction and deprivation, for improved methods of timber construction resistant to 'all hazards at a place' is now open.

The Hurricane Relief Committee reported its recognition of the need to improve typical conditions, if resources and capacity for local disaster mitigation were to be increased. The report of the Official Development Assistance (ODA) Technical Assistance Assignment, among other notes, identified some of the processes that have led, or may lead to, increased disaster vulnerability. It was suggested that there are serious shortcomings within international aid, both development and relief aid seeking either to improve 'normal' conditions or to ameliorate disaster – or both.

The most obvious products of development aid in Tonga are in constructing wharf facilities for tourists and goods, constructing hospitals and schools, developing commercial fisheries, and developing agriculture for animal husbandry and forestry (Kingdom of Tonga, 1976). Commercial enterprise has provided a satellite communication earth-station and an extended airport, while attempting to establish an oil extraction industry, so not always the most environmentally sustainable. In addition to training programmes and advisory and technical assistance programmes, the emphasis of development aid has been on capital expenditure on projects of a physically identifiable kind. Is it in the nature of current policies of international aid that results must be visibly recognizable and therefore more readily identifiable with their donor agency?

This kind of aid has led to a burden of maintenance and recurrent costs which falls on the national government and has to be paid for from the national budget. Building and infrastructure maintenance – and the provision of small buildings, additions, and alterations to capital-intensive projects – place a burden on national resources which leads to a run-down of maintenance generally.

This may explain the reasonable temptation to direct funds from relief aid to small-scale building improvements as well as to repairs. There would seem to be no fault in this as far as the Tongan administration is concerned. The lower the standards of maintenance in buildings or infrastructure, the greater the likelihood of damage and consequent loss during hazards. With more development funding for maintenance and small-scale projects, the greater will be the national and local capacity for vulnerability reduction and avoiding disasters.

Programmes of development expenditure require a widespread multiplicity of small projects. One possibility (identified above) is in water catchment and storage systems. 'Improvement' is clearly synonymous with 'development' in this context.

Another recommended programme is developing commercial fishing, probably undertaken through village co-operatives. Improving local fishing industries provides an increase in alternative food supplies. By its infra-structure, it also provides the means for locally initiated inter-island exchange which has been the traditional life-blood of survival in disaster. Spontaneous assistance from less affected islands to those that have suffered more is an established system of extended mutual aid which has become eroded and largely destroyed by over-emphasis on centralized government and external relief or aid.

Whether development programmes are devised under budgets for vulnerability reduction, disaster reduction, disaster risk reduction, disaster risk management, basic needs, sustainability, or others is immaterial. What is important is that they are implemented and that their role in addressing disasters and disaster risk is recognized by both donors and recipients. Against a background of long-term accretion of vulnerability, the need for post-disaster assistance is not disputed. What has to be examined is the form that assistance takes and its integration into short- and long-term uses and effectiveness.

Examples of useless relief are a part of folklore and are held in perpetuity. In Tonga after the drought and Cyclones Anne in 1977 and Ernie in 1978, local expatriate officials of an international non-governmental organization appealed to their parent body for vitamin tablets. A representative was sent to determine the veracity of the appeal. By the time the representative's report was received, 1 million vitamin tablets had been despatched. Despite the reported conclusion that the cyclone survivors were nutritionally fit and healthy, and despite Tongan Ministry of Health agreement with those findings, the tablets were distributed. With a vitamin tablet supply for three months suddenly appearing, the burden on local administrative resources was colossal. Tongan cultural tradition prevailed to not give offence by refusing a gift. Post-disaster assistance placed a giant burden on administrative infrastructure at a time of emergency when those local resources should have been more effectively used on matters of higher priority of need.

Some relief aid may have negative effects where it is not offered in specific response to locally identified needs. The availability of such relief supplies may create future artificial needs or dependency on them. Dependency may be psychological or practical. It is often difficult to identify.

Is the distribution of canned fish from Japan, another gift, a result of a shortage of locally caught fish or is the local inadequacy of fishing partly a result of the easy availability of canned fish? Does the monthly distribution of flour, sugar, and dried milk over nine months, as gifts from Australia, have a bearing on feckless behaviour in local garden management? There are numerous Tongan administrators who would say that it does.

Dependency comes in many forms, not all of which can be blamed on disaster relief and not all of them present in Tonga. Dependency on cash, cash cropping, the need to work in paid employment, consequent migration, depletion, and mismanagement undermine development and perpetuate dependency. This may, in turn, exacerbate vulnerability to a far greater degree. The relationship of disaster relief to these negative aspects of development, in tandem with the positive aspects, must be understood if integrating relief aid with development aid is to succeed.

Whatever the causes and origins of dependency, vulnerability can only increase as a result. The greater the degree of dependency, the less the capacity for self-reliance. In disaster, dependency is exposed through the disappearance of the dependency prop, in cases where former systems for self-reliance have deteriorated due to a hitherto dependent condition.

Examining the effectiveness of relief aid might reveal some of the negative by-products, might create opportunity for longer-term presence by executive representatives of governmental and non-governmental donor representatives, and might reveal opportunities for continuing involvement by donors of relief aid in programmes of basic needs development that would reduce disasters. Where this already occurs due to the presence of some representatives, it does so apart from, and unrelated to, the major development programmes. There is a lack of integration not only of relief and development aid in this sense, but also between small-scale and large-scale development projects and programmes. Integration is a mutual and two-way process.

Once again, the pragmatic redirection of relief-aid funds into small-scale improvement measures can easily be understood in this context. The relief-dependency-vulnerability-relief process must be broken. Inherent structural weaknesses that create the need for relief palliatives must be exposed and rectified.

In Tonga, it is relevant to distinguish between financial relief aid, which has found an appropriate if not totally logical use, and material relief supplies. It is then relevant to pose the question of whether relief supplies, of the kind there have been in the recent past, are necessary at all. Some cases of destitution and severe need will be found, but it will be necessary to determine whether those cases were caused directly by the disaster in question or whether they are a product of 'normal' conditions. That there is a clear relationship is understood. It is disaster relief which is here the subject of enquiry.

Tonga is known for its ceremonial feasting. Rutherford (1977: 78–79) compares the social (including economic) impact of food shortage resulting from cyclones with the social (including economic) impact of traditional Tongan feasting:

> The land produced for itself a wide variety of plants and trees. Some agricultural products were cultivated yams, bananas, and plantains for food; and the paper mulberry and the pandanus for cloth and mat making ... *Kava* was cultivated for the use of the chiefs and for ceremonial purposes. Pigs and fowls, the only domesticated animals, were left to scavenge for food and to breed at will. Although the Tongans were excellent farmers, aided by a rich soil and favourable climate, famines were frequent. They were caused on occasions by unusually dry seasons, or by devastating hurricanes. More often than not, however, shortages of food resulted from excessive consumption of food at *inasi* ceremonies, weddings, funerals and voyages to the outer islands. At the marriage of the Tu'i Tonga, for example, food was stacked in heaps ... Some attempts were made to lessen the frequency and severity of famine by declaring certain foods *tapu* following large-scale feasting. The *tapu* was also employed before some anticipated ceremony or festival to ensure that ample food was available at the appointed time. At these times of *tapu* the common people suffered and were driven to seek edible plant roots in order to survive. There appears to have been some concern to over-produce in order to meet the demands of ceremonial and obligatory presentations of food, but only limited attempts were made to store food for lean times, the exception being the preservation of bread-fruit in pits and storage of yams in specially constructed shelters.

The impact of feasting on the consumption of food is still recognized. As recently as the 1977 drought, a government circular was issued to district and town officers on how not to waste food. Feasting was not to be *kai pula* but *kai peleti* (on plates) and by 'plastic bags'. Whether 'wastage' is avoided or not, if Tonga can absorb the extremes of feasting to the considerable extent it does through social coping mechanisms, then it may have similarly absorbed the impact of environmental extremes in the past, of similar impact and lesser frequency, and could do so again in the future.

An item in the *Tonga Chronicle* of June 1977, under the heading of 'New Zealand Aid for Ha'apai', reported a cheque for T$24,000 given by New Zealand to the 'hurricane' relief programme. Indented within the same column space was a short account of the royal feast given to 800 guests in honour of the King's 60th birthday. A spokesperson from the feasting committee said 1,462 suckling pigs and 1,223 chickens were roasted for the royal occasion. There were also enormous amounts of seafood and other delicacies. At market prices of T$15.00 per suckling pig and T$3.00 per chicken, the cost of those two items alone would have exceeded the relief donation from New Zealand by T$1,599.

In the Government of Tonga in 1975, the Central Planning Unit was created within the Ministry of Finance as part of the preparation of the Third Development Plan 1975–80 (Kingdom of Tonga, 1976). It later became the Central Planning Department. The report of the Technical Assistance Assignment recommended that all matters pertaining to development (that is, improvement) arising from the occurrence of 'natural disaster' should be handled by the Development Planning Department. The report also suggested that the department may become more closely and effectively able to plan to take environmental hazards of all kinds into account. As a further recommendation for institutional matters, it was proposed that the Hurricane Relief Committee should be renamed the Disaster Relief Committee, should continue to have responsibility for relief after all types of disaster, and should take on additional responsibilities for preparedness matters. The Prime Minister of Tonga chairs the Relief Committee.

In any country, but particularly in archipelago countries, disaster may be localized in its impact. While none of the 36 inhabited islands of Tonga can be said to be immune to environmental hazards, occurrence lacks regularity in each one. Nationally, the country as a whole has to cope with 'all hazards at a place', the place being Tonga. This must not be construed to imply a sole responsibility by central government for disasters, but rather a capacity for initiating locally managed coping mechanisms planned within national frameworks for the reduction of vulnerability and, where and when necessary, the administration of integrated relief. Regenerating local coping mechanisms under governmental initiation and supervision, where these have been eroded, local interdependence, and self-reliance will arrest those processes that have hitherto accelerated dependency on central government and which have brought about periodic national dependency on international relief aid.

Volcano in Tonga

This example was edited from Lewis (1979b). This account of a volcanic eruption and subsequent evacuation in an island of Tonga was given by Town Officer, Moeake Takai, who kept a diary of events at the time, and to whom Lewis (1979b) is deeply indebted. Acknowledgement is made of the permission granted by the UK's Ministry of Overseas Development and the Government of the Kingdom of Tonga for this example's original publication. The experiences of the inhabitants of the island Niua Fo'ou during the volcanic eruption, the subsequent evacuation, and of the return of some of them, are also recorded in detail in Rogers (1986).

The island of Niua Fo'ou is an active volcano, situated at the extreme north of the Tongan island group, almost 640 kilometres from Tongatapu and the capital Nuku'alofa, 168 kilometres west from Niuatoputapu which is the nearest island, and 344 kilometres north-west from Vava'u which is the nearest and northernmost island sub-group. Their location at the extreme north of the island group places the islands of Niuatoputapu and Niua Fo'ou roughly midway between Fiji and Samoa. For European sea voyagers, these islands became an important 'halfway house' for ships taking on stores and water. The early Dutch and Spanish explorers made use, or attempted to make use, of these islands in this way, as they had been for at least 1,500 years previously by ocean voyagers between Fiji and Samoa.

This strategic location has probably accounted in the past for the comparatively large populations of each of the two islands. The ships of the Dutch explorer Jacob Le Maire were attacked in 1616 by 1,000 people from Niuatoputapu and, later, by 'warriors in 14 canoes' from Niua Fo'ou.

Niuatoputapu is 18 square kilometres in area. Niua Fo'ou is 49 square kilometres in area, including a 15-square-kilometre lake, and is volcanic, rising to 179 metres above sea level (Figure 6.2). It has no natural harbour and for

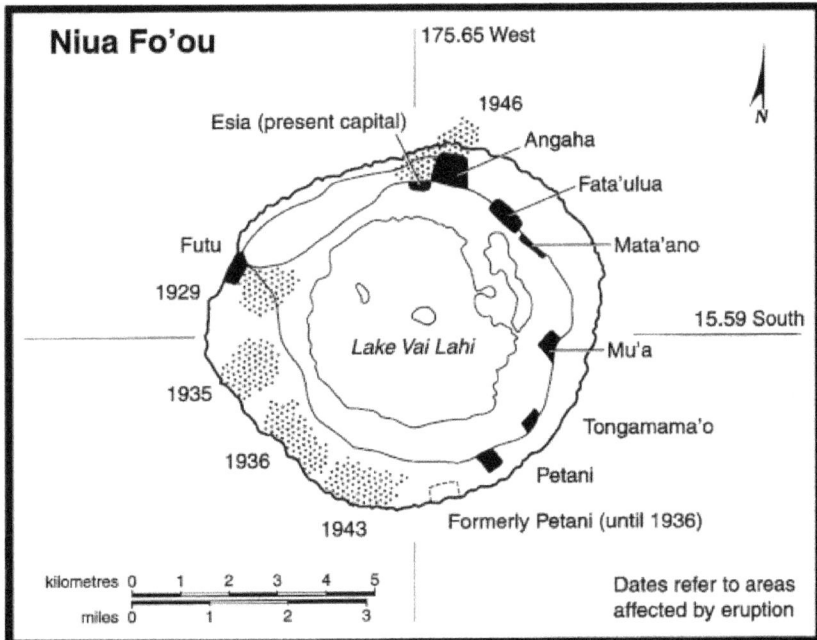

Figure 6.2 Niua Fo'ou's areas affected by volcanic eruptions

many years was called 'Tin Can Mail Island', because mail was dropped from passing ships in sealed tins and retrieved by swimmers. In 1946, Niua Fo'ou's population was 2,500.

It would be interesting to know what the effect of earlier eruptions in history has been on this island's large population. Records in English have been traced back only to 1929, when Niua Fo'ou erupted in July of that year and the village of Futu and many houses and plantations were destroyed. The need for improved communication was stated by the government as a result of this eruption. A wireless station was established soon afterwards.

Eruptions came not from the peak, but from surrounding slopes to the sea. They occurred again in 1935, this time without damage; in 1936, destroying the village of Petani; in 1943; and in September 1946, as a result of which, although there was no loss of life, damage was extensive. The wireless station was destroyed, as were other government buildings, dwellings, and plantations, for the second time during Queen Salote's reign. The decision was made by the Queen and her Government to evacuate the whole population in two stages, first to Tongatapu and then to the island of 'Eua.

In 1977, 'Eua suffered great damage from an earthquake. In the following year, the Government of Tonga requested technical assistance and it was during this assignment that a visit to 'Eua to inspect earthquake damage provided the opportunity to seek out whatever recollection was available of the eruption and evacuation of 1946.

Moeake Takai was Town Officer in Angahā, 'Eua in 1977. Aged 20 at the time of the 1946 Niua Fo'ou eruption, he had always kept a diary and still does. With reference to his diaries, he described the events of 31 years earlier, sitting in front of his house in the moonlight.

There was a full moon on the evening of Monday, 9 September 1946. In the principal village of Niua Fo'ou, Angahā (same name as the town of 'Eua), there was a brass band practice at the Catholic Mission. Moeake Takai and his friend John Malekamu went to football practice. At 7:30 p.m., they felt the first earthquake, then there were two more and a total of probably 10 or 12 minor tremors. The 14 people at band practice stopped playing and, in fear of an eruption, went to their homes. (Three years previously, there had been an eruption on the far side of the island after only one earthquake. On that occasion, people had stayed where they were.) Twenty-five minutes later, at 7:55 p.m., there was a loud roar from the western side of the village.

Moeake Takai ran home. John Malekamu, who was operator at the government wireless station, reported for duty. Moeake Takai's mother and father had left their home and had joined others in climbing up the mountain away from the village on the coastline. Moeake collected his wife and did the same. People were crying and praying, calling to one another and shouting to find one another. There was a great deal of noise. Eventually they looked back, but their village, the principal village on the island, had all gone. Where it had been was engulfed in black smoke.

Climbing up the mountain from the village, as instructed by the police and the district officer, facilitated escape from likely eruptions nearer the coastline. By 11:00 p.m., everyone was on the mountain, including the district officer, the three police officers, and the doctors, but with the exception of the wireless operator. As moonlight shone golden on white steam and black smoke, ministers of all churches conducted prayers together with the people, government officers, leaders, and chiefs.

At about 3:00 a.m. or 4:00 a.m., the eruption ceased and Moeake Takai went down to look for his friend, the wireless operator. John Malekamu had sent out SOS signals for help and had left the wireless station only when lava was 9 metres away, just before its destruction. Exhausted by the intense heat, he had run and finally collapsed under a tree, where he was eventually found by his friend. Having realized that whether he lived or not was now 'up to God', he survived and was taken to join the rest of the island community up the mountain. He was able to report to the police the extent of destruction in the village. At sunrise, all joined in giving thanks to God for their deliverance – without casualty.

Among the 2,500 people on the mountain sides were four nuns, one each from Belgium, France, Holland, and the USA. The one from the latter had her national flag, which was raised on the highest tree to attract attention.

The eruption had commenced on the Monday evening and all the island community was gathered on the mountain sides by Tuesday, the following day. They remained there throughout Tuesday, Wednesday, and Thursday. On Friday 13 September at 10:00 a.m., they heard a plane. A US Navy plane flying from Pango Pango in American Samoa to Na'adi in Fiji saw smoke still rising from the island and the waving of clothes on the mountain sides. They reported the situation at Na'adi. A message was sent to the Tongan government at Nuku'alofa where none of the SOS messages from Niua Fo'ou seemed to have been received. The people remained where they were throughout Friday and until Tuesday, 17 September, when a government ship was at last sighted, one week and a day after the eruption. A cargo ship also arrived on the same day. At 4:30 p.m., a government officer arrived on the mountain to ask the people to move down again.

A meeting was arranged between government officials who had arrived from Nuku'alofa, the Chief of Niua Fo'ou who had been in Nuku'alofa, and leaders of the island communities. On the following day, a public meeting was arranged, where a government official expressed the need to evacuate the entire population to Tongatapu. The island communities are divided between four chiefs. When the time came to vote on the issue of whether to agree to the government evacuation or not, three chiefs and their communities of 1,800 people voted in favour of evacuation and one chief and his 700 people voted against evacuation. The majority vote in favour of evacuation meant evacuation for the whole island population of 2,500 people.

Saturday 21 December was fixed for the commencement of evacuation to Tongatapu. The police magistrate from Nuku'alofa remained at Niua Fo'ou as chair of the Evacuation Committee while other officials returned to the capital. Although there was, therefore, three months to prepare for evacuation, there was much work to be done. All surviving dwellings were to be taken down to permit reuse of building materials. All material had to be stacked, ready for loading and embarkation.

When the day came, loading began at 6:00 a.m. and continued until 5:00 p.m. The 2,500 people and building materials were transported to Nuku'alofa in one day. No animals were permitted to be taken, no food, and no sewing machines, only suitcases for clothing and personal belongings. Each person had been allocated a number and each number was checked as embarkation progressed. It was efficiently ordered, but many people were crying and very upset.

There had been, in fact, two eruptions, one adjacent to the principal village on land and the other just offshore. The landing place between these two eruptions had been totally destroyed. Three boats came from Nuku'alofa for the evacuation. One was loaned by the US Government and another, the *Matua*, came from the Union Steamship Company of New Zealand. These two ships had to anchor 1.2 kilometres offshore. The third boat, a small wooden craft called *Hitofua*, was used to ferry all passengers and goods from shore to ship.

Twenty-one men and one woman were left on Niua Fo'ou to tend crops and what property and belongings remained. They were there from December until the following April. Life for them must have been particularly difficult and they were eventually taken to Samoa by a Seventh Day Adventist schooner. From there, they were taken to Nuku'alofa, still in the charge of the minister on the boat to Vava'u. The woman was taken ill and died on board.

Tongatapu was to be only a transit stop. In September 1948, the move began to the island of 'Eua. The distance from Nuku'alofa is 40 kilometres, but only the contingent of 1,800 people who had voted, with their three chiefs, in favour of the evacuation agreed to go on to 'Eua. The other 700, with their chief, stayed in Tongatapu until 1959, when their requests to return to Niua Fo'ou were recognized, and the government agreed to assist their return.

The island of 'Eua, with an area of 87 square kilometres, is one of the largest in the Tongan island group, but even now has only 4,000 people, 4 per cent of the national total. The island is mountainous, rising to just over 300 metres, naturally forested and with freshwater springs. 'Eua is larger, more fertile, and nearer to the capital than Niua Fo'ou, but the first 10 years were a very difficult time for the newly arrived population.

Agricultural land had to be cleared and crops and planting material had to be established. Forest timber, in government ownership, was not freely available and there were few coconut palms available for building. In 1957, a new sawmill was built with New Zealand development aid and a forestry scheme was established, under which one-quarter of all timber felled on farmed land was made available to the allotted occupier. This marked a turning point in the island's relative prosperity and standard of living. In the intervening 10 years, it had probably been severe economic hardship in unfamiliar surroundings that caused 74 men to sail to Niua Fo'ou in 1950 to work on copra production. They stayed on the island for one year, and then returned to 'Eua, being replaced by another working party in 1951, out of which 24 men stayed. In 1952, about 20 men stayed, and again in 1953. Moeake Takai joined one of these working parties and briefly reflected on the moving experience of a return to his native island. Animals had been untethered and freed by the group of 20 who stayed in 1947, and had since gone wild. The horses responded to the long-forgotten sound of water buckets and allowed themselves to be mounted to join in the work of coconut collection.

There was no permanent settlement on Niua Fo'ou from 1947 until 1959 and all land reverted to government ownership. It was probably the work of the copra working parties that encouraged the government to assist the permanent return of the contingent from Tongatapu. Copra is the principal export commodity of Tonga as well as the principal cash crop of the majority of islanders. In 1977, in spite of government assistance for the return of the 700 people from Tongatapu, land on Niua Fo'ou had not been allocated by central government under the Tongan tax-allotment system for life tenancy by farmers.

The indications are that the evacuation of 1946 was ad hoc and unplanned, and that the decision to carry it out was precipitate. The apparent lack of forethought about the ultimate relocation of evacuees must have made their plight far more onerous than it need have been, and their ultimate resettlement a much longer process than necessary.

Tonga gives serious attention to its hazards. The 1977 measures for disaster mitigation recommended co-ordinated and integrated preparedness measures, attention being drawn to the significant aspect of contingency planning for the evacuation of populated volcanic islands. Preparedness planning indicated the need for policy decisions concerning temporary or permanent relocation of communities as part of a context of development planning, suggesting the need to arrest spontaneous movement of people from outer islands to urban centres.

Infrastructural and administrative development of Niua Fo'ou was planned to provide an airstrip by 1980 and a six-bed in-patient ward for the dispensary. The absence of secondary schooling, commented upon in the Third Development Plan, is a significant cause of migration to larger islands. Additional services such as these would reinforce the island's resources during a major disaster. Local and national disaster preparedness, serving to co-ordinate and generate infrastructural development, may do more to remove resistance to living on a hazardous, active volcanic island.

A multi-hazard history of Antigua

This example was edited from Lewis (1984a) and is based on some of the annexes to a report to UNCTAD (United Nations Conference on Trade and Development) made at the request of UNDRO (United Nations Disaster Relief Coordinator) (Lewis, 1982; UNCTAD, 1983).

Antigua experiences earthquakes, droughts, and hurricanes, among many other hazards. To isolate for study each of these hazards before or as they occur would be to ignore the interrelationships between the after-effects of one and the effects of the next. Moreover, there will be conditions arising from factors outside the disaster spectrum which bear upon, and are themselves affected by, all of these phenomena.

Such interrelationships suggest a human ecology and disaster ecology (Chapter 9, 'Disasters: Monitors of development') which must be recognized if environmental balance and compatibility are to be maintained, particularly in respect of hazards. This documentary analysis of part of the colonial era in Antigua has to conclude for the time being with questions concerning the environmental effectiveness of superimposed systems of administration which, with incomplete knowledge of comparable natural hazards, assumed sectoral separation for their administration, as well as for everything else.

Abstraction of hazards from their historical contexts may have the misleading consequence of attributing a seriousness that external observers might exaggerate – or vice versa. In their contexts, some hazards that would perhaps be serious elsewhere are not locally considered serious. Local interpretations and perceptions of hazard must be one basis for their environmental evaluation and assessment, in addition to any wider implications. The earthquake of 1843 in Antigua had a serious effect upon the emergent communities of then only recently emancipated enslaved people (Woodcock, 1843). Meanwhile, drought in Antigua would not have been considered drought in Cape Verde, as the people in the latter are used to, and capable of, resisting far greater extremes (UNCTAD, 1983).

Drought in Antigua meant loss of sugar production and other exports, of serious consequence to colonial administrators. In this respect, a distinction has to be made between local administrators and those in the corresponding metropolis, who were often in conflict, especially about how the so-called 'natives' were to be treated after a disaster (UNCTAD, 1983).

In Antigua, tremors had been a common occurrence during the 18th (and perhaps early 19th) century. On 16 May 1778, according to Luffman (1789):

> ... the earth shook violently three or four times ... many of the whites as well as negroes were much alarmed and ran out into the street.

Rev. H. Cheesborough (this spelling is from UNCTAD, 1983) from the Wesleyan Methodist Missionary Society (WMMS), wrote on 10 February 1843:

> At 20 minutes before 11 o'clock on Wednesday morning the 8th February [1843] Antigua was visited by a dreadful earthquake ... there arose clouds of dust from every part of the town, the crash of falling buildings was heard, blended with the piercing shrieks of the people and accompanied with that horrid heaving and trembling of the earth beneath our feet ... Almost every piece of masonry in St. John's is in ruins.

Woodcock (1843) describes:

> The stone dwelling houses and stores were crashed and crushed … the wooden buildings waved to and fro … The damage done is immense. In the capital (St. John's), some of the finest stores are a mess of ruins … and in many parts the earth is opened, forming deep fissures.

In the capital, St. John's, the courthouse, police office, arsenal, new jail, barracks, Register Office, treasurer's office, just-built Governor's Secretary's Office, and Colonial Bank were significantly damaged. All the stone buildings on Barbuda (except one schoolhouse) were destroyed. On Antigua at the dockyard of English Harbour, according to Woodcock (1843), the:

> wharves all rocked and rent; in some places they have sunk down to the margin of the sea, in others they are literally heaved up …

Five stores built since the fire of 1841 and seven others, three taverns (one three-storey in brick), a brass and iron foundry ('the only one of its kind in the West Indies'), a bakery, private dwelling houses ('that is those built of stone or brick'), 'almost every kitchen and oven on the island', and cisterns were destroyed or very severely damaged. All the 172 sugar mills and estates received damage. Thirty-five were entirely destroyed, 82 irreparably damaged, 52 partially damaged, and 'works, dwelling houses, labourers' cottages attached to those mills shared their fate in equal proportions.'

Numerous 'free-villages' built by their own labour by formerly enslaved people were destroyed (slavery had been abolished by Great Britain by a law passed in 1834). Woodcock (1843) writes:

> Many of the estates that have fallen prey to the earthquake have been established since emancipation, by men who have exerted themselves to the utmost … and how they will be able to rebuild them it is impossible to say. Indeed it will take many years to restore Antigua to its former position.

St. John's Cathedral was badly damaged and declared 'unfit for public service'. Several parish churches were destroyed or badly damaged, as were eight chapels or mission houses, one 'not much, being a wooden structure'. The largest, the Ebenezer Chapel, required £3,000 to be rebuilt, according to an estimate from HM Civil Engineer, Keightly (this spelling is from UNCTAD, 1983) on 18 February 1843, to the WMMS, who further advised:

> To rebuild in stone would require less by about £500, and though the building would be liable to be damaged by earthquakes it would be less exposed to the ravages of fires and hurricane which are of more frequent occurrence.

St. John's had been destroyed by fire in 1841 and it seems that much rebuilding had been completed in 'fire-proof' masonry. It is a source of contemporary comment that masonry buildings suffered most damage in the earthquake of 1843. Many houses were left with their outer masonry walls collapsed and with the inner wooden walls supporting the roof; houses built entirely of wood remained standing. Again from Keightly:

> Nearly all our [Methodist] members in both town and country, are sufferers ... some of them to an almost ruinous extent. Even the labourers, of whom a large proportion had invested the savings of eight years [since emancipation] of toil in the dwellings they had built have been reduced to such a state of destitution by the destruction of their tenements as to be literally homeless and penniless ...

Various estimates of deaths ranged from 12 to 40. The total cost of damage to the island, including the loss of the sugar crop, was placed at £2 m.

An Act was immediately passed requiring (Woodcock, 1843):

> inhabitants to pull down all injured buildings, in order, if possible to guard against any further accidents. In case of neglect, a committee is appointed to do so, and £100 sterling granted to defray expenses, to be refunded by each individual, either in money or by sale of a part of the broken fragments.

A grant of £500 was placed at the disposal of the committee to support the cathedral roof. The restoration of some of the parish churches commenced in 1845. The repair of those more seriously damaged was completed with government funds by that time. A new cathedral was finally completed in 1846 with the government expenditure of £35,000 being a (Department of the Colonies, 1847):

> ... heavy drain on the public resources; and the effects of this extravagance will, I fear, be sensibly felt for some time to come.

Methodists received nothing from public funds, yet Keightly explains:

> ... all is bustle and activity in the Establishment. The Legislative grants large sums of money for repair and rebuild ... church after church rises from its ruins.

In spite of increased expenditure for relief and reconstruction, the necessary increase in imported materials produced duty revenue for government funds. An excess of revenue over 'a very liberal expenditure' and a balance in hand at the end of 1845 of £13,717, 11 shillings, and 10 pence (20 shillings = £1.00; 12 pence = 1 shilling) was recorded (Department of the Colonies, 1845):

> The increase in the actual receipts has arisen for the most part, from the augmented consumption of dutyable goods, and particularly the productions of the United States; although the declared value of imports generally was less in 1845 than the preceding year ... the net excess of expenditure amounts to £8,232 sterling, which has been caused, in great measures, by the unavoidable and heavy expense incurred in rebuilding the Cathedral and restoring other public buildings ...

Table 6.1 Antigua's exports in 1844 and 1845

		1844	*1845*	*Deficit*
Sugar	Hogsheads*	15,357	11,809	3,548
	Tierces	1,562	1,012	550
	Barrels	4,512	2,745	1,767
Molasses	Puncheons	9,020	8,780	240
	Hogsheads	127		127
Arrowroot	Boxes	665	407	258
	Barrels	104		104

* A hogshead was 15 hundredweight (762 kilograms in total using that time period's UK definition of 'hundredweight') on average; three tierces = 2 hogsheads; and 1 hogshead = 8 barrels. A puncheon was a large cask holding 72–120 gallons (327–546 litres using the conversion from imperial gallons).
Source: Department of Colonies, 1845.

No record was available of how the decision was taken to rebuild the cathedral from public funds, but the cost of rebuilding was a source of irritation to the Governor. There was an accompanying decrease in the value of exports for 1845 of £107,530 (Table 6.1) indicating 'a considerable failure in the produce of island staples'. The year 1846 saw a diminution in both imports and exports compared with 1845 (Department of the Colonies, 1846):

> Falling off of imports appears to be chiefly attributable to a diminished quantity of supplies being introduced in the past year from the United States; arising partly perhaps from the more contracted demand for them than in previous years, when an unusual quantity of supplies of various kinds was required for the restoration of damages occasioned by the earthquake of 1843, and partly perhaps from the very short crop of 1846 causing money to be less freely circulated.

The Colonial Report for 1847 is unusual in including a detailed statement of accounts comparing 1847 with 1846. Significant increases in expenditure are shown for highways, purchase of land, and 'cost of iron tanks for Courthouse' (rebuilding). There are decreases for 1847 shown, among other items, for forts and parishes, indicating perhaps higher expenditure in 1845 more closely following the earthquake. The largest item of decrease (£1,940, 16 shillings, and a halfpenny) is in fact against the item for 'Expenses from earthquake' with an aggregate expenditure (1846/1847) of £9,791. Revenue accounts showed increases on almost all duties and licences, and the marked decrease in tariff duties. 'Expenses of Earthquake' for 1847–48 were £2,060, and that year showed an even more marked falling off of post-earthquake reconstruction expenditure.

Parliament in London sanctioned an advance to Antigua in 1844 'towards remedying the destructive consequences of the earthquake in the preceding year'. At the end of 1854, the consequent public debt was £65,000 (Governor MacKintosh, Department of the Colonies, 1855):

> the reductions which have been lately conceded by HM Government by the amount of the annual instalments of repayment of the principal, from one tenth, to one twentieth, and of the interest from a rate of 5 to one of 3 per centum, have rendered this obligation a comparatively light and easily man- ageable one.

Reading between the lines of the Department of the Colonies reports, these concessions had been hard fought for and the obligation eased only temporarily. Governor Hamilton (Department of the Colonies, 1856) wrote:

> The heaviest liability under which the Colony suffers is the loan from Her Majesty's Government on the occasion of the calamitous earthquake of 1843. I do not now allude to the bulk of the amount lent, which was appropriated to the relief of the necessities of the individual sufferers, but to that portion of it which was retained for the public service, and was expended in the repairs of public buildings ... the strain of this engagement is only now beginning to be felt.

The advance was made available in the form of loans by the Antiguan administration to borrowers, who were due to repay by instalments to coincide with Antigua's 10-yearly repayments to the UK Treasury in London:

> Had the petition to HM Government been for the remission of the portion which must be raised by taxation on a community only just recovering from the struggle of competition between free-labour and slave-grown sugar, their proceedings would at least have met with sympathy, even if they had not met with concurrence.

In 1860 (Department of the Colonies, 1861):

> ... the debt to the Government has been reduced to £14 857 yet, as no separate provision has been made for the liquidation of any part of it, and as the ordinary income of the Colony was inadequate for that purpose, the means by which it has been reduced have been obtained by local loans, indicated by the debt due to the Savings Bank and issue of Treasury Notes. By the subsisting arrangement the debt to the Government is to be reduced in 1865 to £10 000 by the payment of annual instalments; and such £10 000 are being paid in moieties in the years 1866 and 1867.

The earthquake loan disappeared from Colonial Reports only in 1868. In 1867, construction commenced of a waterworks which continued for three years at a cost of £30,000 and a capacity of '500,000 gallons' (2,273,045 litres). This measure of attention to recurrent drought had had to wait until the burden of the earthquake loan had disappeared.

Throughout the period of colonial administration in Antigua the most important crop was sugar cane. Its success or failure in any year was the indicator of success or failure of the colony. Although Colonial Reports make reference in varying degrees to living conditions and other social factors, there is an overriding concern for income from sugar production. The success of a Governor's term of office depended on revenue.

International fluctuations in the price of sugar itself had a much more serious impact than any other factor up to about 1900. Low prices often confounded high production. In 1895, when very low prices accompanied very low production, it seemed that the sugar industry was doomed to extinction, saved only by a rise to average production in 1896 (Watts, 1906).

Before 1898, cane disease was the prevailing factor influencing production. It took many years of experience to distinguish the effects of disease and drought, but successful experiment with resistant cane brought disease under control by 1898. Thereafter, the relationship between rainfall and sugar production became clear, though still masked in small degree by changes in agricultural methods, variations in acreage, new varieties of cane, and factory efficiency. Sugar production in the years immediately following 1900 was below average, due entirely to deficient rainfall and the damage caused by an 1899 hurricane. Thereafter, the construction and equipping of centralized sugar factories, and the introduction of mechanized ploughing and transportation, indicated a confidence in the future of the industry which, as it turned out, heralded a period of increasing annual average production.

The relationship between rainfall and sugar production was examined in a study of 1930–54 (Auchinleck, 1956; Table 6.2) which assumes (applying more recent understandings):

- All other confounders were of limited influence.
- The only lag time of significance between rainfall and impact on sugar is one year.
- Drought results from only rainfall variations without water use influencing it (see Wilhite and Glantz, 1985).

Table 6.2 Rainfall and sugar production in Antigua, 1930–54

Rainfall of preceding year	No. of years	Sugar production: yearly average (tons)
Below 0.76 metres	1	4,442
0.76–1.02 metres	4	15,626
1.02–1.27 metres	7	19,041
1.27–1.52 metres	9	20,010
1.52–1.78 metres	1	27,713
Above 1.78 metres	3	28,657
Average 1.29 metres	Total 25	Average 19,760

Source: Auchinleck, 1956.

- Multi-decadal climate variabilities are of limited consequence, so short-term and long-term averages are meaningful.
- The values selected to divide the table rows are meaningful.

The average rainfall for the longer period of 76 years (1874–1949) was lower, at 1.1 metres, than that in Table 6.2, although statistical significance ought to be checked. Years of rainfall substantially below this average (again, without a statistical significance check) were 1874, 1875, 1882, 1890, 1905, 1910, 1912, 1920, 1921, 1922, 1923, 1925, 1928, 1930, 1939, and 1947. In addition to these 16 years of apparently severely low rainfall, there were a further 17 years with rainfall below average. As Antiguan rainfall was gathered from a number of measurement stations, it is certain that some local conditions were worse, and some better, than the national averages. There is also no guarantee that all stations were calibrated the same. Over the same 76 years (1874–1949) there are, however, only 14 years where drought has been a significant claim in the Colonial Records. It can perhaps be accepted, therefore, that drought conditions, when officially reported as such, were economically and socially serious in the national experience.

Drought in 1863–65 likely had an impact on the mortality rate of 47.8 per 1,000 population. A total of 5,222 deaths, 14.4 per cent of the population, was recorded for this period. The sugar crop of 1874 was the smallest since 1864, and the total value of all exports fell accordingly from £170,977 in 1873 to £106,705 in 1874 (Table 6.3).

Subsequently, at the end of 1912, Antigua had (Colonial Office, 1913):

> suffered from three successive years of drought, which caused considerable distress in country districts … The drought culminated in an almost complete failure of [water] supply in St. John's, and for some days an acute water famine prevailed.

The beneficial effect of hurricanes in bringing rainfall and ending a three-year period of serious drought was apparent in 1924. From Colonial Office (1925), 'Hurricane brought damage of several thousand pounds but also brought relief in the form of welcome rains'. Rainfall for the year was 1.06 metres, 0.25 metres above that of the preceding year, the heaviest being on 27 August preceding the hurricane of 28–29 August.

Hurricanes over and near Antigua have frequently brought beneficial rain and, to those engaged in sugar production, the benefits of employment and income. Hurricanes' immediate consequences have nevertheless sometimes

Table 6.3 Antigua: exports and imports 1871–74

	1871 £	1872 £	1873 £	1874 £
Imports	175,740	200,577	169,156	146,758
Exports	247,630	53,190	170,977	106,705

Source: Department of Colonies, 1875.

been serious, most significantly in 1681, 1772, 1780, 1792, and 1804, with a total of 22 collated for 1664–1846 (Garriott, 1900).

The hurricane of 1848, though of serious impact, received scant mention in the Colonial Report for the year, which was still preoccupied with the aftermath of the 1843 earthquake. The hurricane of 8 September 1899 caused damage to houses, but no reported loss of life, though 'much damage to the huts of the labouring classes, who consequently suffered from exposure and distress' (Colonial Office, 1899). Its part in the run of poor years of sugar production after 1900 is mentioned above. The hurricane of 28–29 August 1924, which ended three years of serious drought, caused 'moderate' damage. A relief fund established by the Lord Mayor of London reached £4,000 which was 'devoted to the relief of peasants and labourers and the reconstruction of their dwellings' in Nevis, Montserrat, Tortola, St Kitts, and Antigua whose share was £1,356, five shillings, and ninepence. Of this amount, a sum of £500 was placed on deposit 'as the nucleus of a fund to meet further similar disasters' (Colonial Office, 1925).

Contributions of clothing and food were sent from other Caribbean colonies, England, the French Caribbean colonies, the government of the Virgin Islands, and the USA. The cost of reconstructing and repairing government property was met partly from a £10,000 grant from the London Parliament and partly from surplus funds (with the total cost not found). Total aggregate revenue for the year 1924–25 was £78,983, eight shillings, and ninepence. Total national expenditure was £85,244, 13 shillings, and ninepence, a rare excess of expenditure over revenue (Colonial Office, 1925).

Following the hurricane of 1928, a special Commission visited Antigua to assess and report upon hurricane damage (Collens, 1928). In 1928, Antigua was the principal seat of government for the UK's Leeward Islands Colony, covering the 'Presidencies' of Antigua, St Kitts and Nevis, Montserrat, Dominica, and the Virgin Islands. Under 'General Observations and Recommendations' their report stated:

1. Peasant houses. We have in all cases taken into consideration the age and condition of the houses at the time of the hurricane, and the ability or otherwise of the owner to meet the total or partial cost of repairs or rebuilding. The allocation of any hurricane funds for such destitute owners can in our opinion be left in the hands of the local authorities.

2. Damage to Government Buildings, Services, Telephone System, Press etc. ... [we] have differentiated between actual damage caused by hurricane effects and damage which may be attributed to normal wear and tear or natural causes ... [and] have endeavoured ... to apportion the estimated cost of renovation or renewals between Hurricane Relief Funds and the funds of the Presidency concerned ...

3. In view of the well-known periodicity of hurricanes in these islands we would recommend that some general form be drawn up for universal

use in each Presidency indicating the nature of damage, and its assessed value and the quantity of nails, lumber, boards, and shingles, if any, issued as relief or estimated as required for reconstruction.

Damage was assessed in categories (a) for private houses (exclusive of estate property); (b) for private houses (requiring some possible assistance); (c) for private houses (poor and destitute persons); and (d) for government property. Total damage assessments for category (c) came to £2,900 and for category (d) to £2,527, a sum £355 less than the local estimate. The Commission recommended special consideration for rebuilding the poor house at a cost of £2,500 (extra to come from Presidential funds), 'as the Poor House is 28 years old having been hastily built to house Boer War prisoners, but never used for the purpose'.

In 1927, the principal author of Collens (1928) amended a (then existing?) hurricane code (Collens, 1927). It focused principally on domestic precautions concerning shuttering for the prevailing wind and warning symptoms of a falling barometer: 'Mutual telegrams (were to be) exchanged between islands of the Leeward Island Colony by the West Indian and Panama Telegraph Company.' A red flag with a square black centre would be hoisted as a storm warning signal at Rat Island signal station. If a hurricane was to be definitely expected (or at night), 'two detonating rockets will be fired in rapid succession from the hill near the Botanic Station'. The 1928 report does not comment on the efficacy of these measures of hurricane preparedness.

In 1950, there were two serious hurricanes in addition to two serious fires in St. John's (Colonial Office, 1950). The first hurricane, on 21 August, brought winds of up to 160 kilometres per hour and severe destruction in rural areas, deaths of livestock, and extensive local damage. Altogether, 488 houses were destroyed and 636 houses were damaged, 'many being rendered uninhabitable'. The second hurricane, 10 days later on 31 August, brought winds of 264 kilometres per hour and references to greater damage in the capital of St. John's than in rural areas. There was considerable damage to government, private, and commercial dwellings and:

> leaving out an account of large houses, which were either insured by their owners or whose owners could afford to repair them unaided, 1,348 small houses were completely destroyed and 2,343 damaged in both hurricanes.

In Antigua, 6,477 people were made homeless. In Barbuda, an additional 84 houses were destroyed, 109 damaged, and 320 people made homeless. The total of 6,797 people made homeless was 15 per cent of the colony's total population.

The UK Government granted £50,000 for relief. The British West Indian Government made gifts of clothing, food, and medical supplies. Jamaica gave £5,000. American and French colonies also gave relief supplies. The homeless sheltered for many weeks in churches, schools, and halls. No further damaging hurricanes were reported in the period up to the end of the colonial administration and the start of self-government in association with the UK in 1967, although droughts recurred.

No significant foreshocks were noted for the earthquake which occurred at 5:51 a.m. local time on 8 October 1974, with a 20-second surface wave magnitude of 7.5 and damage at Modified Mercalli Intensity Scale VIII (Tomblin and Aspinall, 1975). That there were no reported deaths was, rightly or wrongly, attributed to the early hour of the event, when few people would have been about, and places of work, centres of congregation and commerce, and public buildings would have been unoccupied (Tomblin and Aspinall, 1975).

Severe damage was inflicted upon government buildings, the port, and infrastructure services of roads, electricity, telephones, and water supply. Government buildings severely damaged and rendered unusable were Parliament, Judiciary, Treasury, Central Registry, two government ministries, the Secretariat of the East Caribbean Common Market, the Public Health Service complex, the library, printery, and prison. The Anglican cathedral, rebuilt after the 1843 earthquake, received some significant damage. The prison was built in 1735 and had been severely damaged in the earthquake of 1843. The list of government buildings damaged in 1974 is very similar to those damaged in 1843, and the reasons much the same, all being unreinforced masonry or inadequately constructed reinforced concrete frame buildings. Half of the total accommodation being utilized for government operations was rendered unusable (ECLA, 1974).

The authorities of a country where droughts of concern are more frequent than damaging earthquakes were quick to make emergency repairs to damaged water mains and dams for drinking water. Principal industrial damage was to the oil refinery, rupturing tanks and pipelines, causing severe pollution and fire risk and, as the island's largest employer, then laying off of up to one-third of the workforce. The private sector suffered severely and an immediate scarcity of bread resulted from the destruction and damage caused to bakeries. Lobster reefs were damaged by the earthquake, with immediate commercial losses to the fisheries sector.

Three areas of concern were expressed for housing:

- The 40 homeless households.
- 800 habitable but damaged housing units without insurance coverage and family earnings were too low to effect repairs without assistance.
- Damaged housing with insurance cover inadequate to compensate for the full cost of repairs.

Housing losses were sustained mainly in the rural areas and mostly to buildings of traditional construction inhabited by the lowest income earners (ECLA, 1974).

The 131 years that had elapsed since 1843 had made the Anglican and Catholic cathedrals, parish churches, and chapels eligible for reconstruction assistance as Places of Historical and Cultural Interest, being deemed essential elements in the country's history. The same period represents a significant interval of seismic quiescence. This quiescence of major earthquakes was not ended by 1974's tremor, which was perhaps two orders of magnitude less than the 1843 event. Yet, still, the damage was significant and disruptive. In 1988, the library remained closed due to the damage in 1974 and remained unrepaired (Kincaid, 1988).

Colonial government was not a monolithic overburden, despite its oppression. Disagreement and dispute between the local Governor in Antigua and the Department of the Colonies in London over post-1843 earthquake loan repayments continued for 25 years. Issues that continue to preoccupy administrators of post-disaster assistance were being debated in the same terms in Antigua in 1928, as was hurricane preparedness. The poorer performance of masonry structures in earthquakes, but their value against wind and fire, was well-known and consequently well-observed in Antigua in 1843.

The interrelationship of all these issues is of predominant importance and would be obscured by hazard-separated studies:

- The effects of a hurricane on a country still suffering from earthquake impacts.
- The influence of fire upon building construction methods that increased vulnerability to earthquakes.
- The beneficial effects of a hurricane ending prevalent drought.
- Delay to water storage programmes caused by the imperatives of earthquake loan repayment.
- The effects of an earthquake on the settlements of recently emancipated enslaved people.

All are evident from these outline histories of hazards in Antigua – and their connections with vulnerabilities.

This complex administration of human ecology interrelationships means that hazards cannot be studied separately when considering disasters. All aspects come together and their interrelationships are revealed in islands (Chapter 2, 'Islands and vulnerability') to a degree not always so easily discerned and identified in other contexts. This characteristic is of crucial importance for management and development planning, in islands and at local levels everywhere.

Cyclone in Sri Lanka

This example was edited from Lewis (1981b, 1984c) and looked at the impact of Tropical Cyclone 21 on Sri Lanka. The research set out to examine the relationship, if any, between socio-economic conditions and destroyed or damaged dwellings, as well as any relationship between population density and damage, on the basis of information available in local records.

The work for this study was undertaken during May and June 1979. This book's first author extends his most sincere thanks to the director and staff of the Department of Census and Statistics, Colombo, for their kindness and co-operation, and in making pre-publication village-level census data available. He also extends his sincere thanks to the Government Agent and *kachcheri* staff in the districts of Batticaloa, Polonnaruwa, Anuradhapura, Amparai, and Matale for hospitably attending to requests for information, both in person and by correspondence; to the Department of Meteorology for detailed information on the cyclone; and to personnel in many other ministries and departments, in Colombo and in the cyclone-affected districts and divisions, too numerous to mention separately. He is further grateful to Mr K.W. Tilakaratne for his painstaking abstracts from the Sri Lanka telephone directory. Most particularly, this book's first author is grateful to Edward Horesh of the Institute for International Policy Analysis, University of Bath, UK, for his advice during the preparation of this study and for his comments on a draft version.

Tropical Cyclone 21 originated as a tropical storm in the south of the Bay of Bengal on 17 November 1978 (Figure 6.3). Moving generally westwards, on 20 November it was classified as a severe cyclone, with sustained wind speeds of over 117 kilometres per hour and, on 23 November at 5:30 a.m. local time, it crossed the eastern coastline of Sri Lanka at Batticaloa. Travelling

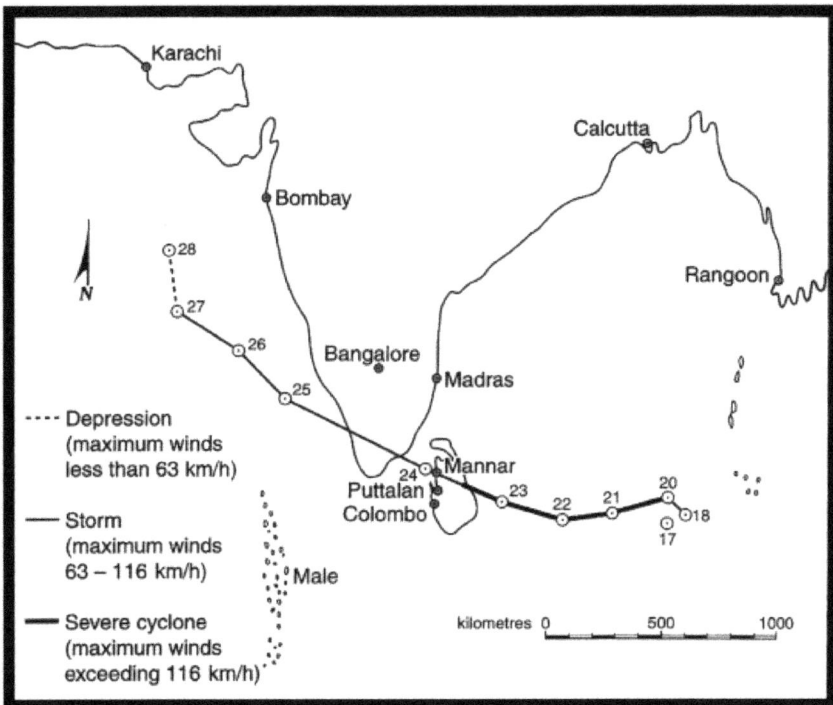

Figure 6.3 Track of Tropical Cyclone 21, 17–28 November 1978
Source: ESCAP, 1979

north-west and moderating to a tropical storm, it continued across the Gulf of Mannar into southern India on 24 November and reduced further to a depression in the Arabian Sea (Meteorological Department, Colombo, 1979, unpublished data).

In Sri Lanka, sustained wind speeds were recorded at 147 kilometres per hour before the weather station at Batticaloa was destroyed. Based on satellite information, the observatory at Colombo estimated the speeds to have been 200 kilometres per hour. Rainfall over the 24 hours (23–24 November) was recorded as 0.30 metres at Batticaloa. Heavier rainfall of up to 0.43 metres was recorded in the Central Highlands brought about by peripheral south-westerly winds of the cyclonic formation depositing rain on the high land. Severe flash flooding thus occurred in many places including Nuwara Eliya and at Ratnapura and Avissawella (Meteorological Department, Colombo, 1979, unpublished data; Figure 6.4).

In all, probably two-thirds of the country was seriously affected, directly by the cyclone, indirectly by severe flooding, or both. Reports from govern-mental and inter-governmental agencies and newspapers seem to have under-emphasized the total effects of the disaster. They focused mainly on the urban centres, where physical damage was most obvious to those making and reporting on disaster assessments and which were themselves the centres of communication.

Damage caused by the cyclone alone covered the whole of Batticaloa and Polonnaruwa districts and parts of Amparai, Anuradhapura, and Matale districts, approximately 20 per cent of the total area of Sri Lanka (Figure 6.4), with approximately 7 per cent of the country's population (Department of Census and Statistics, 1978). Reported to be between 800,000 and 1 million (OFDA/AID, 1978; UNDRO, 1979), the numbers of people affected by cyclone and flooding were another 7 per cent of the national population.

International disaster comparisons at the national level are important for understanding the administrative and infrastructural burdens upon national governments. Equally important are comparisons of disaster impact at subnational administrative levels. The first administrative burden of disaster falls upon affected local governments. The burden of only localized disaster upon local government administration and local government area populations can be considerable. Local government administrations rely on governments at wider jurisdictional levels when disaster recovery exceeds local resources. Where reliance upon central governments exceeds national capacity, then the central government itself may become reliant upon external resources of disaster assistance.

Sri Lanka is divided into 22 districts, each administered from a *kachcheri*, or secretariat, headed by a Government Agent (GA). Each district is subdivided into several divisions, directly administered by an Assistant Government Agent (AGA). Each AGA division is further subdivided into a number of smaller areas containing one or more villages, each represented by a *grama sevaka* (village head).

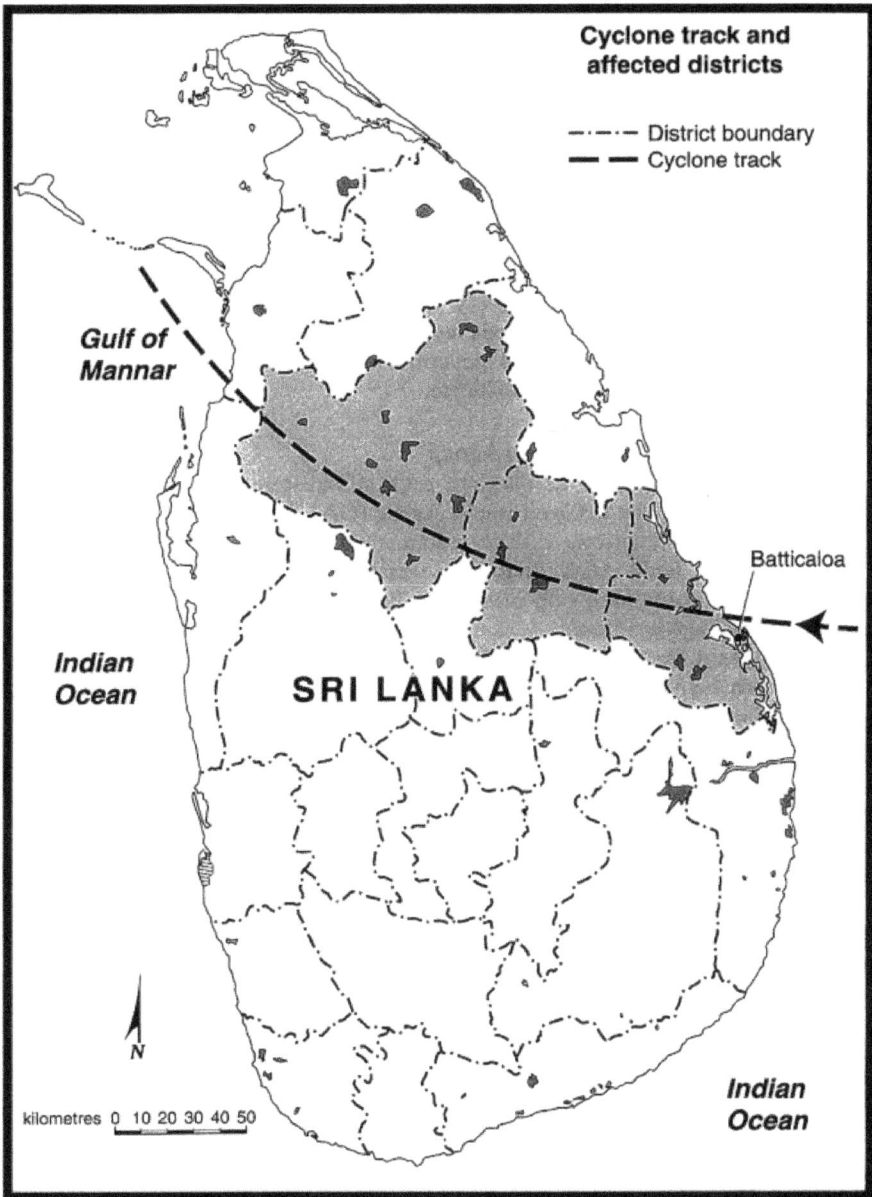

Figure 6.4 Tropical Cyclone 21's track over Sri Lanka
Source: Meteorological Department, Colombo, 1979, unpublished data

A significant feature of the 14 damaged divisions in four districts (Figure 6.5) is the much higher rural, compared to urban, population (Table 6.4). There are seven urban districts (municipal and town councils), with a total population of 108,122 (1971), but there are 992 villages with a total population of

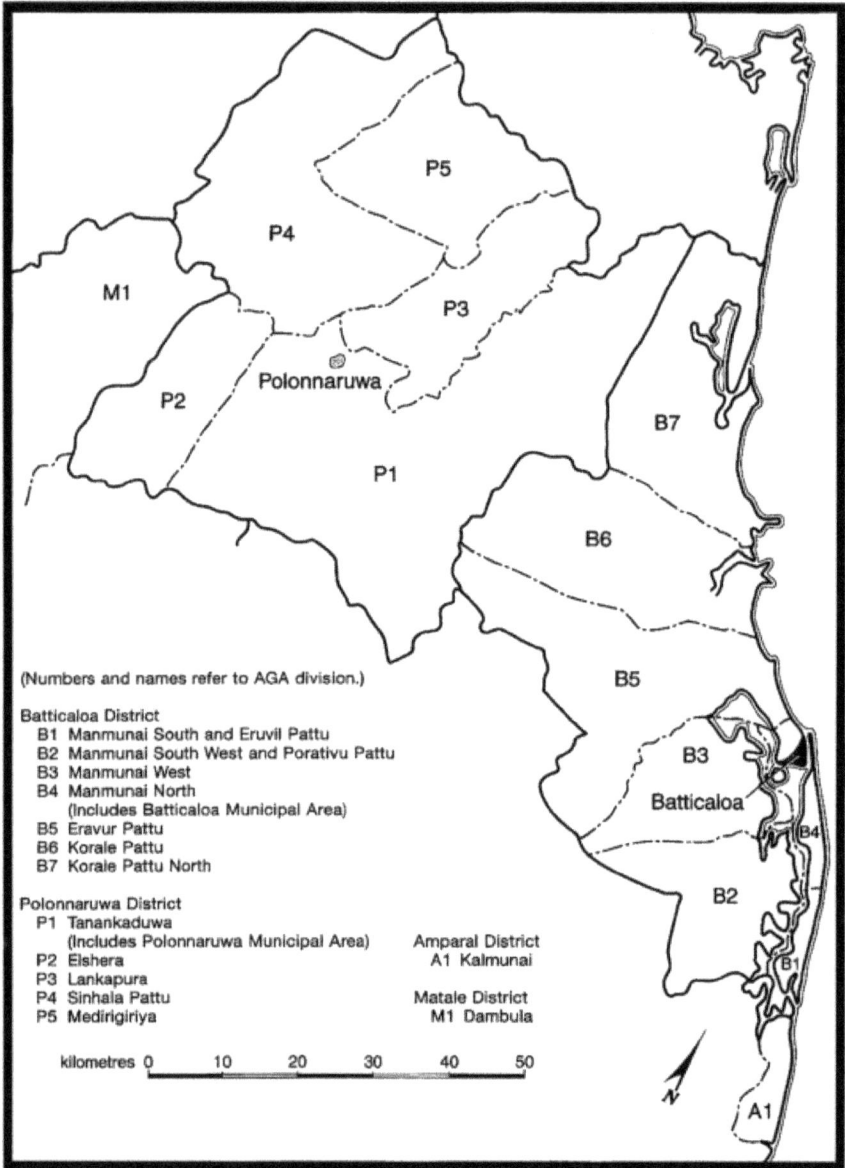

Figure 6.5 The Assistant Government Agent divisions of the most affected districts of Batticaloa and Polonnaruwa, and Dambula and Kalmunai of Amparai and Matale districts

438,963 (1977). The density of rural populations, in divisions without urban areas, is in many cases higher than that of divisions that do have urban areas (for example, B1's population density is higher than B5's). Definitions of 'rural' and 'urban', and the existence of a clear delineation between the two, can be questioned.

Table 6.4 Area population, settlement, and densities by damaged district and division

District and division	Area to the nearest km²	No. of urban areas[a]	Total urban population (1971)[a]	No. of villages	Total rural population (1977)[ab]	Rural population density (per km²)	Total population	Overall population density (per km²)
Batticaloa								
B1	45	0	0	26	33,984	753	33,984	753
B2	291	0	0	102	38,315	131	38,315	131
B3	278	0	0	109	13,306	48	13,306	48
B4	71	2	52,549	36	24,963	352	77,512	1,092
B5	588	1	16,959	95	30,432	52	47,391	81
B6	772	0	0	185	54,979	71	54,979	71
B7	419	0	0	93	9,295	22	9,295	22
Polonnaruwa								
P1	1,503	1	9,684	82	38,266	25	47,950	32
P2	366	0	0	31	21,611	59	21,611	59
P3	392	0	0	35	32,690	83	32,690	83
P4	P4+P5: 1,163	1	6,603	57	35,984	P4+P5: 63	42,587	P4+P5: 69
P5		0	0	52	37,464		37,464	
Amparai								
A1	22[d]	1	19,180[c]	16	37,511	1,704	56,691	2,575
Matale								
M1	438[e]	1	3,147	73	30,163	69	33,310	76
Total/overall	6,348	7	108,122	992	438,963	69	547,085	86

Sources and notes:
[a] Department of Census and Statistics, Colombo.
[b] Department of Census and Statistics, Colombo, basic village-level statistics 1977.
[c] Department of Census and Statistics, Colombo. In 1971, Kalmunai was a Town Council area before being made an AGA division. Reference to 1971 figures may reflect a higher urban value than the present actual urban area with Kalmunai AGA division.
[d] GA *kachcheri*, Amparai district.
[e] GA *kachcheri*, Matale district.

Total numbers of houses destroyed and houses damaged by division and district (Table 6.5) exceed, in all divisions except for P5, the figures for total housing stock by very much more than any margin of error or increase in urban population since 1971. Figures of damage are in excess of totals for housing stock by an average over all divisions of 50 per cent. Figures concerning housing stock per population relate very closely to national average family size and are therefore assumed to be accurate. Due to the lack of control in the collection process, figures on damaged and destroyed housing have been consistently overestimated or exaggerated. Although analysis is not reliable, the figure of destroyed housing has been used for comparing with population density and socio-economic indicators.

As a truism, any indicator at any scale has advantages and limitations, with indicator theories offering plenty of baselines and directions for disaster indicators. In attempting to formulate and apply indicators for measuring progress on disasters at multiple scales, some data remain notoriously difficult to collect accurately, precisely, comprehensively, and comparably. For example, personal income, assets, expenditures, and loans are often closely guarded, especially in small communities. Income, assets, and expenditures might be exaggerated to appear more affluent or might be underreported to avoid taxes and theft. Loans might be exaggerated to elicit sympathy or might be underreported to avoid embarrassment at being indebted. Different people respond differently to similar financial circumstances.

For understanding disasters and, notably, vulnerabilities, most data selected for indicators can be interpreted as local capacities, capabilities, abilities, and resources. They are exactly what is needed for local disaster prevention and vulnerability reduction through development, in addition to their usefulness in measuring change in local progress.

In seeking to examine any relationship that there may be between local societal indicators and the distribution of disaster damage, retrospective analysis of disaster will require information of the pre-disaster condition. Any method of assessment of progress that depends upon only post-disaster observation is unlikely to be applicable in retrospect, and will not work at all where the very elements for observation have been destroyed, damaged, dislocated, or made inaccessible by the disaster. On the other hand, a local survey for prospective analysis of near-future disaster damage requires the pre-selection of a location in which disaster is likely to occur soon. While any location would be expected to experience a disaster at some point, given the lack of vulnerability reduction for so many people in so many places, exactly when a disaster could occur is rarely certain. Hoping for a disaster is unethical and unwarranted (aside from being impracticable for short-term research purposes). A survey now of vulnerabilities and potential disaster damage, however, ought to always be priority, precisely to identify areas of particular vulnerability which require (resources for) disaster prevention and vulnerability reduction through development.

Table 6.5 Destroyed and damaged housing units by district and division

District and division	Area to the nearest km²	No. of housing units	Housing density (per km²)	No. of urban housing units (1971)[c]	No. of rural housing units (1978)[d]	No. of housing units destroyed[a]	% housing units destroyed	No. of housing units damaged	% housing units damaged
Batticaloa									
B1	45	6,019	133	0	6,019	4,812	80	2,768	46
B2	291	6,928	24	0	6,928	3,347	48	7,444	>100
B3	278	2,282	8	0	2,282	2,605	>100	834	37
B4	71	10,779	152	6,233	4,546	5,128	48	11,905	>100
B5	588	11,737	20	7,265	4,472	9,983	85	4,033	34
B6	772	10,412	13	0	10,412	8,744	84	3,719	36
B7	419	1,809	4	0	1,809	1,792	99	615	34
Polonnaruwa									
P1	1,503	8,802	6	1,516	7,286	12,887	>100	6,625	75
P2	366	3,610	10	0	3,610	867	24	3,687	>100
P3	392	4,874	12	0	4,874	5,150	>100	2,322	48
P4	P4+P5: 1,163	7,038	P4+P5: 12	1,273	5,765	3,000	43	6,240	89
P5		6,536		0	6,536	863	13	4,500	69
Amparai									
A1	22[b]	10,332[e]	469	3,473[e]	6,859	465[b]	5	12,015[b]	>100
Matale									
M1	438[c]	6,048	14	610	5,438	1,064[c]	18	5,903[c]	98
Total/overall	6,348	97,206	15	20,370	76,836	60,707	not calculable	72,610	not calculable

Sources and notes:

[a] GA *kachcheri*, Batticaloa and Polonnaruwa.
[b] GA *kachcheri*, Amparai district.
[c] GA *kachcheri*, Matale district.
[d] Department of Census and Statistics, Colombo, basic village level statistics, 1977.
[e] Department of Census and Statistics, Colombo. In 1971, Kalmunai was a Town Council area before being made an AGA division. Reference to 1971 figures may reflect a higher urban value than the present actual urban area with Kalmunai AGA division.

Irrespective, retrospective, post-disaster research was the only option available in Sri Lanka, six months after the cyclone of November 1978, demonstrating what such work does and does not offer. The purpose was, as best as feasible, to assess the relationship between the distribution of disaster damage and local socio-economic indicators. The first step was identifying the local unit of area administration at which data in both socio-economic indices and disaster damage were available.

Because parts of districts were affected and because only two whole districts were involved, data at district level were insufficient for any realistic comparison. Records of disaster damage had been made in some detail for districts for the purpose of reporting to the central government in Colombo (Government of Sri Lanka, 1978). These records had been prepared on the basis of information gathered by the *grama sevakas* and AGAs in turn, and collated by the GA in each district *kachcheri*. The smallest unit at which data on disaster damage were locally available in written form was the AGA division (Tables 6.4 and 6.5).

Possibly the most useable statistics available for socio-economic indicators for AGA divisions are from the Basic Village Statistics Survey made in 1977 (Department of Census and Statistics, 1978). These surveys give figures for, among others:

- Population by age and sex.
- Population by major occupation.
- Unemployed population by educational status and sex.
- Distribution of housing units, households, number of villages with electricity, and total number of villages.
- Distribution of families by land ownership.
- Numbers of fishing craft owned by villagers.
- Distribution of livestock and poultry.
- Distribution of industries (large-, medium-, and small-scale).
- Number of institutions by type of cottage industry.
- Number of housing units by type of cottage industry.

Attempts to determine other indicators applicable to, or compatible with, AGA divisions were unproductive in most cases:

- Land use did not have figures available.
- Figures for the registration of motor vehicles and tractors were available by districts only.
- Figures for the registration of radios, if reliable at all, were collated via post offices, the location of which is not related to GA or AGA administration, plus registrations could be made at a post office in one area by persons residing in another.
- All health statistics are based on health administration areas, which are different from AGA districts or divisions and, although considerable, were not therefore compatible with information on disaster damage.

There was an apparently direct relationship between socio-economic measurements and the incidence of malaria, for which statistics are normally very detailed as part of anti-malaria programmes. Further research and analysis would be necessary to determine how far data covering the distribution of malaria incidence could be used as a socio-economic indicator itself (Ruberu, 1976; Visvalingam et al., 1972).

Some figures were available on costs of agricultural production and farmers' incomes, but for districts only. Other figures which had been prepared were not relevant to the areas affected by the cyclone. There are no official figures on the stock of telephones by division, but information on the number of telephones per AGA division was abstracted from the telephone directory (Sri Lanka Post Office, 1978; Figure 6.6). This is the only information used at national level as a non-monetary indicator of wealth that is usable at AGA division level (United Nations, 1977).

From village-level survey statistics, available per AGA division, some were not of use or were inappropriate as indicators of wealth. Population figures, distribution of housing units, and total number of villages were basic data. Households per housing unit were unreliable as an indicator of wealth without more information on social norms. Number of fishing craft were not representative overall, being more significant to coastal areas. Distribution of industry itself and cottage industry institutions were considered of little value without additional information on numbers of people employed and from which AGA divisions. Number of pigs and number of cows per person were omitted, being unrepresentative due to cultural constraints, although numbers of poultry,

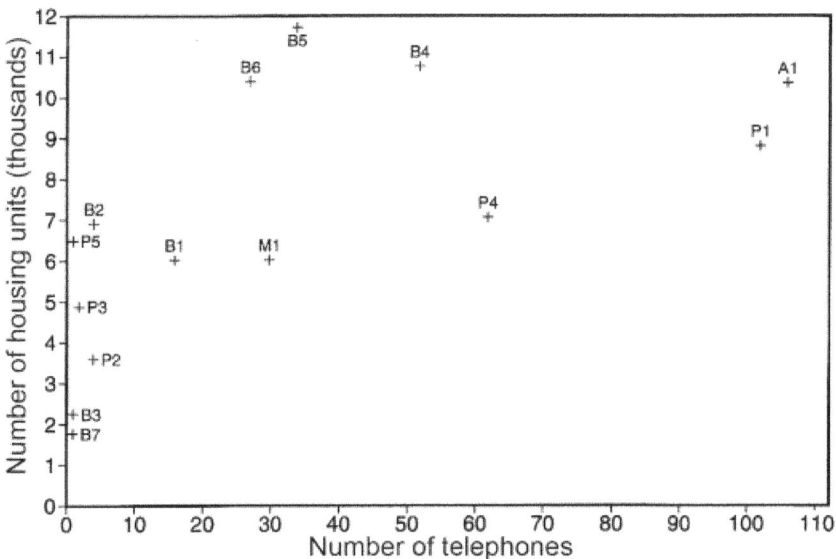

Figure 6.6 Number of housing units and number of telephones

goats, and water buffalo were used. The figure for 'tractors in use' is very low (United Nations, 1977) and ownership of water buffalo is therefore significant as an indicator of wealth.

The indicators finally selected were:

- Percentage of unemployed per employable population; that is, 15–54 years old, plus over 55 years old age groups.
- Percentage of landless families.
- Percentage of landless families plus families with less than half an acre.
- Number of poultry per person.
- Number of goats per person.
- Number of water buffalo per person.
- Percentage of villages with electricity (indicating an overall capacity per village to pay for electricity).
- Number of telephones per division (indicating an individual ability to pay).

The selected indicators and their corresponding values for Batticaloa district rural areas are given in Table 6.6.

As indicators do not necessarily have equal significance, some weighting is necessary before indicator values per area can be computed to a single indicator factor. To find a method of weighting that is other than arbitrary has caused considerable difficulties (Beckerman, 1966). Beckerman's (1966) method is to find which national non-monetary indicators are highly correlated with aggregated national accounts. This method obviously cannot be made to apply for areas smaller than the national, but it is possible to determine which indicator most closely represents all the others for each division.

A computer program to determine the correlation matrix and therefore the most representative indicator was applied to the values in Table 6.6.[1] Correlation output and correlation matrix are given in Table 6.7. The highest correlation between the eight selected indicators is the percentage of villages with electricity and the number of telephones per division, but even these are not significant at the 0.05 level. The percentage of rural dwellings connected to electricity is very low, at 2 per cent in 1970 (World Bank, 1976). The percentage of villages served can therefore be assumed to be very low and so was discounted. The distribution of telephones by individual dwelling or business is in any case a more accurate indicator according to cultural norms, although the standard deviation is large for the mean.

The 12 divisions within Batticaloa and Polonnaruwa districts, crossed by or closely adjacent to the track of the cyclone, have been used as the basis for analysis and comparison, with the addition of two adjacent divisions, Kalmunai in the coastal Amparai district and Dambulla in the inland Matale district (Tables 6.4 and 6.5). Figures for each AGA division obtainable from the district GA *kachcheris* were numbers of deaths, numbers of houses destroyed, and numbers of houses damaged. In some cases, house figures were divided between masonry houses and non-masonry houses. For Batticaloa district

Table 6.6 Selected indicators: Batticaloa district rural areas (to two significant figures)

	Unemployed %	Landless %	Landless + < ½ acre (0.002 km²) %	No. of poultry per person	No. of goats per person	No. of water buffalo per person	Villages with electricity %	No. of phones per div.[b]
	UE	LA	LH	PO	GO	BU	EL	TE[b]
B1	18	14	82	0.85	0.13	0.11	27	16
B2	4.5	22	30	0.69	0.31	0.44	2.9	4
B3	24	33	43	1.4	0.99	0.38	0.92	1
B4	15	13	85	1.7	0.16	0.002[a]	31	52
B5	13	22	57	1.2	0.16	0.19	9.5	34
B6	7.4	23	74	1.4	0.50	0.34	4.9	27
B7	20	41	63	1.3	0.45	0.20	1.1	1

[a] Two significant figures are not available
[b] An exact number, so not two significant figures

Table 6.7 Correlation output and correlation matrix (to two significant figures)

| Selected social indicator | Correlation output | | |
	abbr.	Mean	Standard deviation
% unemployed	UE	15	6.9
% landless	LA	24	9.9
% landless + < half acre (0.002 km²)	LH	62	20
Number of poultry per person	PO	1.2	0.35
Number of goats per person	GO	0.39	0.30
Number of water buffalo per person	BU	0.24	0.16
% villages with electricity	EL	11	13
Number of telephones	TE	19	19

| | Correlation matrix | | | | | | | |
	UE	LA	LH	PO	GO	BU	EL	TE
UE	1.0	0.39	0.16	0.32	0.44	−0.31	0.068	−0.24
LA	0.39	1.0	−0.45	0.075	0.65	0.45	−0.82	−0.69
LH	0.16	−0.45	1.0	0.50	−0.45	−0.82	0.75	0.65
PC	0.32	0.075	0.50	1.0	0.23	−0.41	0.18	0.56
GO	0.44	0.65	−0.45	0.23	1.0	0.62	−0.65	−0.57
BU	−0.31	0.45	−0.82	−0.41	0.62	1.0	−0.84	−0.67
EL	0.068	−0.82	0.75	0.18	−0.65	−0.84	1.0	0.69
TE	−0.24	−0.69	0.65	0.56	−0.57	−0.67	0.69	1.0

only, the numbers of destroyed and damaged weaving centres and handlooms were obtained.

Damage was, of course, widespread sectorally as well as geographically. Besides damage to housing, there was damage to agriculture, fishing, industry, and non-residential infrastructure. The number of houses destroyed is selected from the available data, not only as a significant aspect of sectoral damage in itself, but also as one that is representative of all divisions and districts. Therefore, it is taken as an indicator (merely an indicator) of overall damage sustained.

At first glance, Figures 6.7 and 6.8 show little positive relationship between the number or the percentage of housing units destroyed and housing unit density (number of housing units per square kilometre). In contrast, there is a tendency toward a negative relationship. Both graphs relate the highest density A1 with the lowest number of units destroyed and B4, the next highest density related to the next lowest number and percentage of housing units destroyed. Both these divisions contain very high population numbers and are characterized by very high housing unit densities, plus both contain urban and rural areas (Tables 6.4 and 6.5). Some discrepancies emerge in the values in Tables 6.4/6.5 compared to Figures 6.7/6.8 due to rounding.

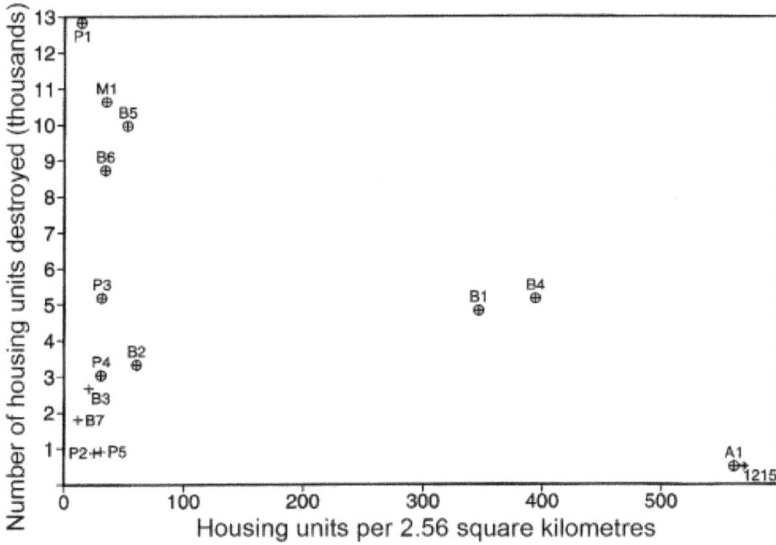

Figure 6.7 Number of housing units destroyed and housing unit density (⊕ means urban or high-density districts; + means rural or low-density districts)

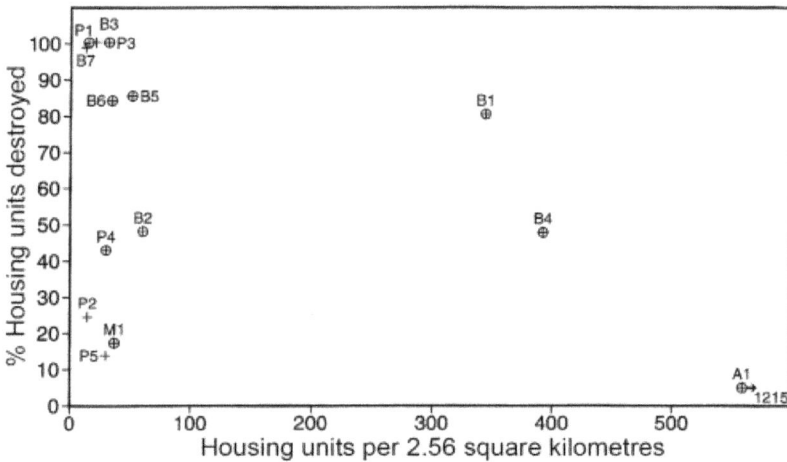

Figure 6.8 Percentage of housing units destroyed and housing unit density (⊕ means urban or high-density districts; + means rural or low-density districts)

When all the divisions containing urban areas are taken on their own, there is a strong negative relationship between density and destruction. There is highest destruction in the lowest densities, P1, M1, and B5; and lowest destruction in the highest densities, A1 and B4. On the same line of the negative relationship, B1 is a high-density non-urban division on the densely populated coastal belt, between A1 and B4 (Figure 6.5). The population density of B1 is higher than that of four divisions containing urban areas. Finally, B2 and P3, also high-density, non-urban areas, are outside this negative value line, but these two may be in the same relationship with each other. P3, with the highest destruction, has lower density and B2 with the lowest destruction has higher density.

The cyclone moderated as it moved inland (Figures 6.3 and 6.4), so wind speed reduced. The greatest wind speeds were therefore at the coast where, in this region of Sri Lanka, most concentrations of population are located. Of the three coastal divisions of highest population density, A1 and B4 show only medium-to-low percentages of houses destroyed. Of the remainder, the higher percentages of houses destroyed (given as 100 per cent or near) are in the low-density divisions of B3, B5, B6, B7, P1, and P3 (keeping in mind the major data limitations).

Lowest density divisions have low percentages of destruction in B2, P4, P2, M1, and P5. For the latter, the environmental factor of cyclone intensity appears to supersede the density factor. All the divisions are inland, B2 with the highest percentage nearest the coast. On the other hand, the significance of A1 with very high density and low percentage of houses destroyed, could be partly due to its distance from the high-intensity centre of the cyclone track. In the divisions of very high density and very low density are the levels of lowest housing destruction, both in number and in percentage. Highest numbers of housing units destroyed are in divisions of intermediate density M1, B5, and B6 (Table 6.5).

Damage and destruction to housing units appear to be lowest in low-density areas. The highest density areas also offer some level of protection. In this cyclone, the highest density areas are the coastal belt which would have received the highest cyclone intensity. Protection afforded by highest density supersedes the environmental factor of cyclone intensity, whereas the 'protection' against high number and percentage of destruction afforded by low-density areas does not. Intensity overcomes low-density 'protection'.

Note that divisions P1, M1, B5, and B6 – and also P3 and P4 with a high number of housing units destroyed – are on the line of highest cyclone wind speed. The cyclone inland might be considered comparable to the cyclone experienced in the divisions in the periphery as the coastline was crossed; that is, the intensity at P1 might approximate the intensity at B7 and B3. There are not sufficient wind speed measurement points to provide enough data to draw isopleths for cyclone intensity. Of the few anemometers, some were destroyed by the cyclone before it reached its peak intensity – and so observed damage is one method used to estimate cyclone strength! Doing so requires making assumptions about infrastructure. The presence of P1, M1, and B5 at the top of the destruction scale (Figure 6.7) is therefore not due, or not only due, to cyclone intensity.

The comparison of the number of telephones with the number of housing units destroyed (Figure 6.9) appears to show conflicting positive and negative relationships until a separation of values is made. From the cluster of six

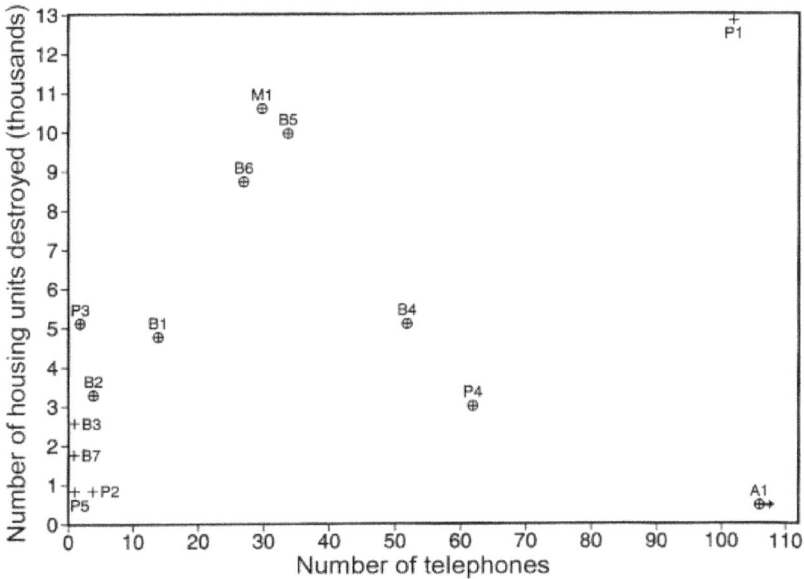

Figure 6.9 Number of housing units destroyed and number of telephones (as a socio-economic indicator) (⊕ means urban or high-density districts; + means rural or low-density districts)

divisions with low density and low numbers of telephones, there is an indication by four more of a positive relationship. The higher the number of telephones, the higher the number of housing units destroyed. To some extent, this can be simply explained by the less definite but totally positive relationship between numbers of telephones and numbers of housing units. But Figure 6.9's top values of the positive relationship, M1 and B5, are the two lowest density divisions containing urban areas, after which all remaining values are similarly urban, yet show a negative relationship. In this latter group, the highest socio-economic indicator has lowest housing destruction. Low-density areas show an increase of housing destruction with an increase in numbers of telephones. High-density areas show a decrease of housing destruction with increasing numbers of telephones. The divisions of highest destruction are in divisions of intermediate numbers of telephones, as in Figures 6.9 and 6.10. P1 appears isolated in these connections, suggesting confounders – as would be expected – for a strict bivariate relationship, as well as limitations in numbers of telephones as a proxy.

The environmental factor of cyclone intensity may be significant in the relationship of the cluster of six low-density divisions (Figure 6.5), but ceases to be significant beyond. Cyclone intensity may predominate in divisions with low numbers of telephones and low damage. The correlation between number of telephones and percentage of housing units destroyed (Figure 6.10) shows neither positive nor negative clarity.

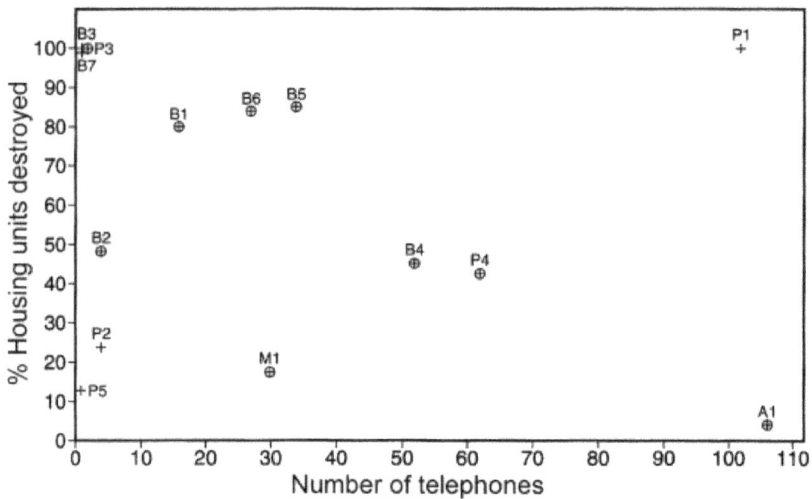

Figure 6.10 Percentage of housing units destroyed and number of telephones (as a socio-economic indicator) (⊕ means urban or high-density districts; + means rural or low-density districts)

Since number of telephones relates positively to total number of housing units, divisions with highest numbers of housing units have the higher socio-economic indicator. Housing unit density itself, therefore, with more definite interpretation of relationships with housing unit destruction, becomes the more obvious key indicator, for either low- or high-density divisions. Nevertheless, the reasons why high-density divisions suffer lower percentages of destruction can be partly explained in terms of higher construction quality; that is, in terms of its socio-economic measure, emphasizing that housing is not equivalent across divisions. Buildings also protect each other. The close compatibility between housing unit density and socio-economic indicator can be simply explained, but not explained away.

Examining the relationship between percentage of housing units destroyed and division area (Figure 6.11) shows two groups of values of negative relationship. Each group shows a higher percentage of housing destruction for divisions of lowest area. The two groups are not, in this case, separable according to density, since each group contains areas of high density and areas of low density. The group of highest percentage of housing unit destruction does contain five of the divisions of highest cyclone intensity. If this grouping would be accepted as significant, then there is a close relationship between a high percentage of housing unit destruction and divisions of smallest area. The smallest divisions suffer higher percentages of destruction.

Deaths in the cyclone (Figure 6.12) were available by division, only in the districts of Batticaloa, Amparai, and Matale. Again, among the highest density divisions of B1, B2, B4, and A1, there is a definite negative relationship. The higher the population density, the lower the loss of life.

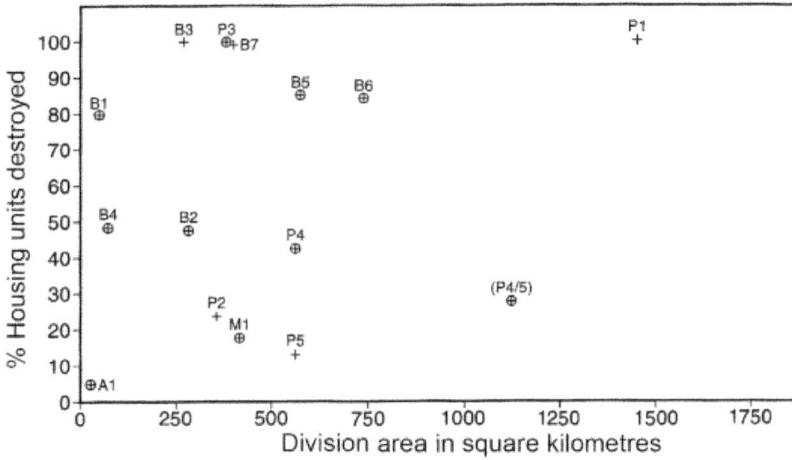

Figure 6.11 Percentage of housing units destroyed and division area (⊕ means urban or high-density districts; + means rural or low-density districts)

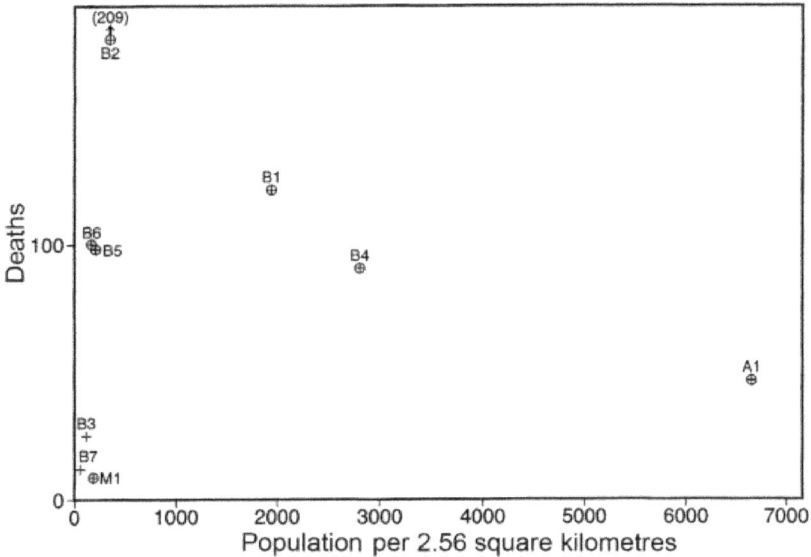

Figure 6.12 Deaths and population density (⊕ means urban or high-density districts; + means rural or low-density districts)

There is no definite relationship, negative or positive, between deaths and number of telephones.

Conclusions, or suggestions, are conditioned by the overriding factor of data incompatibility and unreliability. The totals of housing units destroyed and housing units damaged exceed the figures for housing unit stock (Table 6.5). Inaccuracy in the gathering of statistics for disaster damage in disrupted working conditions, as well as intentional exaggeration or downplaying of disaster damage for political or practical purposes, are common. That either factor is present here is a small contribution to the stock of arguments for the impossibility of achieving an adequate database for post-disaster assessments based solely upon post-disaster observation. Furthermore, some of the maps required for identifying division boundaries – subject to considerable and recent readjustment and displayed on walls of administrators' offices – had been destroyed by rain after the administration buildings lost parts of their roofs.

Conclusions and suggestions offered from these analyses can nonetheless be attempted for discussion, noting that they should not be taken as definitive. Although the strongest definition of relationship is between the socio-economic indicator (number of telephones) and number of housing units destroyed (Figure 6.9), because of the obvious positive relationship between number of telephones and number of housing units in a given area (Figure 6.6), housing unit density, in this case, could be the key indicator. Number of telephones is valid as a socio-economic indicator, but is not sufficiently representative and has been swamped by the more significant housing unit density. The two remain compatible. If problems in data collection and reliability in another study could be overcome, then it would be worthwhile to make another attempt to apply socio-economic indicators.

Number and percentage of housing units destroyed increase with housing unit density in lower density areas, but decrease in higher density areas, even though the high-density areas are coastal, where cyclone intensity was highest. Hitherto, it has usually been assumed that areas of highest population density will suffer greatest losses; that is, that high-density areas have the greatest vulnerability. These analyses now show that low-density – that is, (usually) rural – areas might potentially contain the highest number of destroyed housing units despite lower hazard. The relatively low number of destroyed housing units in high-density areas is not always explained by those areas all being of high socio-economic measure (numbers of telephones), nor by their location in areas where cyclone intensity was lowest. Not all high-density areas have a high socio-economic indicator value, and the highest density areas are coastal. Possibly, design, materials, construction, retrofitting and/or maintenance are different. Possibly, buildings protect each other from cyclone hazards, although when a building fails, its debris might catalyse the failure of other structures leading to more debris and a possible chain reaction. Additionally, the highest percentages of destroyed housing units are in the divisions of smallest area.

The obviousness of damage to buildings in a concentrated urban area and relative ease of access for reporters, assessors, and administrators to-and-from urban centres, should not obscure the possibility for much greater social significance of damage to infrastructure in non-urban areas, which may not be so easily accessible, but which may contain larger numbers of people. Specific measures will be required to reduce, overall, this high incidence of housing destruction and damage, as part of vulnerability reduction and development. Whereas urban centres will usually be centres for administration, transport, supplies, and communications, these and all other services must be provided on behalf of, and with the participation of, the rural areas as well. Measures should correspond realistically to areas of need, without neglecting anywhere or anyone. These measures should additionally recognize the greater scale of potential need in the smaller administrative areas.

Vulnerability in Chiswell, Dorset, UK

This example was edited from Lewis (1983a) which itself updated Lewis (1979c). This book's first author extends his thanks for assisting in the preparation of Lewis (1979c) to Mr K.G. Anderson of the Wessex Water Authority; Mr Stuart Morris of Weston, Portland; and Mr Rhys Davey, Chairman, Chiswell Residents' Action Group. Special thanks are due to Dr A.P. Carr of The Institute of Oceanographic Sciences for his comments on a draft.

Disastrous manifestations of hazard are usually not unique events. In analysing the causes and effects of these occurrences, there are problems for analysts, academics, and policy-makers in understanding the long-term perspective as the context for recent circumstances and future policies. Understanding will necessarily be made initially more complex by the variety of standpoints of different groups in the affected location and of wider communities.

Physical permanence of a community cannot be assumed in a changing environment. Vulnerability to the sea has increased during the centuries of Chiswell's existence in Dorset, southern England, and is continuing to do so. Understanding this changing state by various groups in society is the key to the selection and effectiveness of interacting measures, whether undertaken specifically against hazard or not.

The extent to which technology can be effectively mobilized and implemented to ensure prolonged habitation may be assessed by detailed analysis of environmental phenomena alongside social interests, adjustments, and capabilities – as well as the inescapable social-environmental inter-twining. Social adjustments cannot be compared until options for them are made available, in the case of Chiswell by the authorities elected for their administration.

The condition of vulnerability is not static. Analysis and assessment of short- and long-term issues together is a multi-disciplinary process calling for a fusion of physical and earth sciences, social sciences, arts, humanities, professions, and political and administrative processes. That these sciences and processes are themselves evolving, and are not static, is as true as for vulnerability itself. All are involved in short- and long-term processes of change and must be integrated with each other for the most comprehensive and effective responses to hazards.

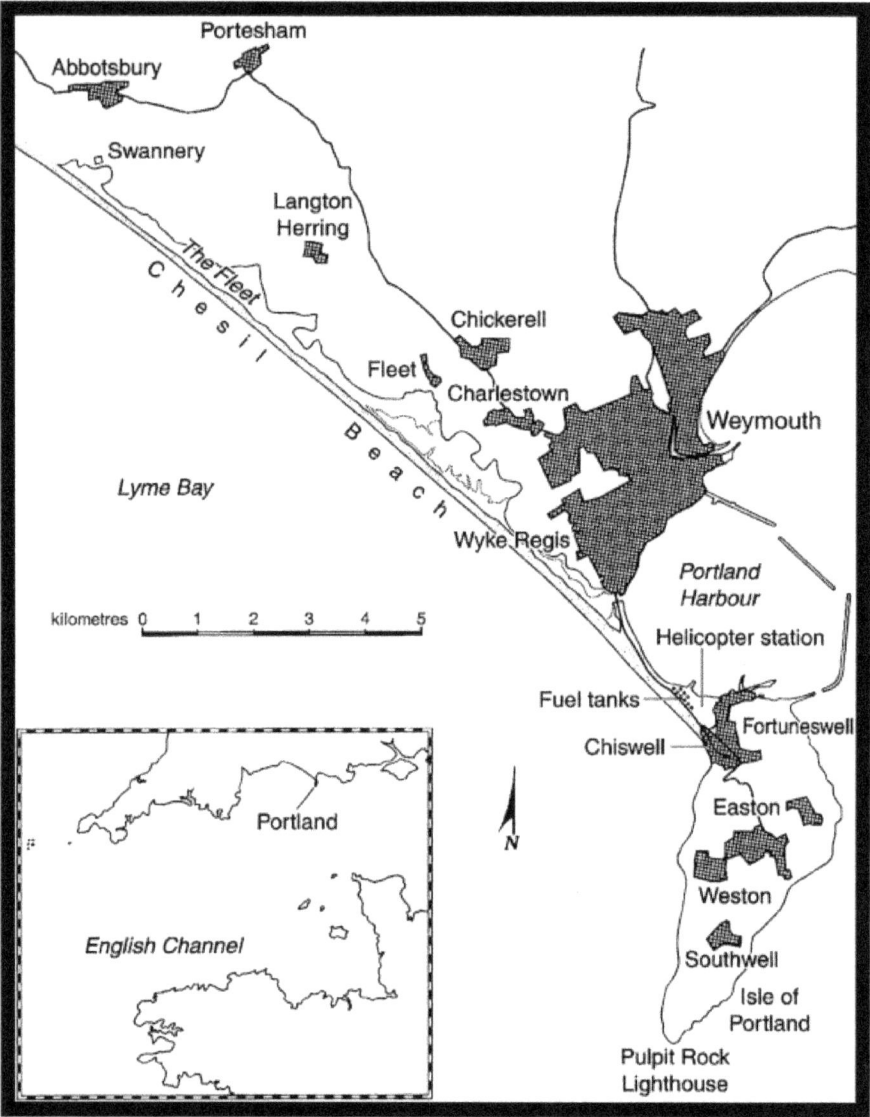

Figure 6.13 Chesil Beach, Dorset, UK

Chiswell is a community of 134 people. It is situated at the foot of the north-western slope of the so-called Isle of Portland, off Weymouth, in Dorset; adjacent to, but below, the much larger village of Fortuneswell (Figure 6.13). Portland is an island but for the shingle bar, or tombolo, and causeway which link it to the mainland. The shingle bar, Chesil Beach, extends for 16 kilometres along the coast of Lyme Bay from a point by Abbotsbury in the north-west to Chiswell itself to the south-east. For nearly 13 kilometres of its total length, Chesil Beach encloses a lagoon, called the Fleet, between it and the mainland. For the remaining 3 kilometres at the south-east end, the sea is on both sides, Lyme Bay on the one and Portland Harbour on the other. It is where the shingle bar joins the Isle of Portland and forms a brief trough between the north-west slope of the Isle and the crest of the shingle where Chiswell community is located.

Flooding by sea water seepage through the shingle, and by sea waves overtopping the shingle bank is frequent in Chiswell. In December 1978 and in February 1979, for example, waves overtopped the bank with such force that several buildings were damaged. In February, the causeway road serving the whole of Portland was breached.

Chesil Beach itself is between 137 and 183 metres wide, but is narrower both adjacent to the cliffs in the north-west and at the extreme south-eastern end. The ridge of the beach progressively increases in height from the north-west to the south-east, with the maximum of 13.7 metres above mean sea level being found adjacent to Chiswell (Carr, 1978).

At the north-western end, the shingle bank had increased in height by about 1.8 metres between 1853 and 1969. Over the central area, from Langton Herring to Wyke Regis, the bank has increased in height by about 1.7 metres. At the south-eastern end, adjacent to Chiswell, there has been a reduction in the height of the shingle of as much as 2.4 metres during this time period (Carr and Blackley, 1974; Carr and Gleason, 1972). Storm waves may periodically destroy the crest, but the overall profile may be maintained by frequent events of small magnitude, encouraging reversion to a potentially more common profile after change from a sudden, large event.

The crucial question is how an expected profile is to be identified compared to measurements of varying reliability taken at different intervals. Vulnerability of Chiswell to storm and flood emerges from short-term changes as well as long-term evolution.

Assessment of vulnerability to overtopping waves requires recognizing the frequent events of small magnitude alongside the rarer extremes. The rare event which may severely reduce the ridge height of Chesil Beach may increase the vulnerability of the Chiswell community to the next frequent event of small magnitude. It may take only small magnitude events to overtop the previously damaged bank. Even though subsequent small magnitude events will help to build it up again, it is of little comfort to the community to know that within several generations everything will be safer, although people died or lost their homes.

After the beach crest was destroyed by the winter storms of 1978–79, the local authority undertook to re-form the crest by bulldozing pebble material back into place, grant-aided by central government. Can the integration of this action into the geomorphic cycle of events be assured? Can the undertaking be more than a temporary palliative in the face of inexorable natural change, on top of which is layered human-caused changes?

There is additional lateral movement of the shingle bank, although landward recession of the bank may have been more rapid in the past than it is at present. There is also some longshore movement along the line of the shingle bank accompanied by sorting of shingle size. The size of pebbles broadly increases toward the Portland end and material is transported by tidal currents and waves from east to west (Carr, 1969). There is also vertical sorting, more active at Chesil which is more exposed to open sea. Larger stones at this south-eastern end cause porosity to be greatest. Longshore movement of shingle is probably less adjacent to Chiswell, where the approach of waves is directly in line with the approach of the sea in the English Channel (Carr, 1969).

The direct approach of more frequent waves is the most likely cause of some landward movement of the beach at this point. Movement since 1852 has been estimated at between 12.8 and 20.1 metres, and may have been greater earlier (Carr and Blackley, 1974; Carr and Gleason, 1972). There was probably a forerunner of the beach 80,000 years ago and a Chesil Beach analogous to the present formation from 6,000 years ago (Carr, 1978). One hundred or even 200 years is a small fraction of the several thousand years since the bank formed offshore and began its inexorable mainland recession.

Recession has increased the vulnerability of Chiswell and especially the causeway at Portland Harbour. The most significant factor of vulnerability at Chiswell is the reduced height of the beach crest, which is now nearer to Chiswell than it was when village settlement commenced. Movement is continuing. Vulnerability of the community at Chiswell to the sea overtopping the beach, and to seepage, is increasing.

In the great storm of 1824, the church at Fleet village, 1.2 kilometres inland from the sea-line of Chesil Beach, was destroyed with several houses, but no lives, lost. By contrast, in Chiswell, 8 kilometres to the south-east, 'upwards of 80 houses' were damaged or destroyed and 26 people died (Portland Flooding Sub-Committee, 1979). Most of Fortuneswell, on the Isle of Portland, is between 30 and 45 metres above sea level, but Chiswell is between 3.0 and 4.5 metres above mean sea level, and below the 13–14 metre ridge of Chesil Beach. When waves overtop the ridge elsewhere along its 16-kilometre length, water runs into the Fleet and eventually into the sea at Portland Harbour. When they overtop at Chiswell, they wash immediately upon and into habitation.

Chiswell's unique location in respect of its direct vulnerability to the sea is matched by advantageous proximity for fishing. Chiswell is the only community on the Isle of Portland with this close proximity, a practical advantage recognized since Roman times. Chiswell was probably established as the principal source of fish for the Isle (Morris, n/d) at a time when the sea was appreciably further away than it is now.

A watercolour of 1805 details the community very clearly as a group of approximately 47 dwellings (Weymouth Local History Museum, c. 1805). Several boats are shown drawn up on the shingle ridge, and the line of the present main street, parallel to the beach, is clearly identifiable. There are also numerous rows and single dwellings at right angles to the main street on the seaward side, rising up the shingle slope. From an image that Bettey (1970) suggests is from around 1830, it is possible to identify approximately

15 dwellings between the main street and the ridge of the beach, which are now no longer standing.

As a principal community on the island, the population and number of dwellings in Chiswell can be assumed to have expanded throughout the 19th century, as did the population of Portland as a whole, due to the prosperity of the quarrying industry for Portland stone and employment on the construction of Portland Harbour. Population peaked in 1901 and then had reduced by just over one-fifth by 1931 (Bettey, 1970). Since then, there has been a gradual increase in the population of Portland which has not been reflected in Chiswell. In 1939, there were 33 commercial premises listed in Chiswell (*Kelly's Directory*, 1939) including six public houses or hotels. In 1979, there were 11, including only three hotels or public houses.

The present population of approximately 134 in Chiswell (Chiswell Residents' Action Group, 1979a) occupies approximately 70 dwellings. As described above, in the great storm of 1824, a total of 'upwards of 80' houses were 'damaged or washed down'. In the storm of 1942, 100 houses were reported damaged (*Western Gazette*, 1942). It is not possible to determine what proportion of the whole community these figures of damage represent, but Chiswell was only recently very much larger than it is today. The decline of 21 per cent between 1901 and 1931 has been followed by perhaps 50 per cent decrease since 1942.

There are two other factors to consider before assessing the role of natural hazard in this decline. Close proximity of Chiswell to major naval, and minor civil, south coast ports created considerable vulnerability to damage by enemy air action between 1939 and 1945. It is reasonable to assume that some war damage, or knock-on impacts thereof, occurred in Chiswell. Post-war planning for Chiswell aimed at 'seaside' redevelopment, noting that rebuilding of derelict or extensively war-damaged properties was not permitted (Dorset County Council, 1964). Most of these and other existing properties were considered to be not in character with their seaside setting. The area was to be tidied up and any reinstatement of properties would conflict with proposals of the local planning authority for the clearance of the area between the main street and Chesil Beach.

There had been storms and floods in 1945, 1949, and 1954 (Morris, 1979), yet natural hazards were generally ignored in post-war planning, which focused exclusively on the architectural and visual aspects of development. The utilitarian quality of much existing construction was considered undesirable, even though it may have resulted from a once local appreciation of sea hazards. Chiswell was to be replanned in the same 'seaside' tradition as Georgian and Edwardian Weymouth.

In the immediate post-war period, damaged buildings were treated as if they were all a result of enemy action. That they included buildings damaged by the sea is likely, just as there are buildings in Chiswell now damaged by the sea in 1978 and 1979, and others derelict and said to have been damaged by earlier storms. What had been the effect of storms on the 'dereliction' and 'blight' that the planners of the 1960s were so concerned about? Storm contributed to the planners' decisions, made between 1945 and 1961, to demolish or close a total of 36 dwellings considered to be sub-standard or unhealthy. There is documentary evidence of the decision (Portland Borough Council, 1962), though not all demolition plans may have been implemented.

'Tidying-up' and refusals for redevelopment 'on the grounds that such proposals represent a piecemeal approach likely to be detrimental to the possible future development of the area as a whole' had a totally negative result. Areas designated as public open space still contain the foundations and some walls of dwellings demolished by people or sea. No 'development of the area as a whole' ever took place, although four new houses were built in 1970. In addition to the arrest of spontaneous change, the removal of seaward derelict buildings has increased exposure to the sea for the remaining buildings (Chiswell Residents' Action Group, 1979a). The few remaining inhabited buildings of the rows that extended at right angles to the main street, up the beach, are protected by the long-standing Cove Inn (Cove House Inn), massive and erect on top of the sea wall and shingle ridge.

Damage to Chiswell by seawater is caused by seepage through the shingle bank as well as by overtopping. In 1824, seawater in the Fleet rose to a depth of nearly 7 metres at the Swannery at Abbotsbury (Arkell, 1965). A sloop was carried over the shingle crest and subsequently relaunched into Portland Harbour. The higher the sea rises up the shingle bank, the greater the pressure of water to cause seepage through the bank, the lesser is the volume of shingle to obstruct seepage, and the larger components of shingle increase the rate of seepage. Finally, the sea overtops the crest aided by storm waves carried on top of a flood tide. When the sea is high, water seeps up out of the shingle bank on the landward side and runs through and between the buildings and dwellings of Chiswell. Waves hurl stones and pebbles, causing their own impact damage to roofs and windows. Flooding is often exacerbated by heavy rain, which has occasionally caused some ponding of floodwater.

There have been 21 documented storms and/or floods since the great storm of 1824 (Morris, 1979). In 1942, seepage through the bank commenced an hour before waves began to sweep over the beach. Slight flooding in Victoria Square, the lowest point, then began to become serious, and that area was eventually flooded to a depth of around 1.8 metres. Waves overtopped the shingle crest, over 100 houses in Chiswell were flooded, and the road and railway (now disused) on the causeway were breached. 'Tin baths were swept from houses' and the suffering of people affected by the floods was compared to people affected by enemy air attacks, being just as deserving of help, but not eligible for assistance from the Lord Mayor of London's Air Raid Distress Fund (*Dorset Daily Echo*, 1942). The storm occurred on 13 December, although the reports of damage were delayed for nine days due to wartime restrictions on news reporting.

On 12 December 1978, Victoria Square was flooded to a depth of just over 1 metre and high seas breached the causeway for five days. Winds were recorded as Gale Force 9, with gusts of up to 112 kilometres per hour. A section of the ridge of Chesil Beach was demolished. Police issued flood warnings in the early hours and residents adopted 'a now familiar routine of taking emergency action to beat the floods' (*Dorset Evening Echo*, 1978, December 12: 16).

On 13 February 1979, before complete recovery from the December storms had been possible, the sea overtopped Chesil Beach without warning at 6:30 a.m. Whereas in the December storm, there had been certain points along the ridge where overtopping occurred, on this occasion there was a continuous sea which overtopped a very long stretch of the beach at a height of between 4.5 and 6.1 metres. 'This had resulted in instant flooding and there was no action which could have been taken to prevent it' (Weymouth and Portland Borough Council, 1979b). Victoria Square was flooded to a depth of just over 1 metre, parked cars were piled on top of each other, electricity and gas mains in the causeway were broken, stones and masonry were swept through breaches in buildings, and 24 people were evacuated from their homes (*Dorset Evening Echo*, 1979, February 15: 15).

The storm which caused the events of December 1978 was local and its results in Chiswell were direct. The February 1979 sea surge resulted from a storm or storms in the Atlantic which, with coincident meteorological and hydrological conditions, sent the sea surge up the English Channel to be trapped by the promontory of Portland. There was no storm at Chiswell when the surge struck, hence the surprise and lack of natural warning when it occurred. Storms such as that in December 1978 are regular occurrences at Portland, with an estimated return period on spring tide of five years, with minor floods as frequent as twice yearly (Dobbie and Partners, 1979). The sea surge, too, was not unique, the previous similar event having been in 1904 and the return period having been calculated as 50–70 years (Dobbie and Partners, 1979).

In its 9 square kilometres (in 2024, the area is listed as 11.5–12.0 square kilometres), and in addition to Chiswell, the Isle of Portland contains four principal communities, two ancient castles, quarries and stone works for Portland stone, coastguard stations, Pulpit Rock lighthouse, a prison, a borstal (which was a type of UK youth detention centre, replaced in 1982), a hospital, a naval helicopter station, an underwater weapons establishment, and dockyard installations and a fuel depot for Portland Harbour. Most of these communities and establishments are elevated and, while exposed to wind, are protected from the sea. Chiswell, almost at sea level, is a very small community seemingly incidental to the island's other activities and uses. Its main street is the one-way main road off the island, which passes through Victoria Square and very near to the naval helicopter station.

The helicopter station was built by the Admiralty in 1962–63 over what had been Portland Mere, which had served the same drainage function as the Fleet still does to the larger section of the beach north-west of the causeway. Earlier maps marked the mere as 'liable to floods' (Ordnance Survey, 1930) caused by the drainage of seawater from Chiswell. The area was little used, but the construction of the helicopter station blocked the natural escape of excess water. Although there are two culverts, they become easily blocked with rubbish and debris (Chiswell Residents' Action Group, 1979a).

There is a two-hour difference between high tides to the west and to the east of the causeway. The mere served as a ponding area for excess water awaiting the ebb of the tide in Weymouth Bay. Even fully operative culverts require the low tide and ponding now takes place in and adjacent to Victoria Square. Such was the volume of water trapped in this way in February 1979 that the 1.5-metre-high perimeter stone wall of the station was demolished (Chiswell Residents' Action Group, 1979a).

Similarly, the conversion of Victoria Square into a roadway intersection has contributed to successive increases in the general road level as a result of roadworks and resurfacing. While this may have had the effect of reducing the depth of flooding in Victoria Square, it further impeded the runoff of excess water from Chiswell. There are houses adjacent to Victoria Square which formerly had up to five steps from their elevated ground floor level to the street, a sensible precaution unheeded by the highway engineers (Chiswell Residents' Action Group, 1979a).

Chiswell's primary long-term flooding concern is from the sea. Secondary flooding concerns from deeper and longer-lying floods are from technological changes over shorter time periods. These changes have been brought about by, or on behalf of, the numerous and significant authorities and institutions that have adopted Portland as a base, and the thousands of people who live or work there.

A sea wall and esplanade were constructed in 1962 for almost half a kilometre from where Chesil Beach runs into the north-east face of the island at Chesil Cove, to a point in line with halfway along Chiswell. Construction was then considered possible only with foundations on clay. Construction on deep, shifting, shingle was more difficult, which accounted for the apparently arbitrary end of the sea wall. Protection afforded to Chiswell by the sea wall is evident in so far as its limited height and extent allow. Since the first publication of this study (Lewis, 1979c), the sea wall has been extended.

The construction of the sea wall reflects acceptance of responsibility by the authorities concerned for Chiswell's safety. The wall is overtopped from time to time, its design height being lower than the adjacent natural beach crest. The construction of the sea wall may be a cause of the natural reductions in height of that beach crest (Carr and Gleason, 1972).

The authority with direct responsibility for storm and flood hazard and its consequences is the Wessex Water Authority, also with responsibility for coastal sea defences. The Weymouth and Portland Borough Council (amalgamated in 1974) has responsibility for evacuation, rehousing, relief, and road maintenance. Both these authorities are able to apply to ministries within the central UK Government for financial assistance, subject to the respective minister's approval within certain proportional maxima. Both authorities have a responsibility for the removal of excess surface water.

Non-governmental organizations involved with raising and distributing relief funds at Chiswell have been the local Rotary and Lions Clubs, as well as the Round Table. Most recently, as a direct result of the December 1978 and February 1979 floods and storms, the Chiswell Residents' Action Group was formed (Davey, 1980). Consultant engineers were appointed by the Wessex Water Authority after the floods of 1979 to assess all available data relevant to flooding at Chiswell and to advise on probable return periods of the storms and floods, on the necessity of further studies, and on options with budget costs that might 'safeguard' Chiswell from flooding.

All four of the measures considered in that report are of engineering construction to prevent flooding by seepage, to avoid overtopping, and to reduce the energy of sea waves. The important need for a warning system is emphasized, but in this regard 'many problems remain to be solved'. The report concluded with a recommendation for further studies and the preparation of a 'full feasibility report', estimated then to cost £150,000 (Dobbie and Partners, 1979).

The Council's activities in the meantime have focused on the drainage of floodwaters, the establishment of an emergency control centre, the use of earth-moving equipment to replace shingle from the rear of the beach to re-form and maintain the ridge height, and to liaise with owners where property has become unusable. A special sub-committee of the Council's Policy and Resources Committee was appointed to consider the problems of flooding, necessary remedial action, and the future of the Chiswell area. Initial priority of concern and the emphasis of actions have been on the construction of physical measures to resist the forces of sea and storm. The need for warnings, which received secondary mention in the engineers' report, has been realized and approached as a matter of co-ordination between local authorities and water authorities with responsibility for Chiswell, and those responsible for other areas further westwards (Weymouth and Portland Borough Council, 1979a).

It was not until 12 April 1979 that consideration was given to Chiswell residents' housing difficulties resulting from the floods (Weymouth and Portland Borough Council, 1979a). As a result, it was agreed that 'positive moves' should be taken with regard to these properties as a first step toward regenerating the area, and to ensure that the community is revitalized. The Department of the Environment within the UK Government was to be approached by the Council for possible financial assistance.

Serious hardship was being experienced by some Chiswell residents unable to live in flood- and storm-damaged properties upon which they were committed to mortgage repayments. Relief on these payments had in some instances been given for three months, an insignificant period of time in relation to the scale of damage and of the damaging events experienced.

While these conditions may not always be directly connected with local authority administration, there is clearly no policy for their general consideration, nor for their co-ordination. Neither is there, it would seem, any policy for engaging in the preparation of schemes for physical protection and prevention of flooding. Decisions for taking such measures are based on an acceptance of moral responsibility rather than as part of a specific policy declared as a result of comprehensive problem analysis. Consideration of social measures, the preparation of flood and storm warnings, and the consideration of means for property purchase and compensation have been secondary. The last in this list was instigated by residents.

The formation of the Chiswell Residents' Action Group (CRAG) itself was partly an expression of frustration and concern due to the absence of a stated policy on social measures. In fact, were a policy for property purchase and compensation to be introduced, a larger proportion of Chiswell residents might have left the area. Local estimates were 20–50 per cent in addition to some who had already left. In May 1979, there were 30 recently vacated domestic and commercial properties in Chiswell, while four were for sale. Social measures cannot be left to the relief funds initiated and managed by voluntary organizations. The impressive £8,000 total of the fund for the two recent floods made possible the allocation of only £140 each to 50 households, with £1,000 remaining in the fund for its recommencement after the next flood.

CRAG:

- Co-ordinated and mobilized local residents opinions.
- Mobilized action for which individuals may have been, or felt themselves to have been, ineffective.
- Produced an 'Analytical Report' concerning the flooding problems.
- Explored possible avenues for compensation or relief, such as discussing possibilities of reduction in property rates.
- Requested and achieved representative co-option as non-voting members of the meetings of Weymouth and Portland Borough Council.
- Formally applied to the Disaster Fund of the European Economic Commission for financial aid for the alleviation of flooding at Chiswell (Chiswell Residents' Action Group, 1979a, b, c; Dorset County Council, 1964).

Although the authorities would claim that they would have similarly attended to the problems caused by flood at Chiswell whether or not there had been a residents' action group, CRAG's activities were taken seriously. The authorities acted in some cases only after approaches had been made to them by CRAG members.

Wessex Water Authority pointed out that they are not obliged to protect communities from flooding. Weymouth and Portland Borough Council was 'firmly of the view that Chiswell must be preserved, and indeed enhanced' (Portland Flooding Sub-Committee, 1979). CRAG stated their objectives to include lobbying for 'a scheme or schemes that will end for all time the danger to Chiswell from flooding' and 'to ensure that the environment of Chiswell reflects the expectations of the people who reside there' (Chiswell Residents'

Action Group, 1979a). All these statements were made before comprehensive analysis of vulnerability to flood had been completed.

CRAG balances the absence of social measures by the authorities for flood alleviation. Neither the authorities nor CRAG have a policy formulated on analysis. Both discharged what they saw as their respective duties on the basis of moral concern after flooding had occurred. It is likely that discussion and negotiation between the two bodies may actually have impeded analytical processes and official policy formulation. Had there been a policy by the authorities to include social measures at the outset, the formation of CRAG may not have been necessary.

There are no figures available for the cost to the local authority of flood emergency services and repairs to roadways and property. The total cost of damage in the storm of 1942 was put at 'several thousand pounds' (*Dorset Daily Echo*, 1942). After storms in February 1972, the total value of 45 damaged dwellings was put at £330,000 (*Western Gazette*, 1972). Total damage from the February 1979 storm was estimated at £250,000 (Observer, 1979). These figures estimate total damage to property in both local government ownership and in private ownership.

To these costs must be added the value of voluntary relief funds which have been established, either nationally, as in 1824 (*Morning Chronicle*, 1824; Morris, n/d), or locally, as in for the late 1970s by the Rotary and Lions Clubs along with the Round Table. The joint fund raised by these three bodies in 1978 and 1979 totalled £8,228 (*Dorset Evening Echo*, 1979, February 15: 15).

The cost of the sea wall in 1962 was £180,000 and investment into the improvement of property since housing legislation around the same time could have been £1,000 each for perhaps half the dwellings in Chiswell, and thus have totalled around £35,000. Were it necessary for central UK Government grant-aid sources to apply rules of cost-effectiveness for proposals submitted to them for sea defences for Chiswell alone, it is difficult to see how they could justify their potential 65 per cent proportion of the total cost of £6 m.

Were sea defence not to materialize, the inhabitants of Chiswell would have to reconsider their collective and individual alternatives. They could either accept continued and increased risk or else move away in the hope of compensation for loss of property or property value. It is this last option which should have been safeguarded in the first instance as a matter of policy. Only when the size of the remaining community is known can any cost-effectiveness be assessed for civil engineering preventive measures.

The fishers who formerly lived in Chiswell accepted in the 1960s recently completed housing rentable from the local authority. Had vacated properties not been reoccupied by newcomers, recent problems would not have occurred to such an extent. Also in the 1960s, UK legislation on housing meant that assistance had been available for owner-occupiers to improve their properties. Where central and local authorities are prepared to be involved in domestic improvements, for the purpose of improving national housing stock, they must surely be prepared to be involved where financial inducement for domestic improvements may have encouraged continued occupation of property in a hazardous location.

Understanding and dealing with such impacts and interactions cannot be achieved through sectoral separation in administration. The planners of the 1960s demonstrated significant social measures which would have more positive results where integrated into a comprehensive policy. Not only was Chiswell diminished, but vulnerability was increased for the remaining people – and similarly for suggestions that Chiswell be protected as an environmental area. Chiswell was apparently a visually attractive place at the beginning of the 20th century and after (Morris, n/d). It has since dealt with enemy action and post-war planners as well as storms.

Preservation will not serve to hold back the encroaching shingle, as has been suggested (Chiswell Residents' Action Group, 1979a). The shingle advances inexorably landwards and Chiswell's problems have increased for that reason and others. People and place are a part of the environment, not separate from it. The sea and shingle, which once created opportunity used by people for the advantageous proximity to the sea, now removes that opportunity. Practical advantages, once predominant, are being slowly supplanted by the disadvantages of hazard, to which conservation would in this case prolong exposure.

Preventive measures against hazard and, more importantly, against vulnerability, through development, must therefore take comprehensive account of the relationship and interactions of people and the environment. That is, human ecology. These 'human ecological' adjustments are needed for the activities of vulnerable people and (in the UK) their elected administrations, rather than seeking only separate technological resistance to hazard. Human ecology is the relationship of society, via its adopted governance and administrative processes, with its social environments – including politics and economics – as its means of effective and comprehensive relationship with its physical environment. That some of society's options with regard to the physical environment are managed and controlled by its administrators must be understood by those administrators. Vulnerability comprises physical and social processes and conditions, interconnected and inseparable. Thus, preventive measures through development must comprise physical and social processes and conditions, interconnected and inseparable.

Warnings are of prime importance in measures for prevention, planning, and preparedness. Examples of warning actions are advice on expected hazards, on what to do and when, on how to secure people and property against flood, on what evacuation and sheltering procedures will be available, on how and where to make contact with authorities, on what measures various authorities will undertake, and on flexibility and adaptability as circumstances change. These actions cover many disciplines, knowledges, wisdoms, skills, and sectors, requiring communication, interaction, exchange, and mutual support among everyone involved.

One additional factor has implications for policy formulation in respect of natural hazard at Chiswell. The population of Portland is 12,500, some commute to the mainland, and others commute from the mainland to the institutional, scientific, military, and commercial establishments on the island. They are all served by the causeway road and by the one-way road approach and exit system to the island which includes the main street of Chiswell. The causeway road and the electricity, gas, water, and telephone utilities and services under it are all afforded protection from the sea by Chesil Beach, as are the naval fuel tanks, the naval helicopter station, and the western side of Portland Harbour.

Vulnerability to the sea is increasing for these institutions and services, as it is for Chiswell. This may make all the difference to considerations of cost-effectiveness for sea defences, which will still be comparatively short-term, or to the possibility of obtaining financial assistance for them. The danger to Chiswell may nonetheless be from increased secondary hazard of floodwaters. There is also the added danger of preventive measures designed for longer return periods permitting and encouraging development of Chiswell, which may bring about larger disaster on the rarer occasion of eventual overtopping. That is, short-term measures to protect from hazard may lead to more development, settlement, and use of land, increasing vulnerability and so augmenting disaster in the long-term (termed 'risk transference'; see Chapter 4, 'Surviving many vulnerabilities' and Chapter 9, 'Opportunities for reducing vulnerability').

Were it not for special consideration for the Isle as a whole, policies by the local authority for the preservation and enhancement of Chiswell would have brought greater demands for protection by the water authority. As the UK's central government is involved in improving housing stock and sea defences, one hand pays for the protection of what the other hand creates.

Similarly, the extraction of pebbles was continuing in 1979 some 40 kilometres along the Dorset coast at West Bay. Removal of aggregate was licensed by the West Dorset District Council, which received a royalty per ton (about 907 kilograms). At the same time, expenditure was being incurred by nearby authorities to combat coastal erosion and flooding.

Long-term decisions have long-term consequences – political, legal, and economic – for individuals, families, their properties, their places, and their communities. As shown by the examples throughout this chapter, this is the story of development and disasters in the context of natural hazards and vulnerability reduction.

Note

1. Time series processor Fortran IV version for the CDC 6600, originally written for the CD6 6400 by R.E. Hall, Department of Economics, University of California, adapted for the 7094 at the Harvard Computing Center by F.C. Ripley and J. Brode (program also available on the Harvard IBM 260/50, adapted for the CDC 6600 at London University by S. Robinson, LSE), Processed at the University of Bath Computer Unit, Bath.

PART THREE

A pattern for development

CHAPTER 7

Comprehensive development and disasters

Or disasters and development?

Because prominent information on disasters focuses on those of large magnitude, perception can be skewed that disasters are rare. In their apparent rarity, a further assumption is that their occurrence is outside 'normal life'. For follow-up activities to be publicly credible, these activities would best be associated with large magnitude disasters that had reached public and popular awareness. Relief measures would need to be on a large enough scale to appear meaningful externally.

These assumptions have influenced governmental, non-governmental, and business measures for post-disaster assistance, in addition to influencing much disaster research. The assumption that disasters are 'abnormal' led to their disassociation from everything else that was 'normal'. Day-to-day 'normality' could continue in the knowledge that disasters could occur and in the assumption that, as there was nothing that could be done about them, changes to day-to-day affairs would be unnecessary and ineffective.

The few exceptions proved the rule. Storm warning systems were arranged and plans were made for their operation in the event of a storm. They remained separate, for rare and occasional use. When not in use, they were out of sight and out of mind. Their operation and management depended upon available resources, with few new demands for unusual or special equipment, and they had little effect on daily routines and affairs. Basically, the antithesis of what a warning system should be (Garcia and Fearnley, 2016).

Perception of disaster as being dissociated from everything else until it happens has had serious, detrimental consequences. Activities of settlement, construction, education, production, commerce, livelihoods, and more could proceed undeterred by the possibility of disaster. When a disaster did occur, these activities would have a significant bearing upon the consequences. Moreover, when disasters happened, it was unfortunate, but apparently no one was at fault and little could have been done.

As a response, disaster-related work indicated that adjustments were necessary so that the impact of natural hazards might be lessened. Adjustments were identified *after* a disaster, but if implemented, would be done so in readiness for another. Adjustments were indicated in a socio-economic context where options and resources for their implementation were available – although availability of options and resources did not always mean that adjustments were actually implemented.

Examining further disasters, it was better understood that what was happening in settlement, construction, education, production, commerce, livelihoods, and more – dissociated as they seemingly were from any awareness of dealing with natural hazards – was having a far greater effect on natural hazard consequences than any adjustments could possibly have. Though adjustments were identified, their implementation depended to a large degree upon either legislation or self-preservation. Meanwhile, activities could proceed in other places where legislation or self-preservation were less relevant or non-existent.

Development and its administration progressed in those other places because they were labelled as being less fortunate, less skilled, and less rich. At the time, the 'poor' places had leaders who accepted development because of external pressure and internal aspirations. This 'development' proceeded uninterrupted by cultures and concerns that were different from those imposing development and that were less articulate in a form that was understood or accepted by those imposing development. Fundamentally, local viewpoints and suggestions were less powerful than external ones bringing development.

In the meantime, the disaster relief lobby had become a large and growing industry, with humanitarian assistance increasing many times over. Nevertheless, 'humanitarian assistance' struggles to cope with disasters that are always reported as becoming larger, more numerous, and more complex – typically without solid metrics and analyses to back up these claims of the trends. Yet no matter how many resources are given to post-disaster aid, it can perhaps be an occasional palliative, but never a long-term resolution.

'Complex disasters' and 'wicked problems' are ever-present symbols. Yet which disaster is not 'complex'? Which policy issue involving disasters is not a '(super)wicked problem'? The phrases obscure reality. Vulnerability is not simple and vulnerability has continued for too long regardless of its (disastrous) consequences. More to the point, its wicked consequences occur because super-wicked people refuse to redress them. The consequences of unconcerned activities in the past have now become the cause of concerns for the future. Humanitarian assistance, though necessary, can never substitute for development that prevents disasters through vulnerability reduction.

Linkage between development and disasters must be made, at minimum, so that the effects of one do not impede the other. Which way round the effects are most felt is a matter of operational viewpoint or political bias. The 'disaster continuum' approach positively attempts to align post-disaster assistance with development by defining the intervening stages of recovery, rehabilitation, and reconstruction. The one, it was intended, should lead to the other, in that obvious and orderly sequence.

That is, disaster leading to recovery-rehabilitation-reconstruction (sometimes with other words), then leading to development is conventionally thought of, perceived, and represented linearly. In reality, they are simultaneous, whether framed as 'build back better', 'build back safer', 'build forward better', 'build forward safer', or any of the other plethora of phrases that promise absolutely to achieve definite improvements this time (despite all previous failures). Each 'stage' overlaps with others in the same or neighbouring places; in responses to the same or different disasters; and by the same or different authorities and organizations. In any case, development will have been taking place, appropriately or inappropriately, planned or unplanned, successfully or not, since human settlement began in the area.

Which way round should it be: 'disasters and development' (as in Cuny, 1983) or 'development and disasters' (adopted for this book to avoid usurping Cuny, 1983)? Which comes first, which should come first, and which has the greater influence upon the other? Most likely, both simultaneously to be mutually supportive. After all, the impact upon development of disasters is frequently deplored, but what of the impact of development upon disasters?

Cyclical concepts

For a specific disaster, the disaster, the reconstruction, and the development are often presented as cyclical. The cycle repeats around several 'disaster events'. Though a disaster may commence a process that leads to development, development has invariably preceded disaster. This development had a bearing on the extent and implications of the disaster that ensued, for better or for worse.

It has thus been referred to as 'the disaster cycle' (Figure 7.1), in which disaster, usually presented as the trigger for everything else, occurred at a place and time, producing a linear sequence of action that cycles back to disaster again. It not only acknowledges that disaster could recur, but demands it. A never-ending cycle flows of disaster, relief, rehabilitation, reconstruction, mitigation, planning, preparedness, and disaster – or other words according to preference.

What the self-centric 'disaster cycle' does not acknowledge is that other activities continue outside, influencing the cycle's stages. Not everything that happens, or that is undertaken, subscribes to this cyclical interpretation of disaster management and disaster risk management. Instead, all activities, by definition, invariably subscribe to the contexts in which they occur, which are the contexts for disaster impacts. Development, and simply change, always takes place, of its own inevitable volition or in a planned and programmed way, the two generally overlapping. Where does 'development' appear in the 'disaster cycle', the 'disaster management cycle', or the 'disaster risk management cycle'? What role for 'disaster risk reduction' within this question?

If a cyclical approach must be adopted, rather than many alternatives such as helices (Walshe et al., 2020) or simply acting to break the cycle (Petal, 2009), then there would not be one 'cycle', but two. It is not a 'disaster cycle', but a 'disaster bicycle' (Figure 7.2).

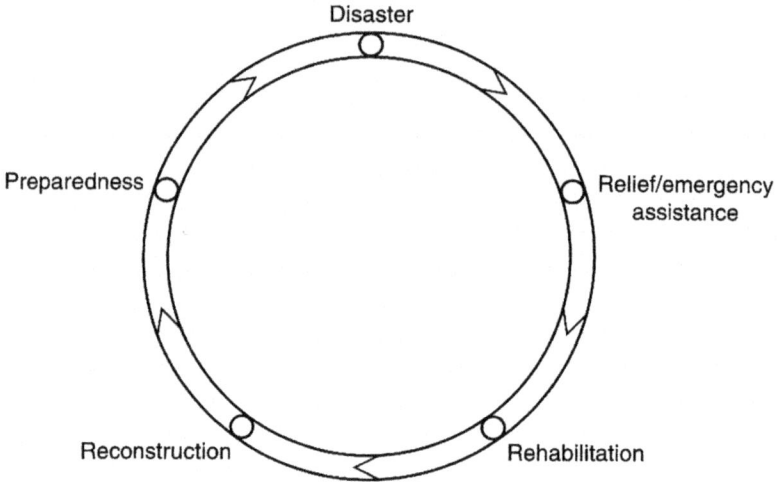

Figure 7.1 A disaster cycle

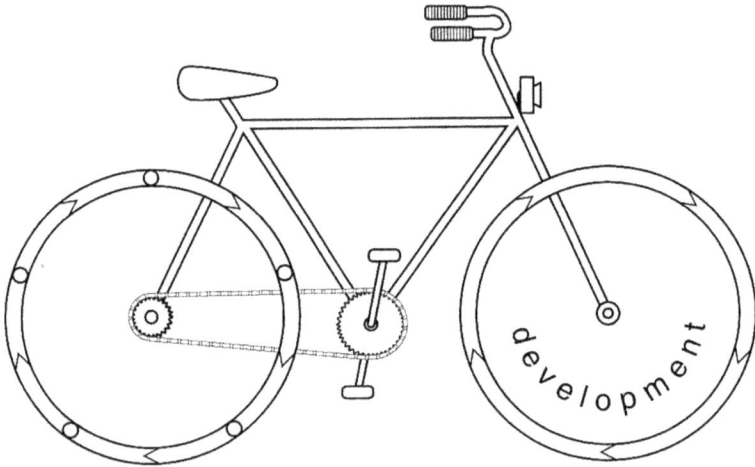

Figure 7.2 The disaster bicycle

The bicycle proffers undeserved credit to this duality. Most bicycles have a single person riding, propelling, steering, and braking. Even tandem bicycles and quadracycles assume that the multiple riders are communicating and collaborating, ostensibly aiming to reach the same destination safely. In contrast, the disaster cycle and the development cycle, by any form or forms, are not driven by the same entity, whether a leader or an organization. Nor are multiple leaders and multiple organizations typically seen to be communicating and collaborating to achieve the same direction at the same speed with the same safety and awareness.

Of overriding (pun intended) concern is that the activities of the bicycle, or multiple cycles/wheels, are implemented by various sectors with various leaders pursuing various mandates at various speeds and with and in various directions. They are rarely co-ordinated or interrelated. Cluster systems and intra- and inter-sectoral meetings and programmes try to do so, with some positive trends. Attendees are still most beholden to those providing the funds and to their buzzword soup of missions, visions, mandates, aims, objectives, and goals. Activities within the disaster and development spectrum/spectra, continuum/continua, and bicycle/multicycles are organized and managed in spaghetti diagrams requiring more than three spatial dimensions to disentangle.

In the meantime, disaster management and disaster risk management have become separated as their own sectors, from all of these already separated activities, just as disaster (risk) research or science has become its own discipline with its own vocabulary, conferences, journals, and assumptions. Of necessity, measures for vulnerability reduction and preventing disasters are widely multi-sectoral and their management is a pervasive part of local experiences and contexts. Yet they have separated from other aspects of development, as other aspects of development display separation from each other. Most crucially, disaster (risk) management has become separated from the development of everyday affairs that create vulnerability and that ought to be used to reduce it.

As a result, the activities of one sector may not necessarily subscribe to preventing disaster or reducing vulnerability, as the latter has been made the responsibility of someone else. By ignorance – too often, actually being ignore-ance, which refers to understanding being deliberately ignored (Streets and Glantz, 2000) – of processes that subscribe to vulnerability, this may actually worsen the situation. Vulnerability has frequently been made, or been made worse, by 'development'.

Questions remain, therefore, regarding the relationship between disasters and development (Cuny, 1983). What kind(s) of development made situations worse and, more constructively, what kind(s) of development would have made situations better? Will the kind(s) of development that improve(s) be used now and into the future? More precisely, without waiting for disaster to start a process that could lead to development, what kind(s) of development is/are required in the first place so as to achieve vulnerability reduction and disaster prevention?

Institutions and policies

As World War II appeared to be moving toward its final phase, the United Nations Relief and Rehabilitation Administration (UNRRA) was formed in November 1943, almost two years before the United Nations itself. As a war so catastrophic was hopefully ending, was any other response conceivable? The urgent and appropriately identified need for relief challenged any concept of how relief might become less necessary in the future, or consideration of how development might reduce vulnerability and make survival and thriving more likely.

UNRRA was followed in 1944 by the International Bank for Reconstruction and Development (IBRD), now the part of the World Bank Group that provides loans. The sequence of words in IBRD's name, reconstruction followed by development, was perhaps framed in response to an (expected) unrepeatable war that had led to IBRD's founding. Was it appropriate to apply the same thinking to presumed-to-be naturally recurring disasters? Where recurrence was regarded as inconceivable – that is, large-scale war (irrespective of World War I being the War to End All Wars) – was deemed separate from where recurrence was regarded as natural (and so 'natural disaster').

There continues to be relief agencies, disaster risk agencies, and development agencies. At the time of writing, these include the United Nations Office for the Coordination of Humanitarian Affairs (OCHA); UN Crisis Relief; the United Nations Office for Disaster Risk Reduction (UNDRR); the United Nations Development Programme (UNDP); and the United Nations Environment Programme (UNEP), plus others. The sequence commencing with disaster and ending with development holds, although at times framed as overlaps, such as the humanitarian–development nexus.

Perhaps amid a world war, legitimate reasons could be formulated to justify post-war assistance as separate from development in a sequential pattern. Now, there is no excuse, given the knowledge and experience since. Notwithstanding noble global efforts (UNDP, 2004; UNISDR, 2004), post-disaster activities and development frequently fail to accommodate vulnerability reduction to all hazards. Disasters do not belong exclusively to 'disaster relief' and neither does disaster response have to wait for a disaster to start.

Vulnerability is pervasive and thus has significance beyond disasters discourse, requiring immediate response to reduce it in order to avert disaster. Vulnerability to wars, conflicts, and violences is vulnerability to natural hazards, human influences on them, and human hazards – and vice versa. Development to reduce vulnerability to one or more reduces vulnerability to others. How many of the ever-expanding plethora of institutions, polices, and nomenclature adopt this baseline? How many accept that basic needs development supporting vulnerability reduction, survival, and thriving serves to increase the quality of life irrespective of hazards and disasters? Yet dealing with disasters remains, and appears to want to remain, heavily institutionalized.

Despite decades decrying it, post-event approaches can be disaster-specific, excluding the possibility of a necessarily wider view which accounts for the multitude of factors that are the root causes of vulnerability and so of disasters. Institutional separation can take 'disasters' away from everything else, implying the absolution of all other sectors, institutions, and policies of their responsibilities in that respect. This approach has been encouraged by, and has followed, international inducement and format, not always developing on the basis of local needs, conditions, and contexts. Consequently, as a result of popular interchange of terms and labels and of common misunderstandings, 'disaster relief' and 'humanitarian aid' have, at times, been assumed to be the total necessary action for disasters – especially unstoppable, unpredictable, unscheduled 'natural disasters'. Disasters, then, need not involve any but the department designated for response and assistance afterwards. This dangerous outcome could not be further from reality.

Institutional separations reflect shortcomings in the understanding of the relationships among vulnerability, disasters, and development. They also deny the opportunity that integration would offer for development for vulnerability reduction and vice versa. Too frequently, preventive measures that are implemented are largely mono-sectoral, mono-disciplinary, mono-hazard, and largely technological or technocratic – despite long-standing warnings about the drawbacks of this approach (Hewitt, 1983; Torry, 1979).

As it has become more and more institutionalized, disaster relief and humanitarian aid have become more obviously separated from those sectors responsible for development which ferment and foment the causative factors of vulnerability. Separate sector policies may negate the possibility of comprehensive strategies to the extent that some sectors may be the root cause of disaster consequences. Post-disaster institutions of the same governments and organizations are then called upon to attend to and to pay for the consequences of disaster. Disaster relief and humanitarian aid have not been immune from recognizing this situation (Cuny, 1983; Davis, 1978; Terry, 2002), yet the contradictory actions continue.

Institutional and organizational separation nonetheless remains a major impediment to integrating development and addressing disasters through vulnerability reduction. Inefficiency, counterproductivity, and retrogression characterize the separation and rivalry among institutions and organizations that have been established to implement various objectives that subscribe collectively but piecemeal to vulnerability reduction – and thus often fail in their task.

Repeating the long-established mantra, programmes and projects across multiple sectors are required for policy formulation, information sharing, information gathering, analysis, research, and action. Vulnerability reduction requires the support of, and subscribes to, development. Development ought to be the paramount vulnerability reduction activity, yet development is not sacrosanct. It must be moulded to adapt to requirements. It is a never-ending process rather than a final product, stage, or phase. The degree by which people and places can absorb, reduce, or change their vulnerabilities, and achieve survival and thriving, is an expression of prevailing conditions. Improving prevailing conditions should represent the point of comprehensive development.

Management for comprehensive development

Since disasters are social processes, post-disaster actions failing to accept this foundation can make the long-term situation worse. This worsening emerges with perceptions of post-disaster actions being merely sequential, stage-by-stage recovery subsequent to a specific 'disaster event'. The same observation applies to pre-disaster initiatives for vulnerability reduction. If taken to be sequential and neatly partitioned in time, in space, or by sector, then pre-disaster work is not likely to be fruitful development. It is certainly not comprehensive development. Instead, post-disaster conditions become part of the social context for subsequent and recurrent disasters.

The automatic adoption of existing and conventional management frameworks, including jargon and cycles, has not had the expected effectiveness in preventing disasters. They can instead be contributary factors to disaster risk creation and vulnerability perpetuation. Theoretical division of many concepts by outsiders and imposition of complicated vocabulary was responsible for separate initiatives for tasks including 'prevention', 'preparedness', 'planning', 'mitigation, 'relief', 'reconstruction', 'rehabilitation', and 'recovery'. Separation meant that they could be exclusive alternatives, but for successful vulnerability reduction and development, all these measures have to be comprehensively applied to, applied with, and integrated into each other, other sectors, and local contributions. For their achievement, they need to be focused locally, not defined and siloed exogenously. They require a (comprehensive) development context to serve integral experience of all hazards, without assumptions of unique, extraordinary, or unusual events.

Processes seen to be outside disaster-related strategies and actions are too often disregarded for dealing with disasters. Conflicts, violences, forced migrations, and their causes and consequences – informal settlements, fear, marginalization, living on poor land, having inadequate livelihood options, oppression, and discrimination, among many others – were presumed to be external to the remit of preventing disasters and reducing vulnerability. As post-disaster work continues, and needs to continue, the call for ever-more resources for post-disaster processes should be accompanied – not drowned out – by calls for resources to deal with the causes that make post-disaster processes so necessary. Vulnerability processes have to be reduced by processes of development, not by the ad hoc application of services that commence post-disaster, or with the identification of, and attendance to, already 'vulnerable groups' – which actually covers everyone.

These points are truisms and should be accepted as such. Sometimes they are, sometimes they are not, and sometimes it is unclear whether or not they are accepted due to obfuscation by the latest buzzwords or buzzphrases. Despite 'the relief-development continuum' being unpicked long ago (for example, Sollis, 1994), we remain today awash with 'the triple nexus' of relief or humanitarian aid, development, and peace or peacebuilding; 'early recovery' to align with development; 'resilient recovery' for development; and much more. The Intergovernmental Panel on Climate Change (IPCC, 2021–2022) offers six different types of 'adaptation', hardly differentiated and hardly differentiable, without ever explaining convincingly the difference from 'adjustment', vulnerability reduction, or development.

The smokescreen of lofty words and colourful diagrams can still place development as the goal once everything else has been accomplished. Less frequent is the recognition of how development contributed to the disaster, notwithstanding laudable efforts seeking to ensure that development lessens disaster impact and is ready for disaster response; for example, pre-disaster recovery planning (FEMA, 2017). How often is Quarantelli's (1976: 1) warning heeded about 'the tendency to think of the last major particular disaster as the case to use to plan and think about disasters in general'?

Management for comprehensive development means moving beyond this tendency in order to recognize that operations of relief, rehabilitation, and development may all be occurring simultaneously within any group or place. They should assist rather than inhibit each other. As the 'disaster cycle' is inappropriate, since the goal should be to break the cycle, 'disaster continuum' is inappropriate, implying that each phase follows the other in sequence. 'Disaster contiguum' has been expressed as all phases being implemented simultaneously, complementing and linking to each other (Audet, 2015). The balance among the phases must be functional, neither political nor for show. Better development can reduce the need for emergency relief; better relief can contribute to development; and better rehabilitation can ease the transition between the two.

The 'relief-development contiguum' appears (OECD, 2010), with variations including the 'emergency-development contiguum', the 'crisis-development contiguum', and the 'security-development contiguum'. With other nomenclature becoming populist along the lines of 'environmental security', 'nature-based solutions', and 'ecosystem-based disaster risk reduction', the role of 'environmental management' becomes important for 'management for comprehensive development'. The environment, after all, contributes major parts of hazards while societal activities impinge on the environment, modifying hazards. Following on from the World Commission on Environment and Development (WCED, 1987) and many precedents, it has never helped development where policies and actions pertaining to nature (often framed as management, conservation, protection, or preservation) are the responsibility of environmental ministries and institutions with limited control over environmental destruction by other sectors. Sometimes, in fact, the job of the environmental ministry or institution is to forgo nature's needs in favour of other sectors! Rather than supporting or not worrying about environmental damage, the ministries and institutions for all sectors should have responsibility for preventing environmental damage and integrating environmental needs into development – not assuming that an 'environmental impact assessment' suffices. Otherwise, environmental management becomes 'after-the-fact repair of damage: *re*forestation, *re*claiming desert lands, *re*building urban environments, *re*storing natural habitats, and *re*habilitating wild lands' (WCED, 1987: 39; emphasis added). Instead, environmental management should be part of the development contiguum.

What closer parallel with development and disasters could there be? Just add in *re*sponse, *re*lief, *re*habilitation, and *re*covery (etymological problems aside)! And never forget 'human security', 'complex adaptive systems', 'social capital', and other such fun.

Vulnerability *re*duction should be made the *re*sponsibility of all development, notably sectors that otherwise have perpetrated and would perpetuate vulnerability. Each should be given guidance sufficient to enable it to understand the implications for vulnerability and development that are incumbent within its activities, intentions, and objectives. Actions should then be focused on management for comprehensive development rather than disaster risk creation and vulnerability perpetuation.

CHAPTER 8

Preventive development for preventing disasters

Equitable practice

While recognizing that vulnerability tends to increase with poverty, marginalization, discrimination, oppression, and many other societal ills, disaster prevention, planning, mitigation, preparation, and preparedness, among other words, sometimes construct their strategies as one-size-fits-all. The effectiveness for and accessibility to the worst-off people and places is not necessarily considered. They are left to disaster relief and humanitarian aid tending to their needs in the aftermath – or not, when these actions, too, do not consider the effectiveness for and accessibility to everyone.

Amelioration of the perceived causes of and reasons for vulnerabilities has to be applied equitably at all times throughout all groups in all places. Responding only to 'events' as they occur, and framing them as events, contributes further to social inequity and imbalance. Starting to consider equity during an emergency is not conducive to ensuring equitable distribution of post-disaster assistance so as not to leave some groups disadvantaged, externalized, or otherized – or with their perception of being so. Nor is it conducive to avoiding markets, trade, and prices being disrupted by the sudden availability of goods and materials. Same with services, such as carpenters, masons, electricians, plumbers, mechanics, and specialized vehicle drivers. There might be an overabundance due to outside post-disaster workers parachuting in, thereby undermining skilled people locally. Or there might be a deficit as everyone with skills is in high demand and is overworked.

Avoiding inequity and disruption requires careful planning, preparation, and management, easiest during non-emergency circumstances. This is the responsibility of development. Once a strategy for avoiding inequity and supporting equity has been reached and implemented, post-disaster assistance, if required, will have a known and acceptable context within which to integrate.

Instances where relief consignments were illicitly (mis)appropriated for the support of warring factions (Terry, 2002) or siphoned off by governments (Olson and Gawronski, 2003) underline the need for the principle and actuality of equity. The aim of war, conflict, and violence is frequently to destabilize, or to exploit destabilization, for the purpose of achieving power – which is, in itself, inequity. Achieving equitable contexts can reduce the risk of certain wars, conflicts, and violences (although certainly not all). Without rigorously aiming for equity, post-disaster actions may contribute not only to vulnerability making for recurrent disasters, but also to local dissatisfaction, unrest, war, conflict, and violence.

Economic interventions on their own can cause and aggravate vulnerability, notably when considering only economics, monetization, or financialization. Wider scopes of livelihoods and social needs, including non-monetary economies, should be considered within any intervention. Losses can be intangible, perhaps cultural heritage, ecosystems, heirlooms, education disruption, less healthcare access, and severing of social networks. Livelihoods can thrive without money or monetary valuation, through trade, exchange, mutual aid, and bartering. Monetizing life and quality of life has long been contentious. Simultaneously, cash transfers are not inherently detrimental. In anticipation of a major hazard and after its consequences, they can bring advantages, from preserving people's savings to injecting economic opportunities into wrecked livelihoods (Tappis and Doocy, 2017). One key to success is understanding and working within each specific context.

Not accounting for context, or assuming that money solves all ills, will continue to contribute to existing inequity, underdevelopment, and vulnerability creation. New such conditions can also be generated. Policies for financial participation in reconstruction, for example, might perpetuate inequitable divisions between those who can and those who cannot participate, no matter the actual need (see the example of Tonga in Chapter 5, 'Disasters creating vulnerability'). Similarities can emerge before a disaster. Insurance of various forms should contribute extensively to vulnerability reduction and to reducing disaster impacts. Many people cannot afford adequate or any form of insurance. Then, when property and possessions are damaged or lost, those who could afford insurance (and whose insurers adequately pay out and support the affected policy holder) are much better off than those who could not, widening inequity.

Accrued conditions of invidious deprivation, perceived disadvantage, and actual disadvantage may lead to animosity and strife, often under cover of more obvious demographic differences. Alternatively, equitable practice for development and disasters can be enacted to assist the establishment and growth of pervasive, comparative, and improving wellbeing, which can be one contribution to reducing and avoiding war, conflict, and violence. Violences aim at disempowering individuals, groups, places, institutions, and organizations. Local participation in development and disasters programmes requires and brings about local empowerment, if done so equitably. Conflict reduction and conflict resolution can be built-in objectives of development and disaster programmes, by explicit acknowledgement of how enfolded conflicts and disasters are, feeding into each other (Peters, 2021), which, in turn, undermines efforts at equitable practice.

Social networks

Equity, by definition, is about people and places, examining individuals in their contexts and in relation to one another. Equitable and preventive development that supports surviving and thriving must, by definition, consider interactions and connections among people and places. This involves social networks.

Bangladesh demonstrates how social networks may facilitate survival and thriving in floods and after tropical cyclones where, without those networks, inequity worsens (Rahman, 1991). The networks facilitate social organization and the greater likelihood of sharing losses and resources to overcome those losses. Social networks have a broad definition and remit, involving people as well as organizations, such as facilitating social networks in Bangladesh to reduce infant mortality (Fottrell et al., 2013).

One significant network in Bangladesh at the time of Rahman's (1991) study was the Grameen Bank micro-credit system, founded in 1976 by Muhammad Yunus. Yunus and the Grameen Bank shared the Nobel Peace Prize in 2006. Yunus was then imprisoned in Bangladesh in 2024 on labour-related charges which he and his supporters explain were politically motivated. He was appealing the charges when, in August 2024, protests brought down Bangladesh's Government and Yunus agreed to head an interim government.

The Grameen Bank makes small credit available to individuals who have formed groups for this purpose among themselves. This facility is extended to the poorest people and to single parents who would be unable to avail themselves of conventional banking services and who are exploited by money-lenders. The Grameen Bank makes possible a degree of self-employment and self-sufficiency among the poor that would otherwise not be feasible. At times of disaster, usual repayments are suspended by the Grameen Bank, while those who have been able to save money have resources to draw upon. The Grameen Bank assists those who have no savings with loans through the group system. Moreover, the members of networks formed by the Grameen Bank's system of credit availability are informally inclined to help each other in further matters.

In these ways, survival and thriving are more assured for more people. Recovery takes a shorter time due to resources available, through self-sufficiency, and due to shorter time periods of self-employment interruption, all of which support thriving. The Grameen Bank's small-credit system supporting and sustaining social networks is development and vulnerability reduction in itself, especially when it tackles corruption (Azim and Kluvers, 2019). It helps further development and vulnerability reduction in the process.

Without people, their relationships, and their connections, there can be neither vulnerability reduction nor disaster recovery. Recovery will be enabled and vulnerability reduction further facilitated by the previous creation through development of positive social networks, for participation ensuring accessible and equitable resources for basic needs. Locally identified, initiated, and led recovery, where equitable, will ensue and feed further and comprehensive development.

Decentralization and accessibility

Perceived need for retaining power and control – political, financial, and others – are drivers toward centralization, inequity, arbitrary decision-making, and less accessibility. It might be by military or authoritarian styles of government, through hierarchical and technocratic systems of management. It might be simply for love of power and control. Localization is diminished and questioners or contrarians are summarily eliminated, violently or otherwise. These actions diminish equitable, participatory, comprehensive, preventive, and localized development and hence diminish vulnerability reduction.

The functional local provision of social networks, infrastructure, resources, and services on the basis of population and need has limited opportunity in centralized systems. Devolution, decentralization, and subsidiarity are required if smaller or more dispersed populations are to be equitably, comprehensively, and functionally accommodated and resourced (see also Chapter 2, 'Islands and vulnerability'). Their political participation, credit and banking facilities, education and health services, food, and potable water exemplify what may not be within the objectives, interests, or reach of centralized systems.

Participatory processes (for example, Chambers, 2002) apply to any place, irrespective of population numbers and densities. Settlements of any size and density can identify their own micro-vulnerability, their own resources to address micro-vulnerabilities, and needs which local resources could not fulfil. The latter would need to be provided externally, with outsiders also considering larger scales to identify macro-vulnerability alongside causes and solutions thereof.

Away from macro-vulnerabilities, participatory processes might elicit that the nearest school is further away than some young children can safely walk and there is no other transport for them. It could be that the nearest health clinic or centre is further away than most people would want to travel or could afford to travel. People may fear to raise issues of unmet basic needs, extortion, or discrimination, due to expectations of retribution and the deliberate continuation of these practices.

The centralization of health services in large general hospitals, or of education in large schools, serves economies of scale by monetary calculations. They are (should be) built to a size commensurate with the area served and the numbers served – and perhaps increased in size to make their service area larger. Conversely, the larger the area served (considering spatial area rather than only population numbers, since higher population densities can still be nearby), the larger the number of people who have greater distances to travel for access to healthcare and education. On the other hand, decentralized health and education services would serve smaller areas, so would be easier to get to, and would each serve a smaller number of people. If the services provided are to be the same everywhere, then accessibility increases and the services are more equitable. How available are specialized personnel, equipment, and services, so that they could be offered multiple times across dispersed populations? That is, direct costs also increase and enough teachers and medical personnel and equipment might not exist. Full understanding of the financial and logistical implications must account for the difficulties and for the benefits accrued from equitable development and vulnerability reduction – most comprehensively, the preventive benefits.

Providing services for health and education assessed on the basis of user needs provokes a different strategy and cost-benefit analysis (if that is an appropriate method) than when assessed from the point of view of the provider. The appropriateness of accessible, small-scale, comprehensive, and equitable services becomes greater when services support vulnerability reduction and disaster prevention. Examples are nutrition and hygiene guidance, preventive medicine, injury prevention, treating minor ailments (to prevent them from becoming major ailments), conducting regular check-ups (to prevent worse conditions), and routine support, such as for pregnancy, childbirth, childcare, exercise, diet, and mental health and wellbeing.

The implications for vulnerability reduction and disaster prevention are significant. A societal interpretation of vulnerability reduction, including preparedness for post-impact survival requirements, requires localized services – or, at least, as localized as feasible. Rather than it being expected or assumed that emergency hospitals would be flown in and set up with external staff, it would be more effective for the day-to-day achievement of a healthy population, for health services to be made accessible beyond an emergency basis. Similarly, education should be day-to-day and safe for all children, so that they contribute to vulnerability reduction and development throughout their entire lives.

A hazard, such as an earthquake or landslide, could suddenly damage or destroy health or education services in the area affected, rendering them inoperative and possibly killing or injuring staff and patients/pupils. Prevention should, theoretically, avoid such scenarios, especially on a wide scale. If prevention has not been implemented, then development is lacking. At least, however, with health and education services distributed according to population, there would be shorter distances to the nearest operational services. Similarly, trained staff would be better deployed, spread among the population, mobile and independent of technical resources. If the hazard destroys the centralized services of a hospital or school, then many more people would be deprived of those services and would have much farther to travel to reach them elsewhere. Or the hazard might crack one bridge across a river or bay, stopping a good proportion of staff from reaching the facility, undermining the service.

Disaster prevention often highlights buildings containing services deemed to be of high strategic value. They can be termed 'critical infrastructure' with prevention prioritizing them over people's homes. A form of preventive development for preventing disasters reduces the number of buildings of high strategic value. It provides more installations and services that, by their increased number and reduced size/centralization, would be strategically less critical. The extreme, which might not be achievable everywhere, would be that all infrastructure is 'critical' because none is. If one structure or transport route is lost, then many others can take up the slack, leaving services uninterrupted. If potable water and energy including electricity were provided locally, then people would understand where the supplies are, locals would be qualified to maintain and fix them, and neighbouring locations should be ready and willing to help where repairs are taking time or personnel incapacitated.

Where enacted equitably and accessibly, decentralization can foster a positive relationship between the people served and the institution or organization providing the service. An ethos can be formed of supporting local representation, involving everyone, and creating an atmosphere of care and a sense of identity and belonging. Decentralizing and improving accessibility, then, are preventive development for preventing disasters.

On resilience – and beyond

Despite the importance of vulnerability and, by extension, reducing it, the word and process have been downgraded by some seeking to promote other concepts, rather than a balance. Prominent among the displacers is 'resilience' or 'resiliency'. The backlash against the various schools of 'resilience thinking' is not an objection to notions of resilience per se. It opposes the confusion created by so many definitions of 'resilience' and the presumption of the need to go solo with resilience rather than being in tandem with vulnerability. Hence, Bankoff and Hilhorst (2022) titled their book *Why vulnerability still matters*.

The text in this section, largely based on Lewis and Kelman (2010), summarizes aspects of the contrasts and connections between vulnerability and resilience in the context of development and disasters. Since Lewis and Kelman (2010), concerns about resilience have been corroborated and have expanded (for example, Horn, 2021; Reid, 2018). Again, the resilience critics do not so much dispute the need to accept, support, and enhance people's own actions, skills, and abilities in dealing with difficulties. It is more about the catch-all assumptions and vagueness in resilience's frequent articulation, leading to adulation overriding reality. These detriments become all the more noticeable when more practical and grounded terms exist such as 'capacities' (Gaillard et al., 2019) and vulnerability reduction.

The alternatives' nuances and power precede the dominance of resilience. They are often submerged under the alleged panacea of resilience, particularly when resilience is seen as the counterpoint or opposite to vulnerability. Such juxtaposition requires examination, as noted by Manyena (2006), especially in the context of studies that do not see vulnerability and resilience as opposites (for example, Timmerman, 1981). As indisputable as people's vulnerability to hazards is people's simultaneous capacity for, abilities for, and 'resilience' in preparing for, dealing with, and recovering after hazards – surviving and thriving.

As a concept in the context of natural hazards, although it appeared earlier (for example, Timmerman, 1981), resilience had perhaps not fully emerged and become fully accepted until the 1990s (for example, Kreimer and Munasinghe, 1991). It did so out of practical recognition of capacity in adversity and as a counter to what had come to be considered the negativity and pessimism of 'vulnerability'. People in vulnerable places were generalized as capable of exercising inherent capacities for 'recovering strength quickly', 'springing back', 'buoyancy', 'bouncing back', 'returning to normal', and 'resuming an original form'. Sometimes, such constructions of 'resilience' were enfolded within the definition of 'vulnerability'.

Often interpreted as the capacity for reversion to the condition that prevailed prior to disruption, disturbance, or disaster, resilience is then concerned with avoiding consequences. Within this interpretation, it is less concerned with causes of vulnerability beyond its capacity and remit, even though vulnerability results from processes perpetrated by humankind and that are therefore controllable by humankind. Causative processes of vulnerability are sometimes considered not to be an issue, except where consequences are currently observable as conditions of individuals or of buildings (for example, Norton and Chantry, 2008). However quickly original strength might be recovered, the same situation could arise again and for the same reasons (see also Glantz and Jamieson, 2000), going round the 'disaster cycle' rather than breaking out of it.

Beyond the purview of some 'resilience' are the reasons that led people, infrastructure, and places to be as vulnerable as they are. As a response to perceptions of 'risk', the concern of resilience is often with exposure or propinquity to sources of hazard. It foregrounds an evident status quo of conditions and their consequences, rather than the causes of that exposure, decrepitude, or disadvantage, thereby diminishing the vulnerability process and focusing on a state of being. This point is discussed and evidenced by Glantz and Jamieson (2000) and Tobin (1999), who show that if resilience involves a return to the pre-disaster conditions, then it is simply a return to the 'resilient' conditions, including vulnerability, which led to disaster in the first place. 'Return to normal' could be the antithesis of preventive development for preventing disasters, because it creates the 'normality' of vulnerability (Hills, 1998; Fordham, 1998).

'Resilience' has never been an exclusive domain of natural hazards or disasters. Prior to and in parallel with its contrast with vulnerability in hazards work, examples are from share marketing, psychology, psychotherapy, political science, materials science, engineering, ecology, and biology among others. Some such interpretations of resilience more realistically relate to an already existing social or administrative structure, from which capacity is generated or in which it is inherent. Organizations and their capacities exist, but require improvement. People's capacity for self-help expresses an optimism to counter the consequences of vulnerability, fostering participation for survival and thriving as amelioration of what otherwise would be helplessness (for example, Paton and Johnson, 2001, 2006).

Resilience as an appropriate strategy against some consequences of vulnerability can be only a partial response against causative processes generated outside of a people and a place and beyond their influence or capacity. Resilience, where it is implied as an appropriate counterpart of vulnerability, does little to help assuage invidious processes, often unseen and unidentified, as the root causes of so many vulnerabilities. Neither vulnerability processes, nor all aspects of vulnerable conditions, can be matched by the exercise of people's capacity – not even with the addition of 'creativity' to its spectrum (Maguire and Hagan, 2007). Resilience, moreover and in all its contexts, may give up, fail, or be overwhelmed. It is less 'community capacity' that is in question than the capacity of resilience itself.

An example is in a study of traditional construction on the earthquake-prone Greek island of Lefkada (Karababa and Guthrie, 2007). It describes vulnerabilities of people in a vulnerable place being increased by local erosion of traditional culture due to resilience. The study observes that, worldwide, while properly constructed reinforced concrete had the initial effect of reducing earthquake losses, its popular use in poor economies and without necessary knowledge led to increased structural failure. Over the same period in Lefkada, traditional use of timber declined in favour of concrete, as did traditional skills. The result was that new buildings in timber came to be at greater risk of failure. Cheaper construction – in timber, masonry, or reinforced concrete – produces vulnerability to earthquake damage.

Karababa and Guthrie (2007) demonstrate how local capacities generated against a specific hazard over several generations were quickly eroded by externally generated economic and other social forces and by changes in population caused by outward and inward movements. New technologies, assumed to be superior, contribute to declining local skills and collective memory that combine to erode the earthquake-resistant culture and consequently combine to increase earthquake-related vulnerability.

People and places are unlikely to be able to maintain resilient cultures against these inexorable pressures, even if they have the capacity to identify them. It required long-term, in-depth analysis by 'outsiders' of Lefkada at the time of the study to begin to expose and to record these changes and their impacts upon vulnerability. Karababa and Guthrie (2007) further observe how the 'revolution' of concrete and steel technologies within construction, coupled with trends of globalization, perceived economies of scale, foreign investments, and other factors, all contributed to undermining past learning. They pose a threat to local seismic construction cultures that will cause mistakes of the past to proliferate. In the absence of alternative action, losses will increase.

What can 'resilient communities' achieve against causative processes of vulnerability which are long-term, under cover, not evident, not known, not understood, or not cared about – exemplified by corrupt construction practices or inept land-use procedures? These problems may be revealed only by damage to or destruction of infrastructure and places, with resultant casualties. What can resilience achieve, except brief amelioration of or temporary belief in having overcome pervasive helplessness? Resilience basically has a small part to play as a counter to the accretion of vulnerability in all its dimensions from multiple and usually external sources. The probable incapacitation of resilience is reason enough why all causes of vulnerabilities and vulnerability processes must continue to be recognized, investigated, and countered.

What usefulness resilience offers is restricted by perception and capacity in any response it may make to interpretations of risk. While a necessarily internal function of its community, its identification of externally perpetrated causative processes of vulnerability would require extension of capacity beyond the confines of its place. Additionally, and frequently identified by vocal and local but impotent opposition, resilience would have to become more meaningful to achieve the removal, reduction, or amelioration of external sources of risk. Currently, resilience is not intended to function in this way and it does not. Processes of exploitation and marginalization, and the exercise of commercial and political greed, impede preventive development for preventing disasters, yet may be regarded as 'external' to consequent vulnerable conditions.

Despite the basis in multiple knowledge forms, including contemporary science, understanding causative processes of vulnerability, their past consequences, and their possible futures are paid insufficient concern by resilience. Increased understanding of vulnerability during past decades means that it should, by now, be possible to implement effective measures against its conditions, causes, and perpetrations. Without such measures, efforts toward risk management and post-disaster assistance will continue only in parallel with the creation and manufacturing of vulnerability. Little account of futures or of pasts is taken in 'resilience' analyses of the vulnerable status quo or of long-term consequences of actions outside of its narrow purview. Future exposures will be considered negligent, as are exposures now of past shortcomings. Adopting a 'resilience process' could contribute, but like vulnerability, there is resistance in 'resilience thinking' to discard the 'state of being' construction.

Resilience building and vulnerability reduction must maintain temporal awareness of pasts and futures, as well as of the present, so that as vulnerability processes (and resilience processes) come to be recognized, negative conditions and consequences are reduced. For resilience to be effective, programmes require wide-ranging inclusion of, for example, training in vulnerability accretion as a process, centralized and decentralized governance, environmental and institutional management, planning, and building construction and maintenance, among other activities. Through these, people and places become aware of the wider contexts that may impinge negatively upon them as well as of ways to counter them. Nor is all local knowledge perfect for these purposes, as shown in Lefkada (Karababa and Guthrie, 2007) and by Tibby et al. (2007), indicating the need for multi-scale combinations.

In fact, no group of people and no place is homogeneous. Local divisions are often used to permit some members to make decisions beneficial to themselves, irrespective of the positive or negative consequences for others. Thus, the vulnerability process continues, with one group – nominally the people with decision-making power and control – perpetuating the vulnerability (and resilience) imbalance to favour themselves. Such divisions can be delineated by place, whether that be informal dwellings in contrast to gated sections of a city, or the poor being forced onto floodplains, unstable hillsides, or volcanic slopes.

Aiming for resilience among people – sometimes suggested as needing to occur through initiatives of empowerment, control, and wealth rebalancing – cannot occur without factoring in place. Seeking potable water, proper sanitation, and safe energy for informal settlements helps to reduce vulnerability – but only to some extent, if the hill on which they reside collapses in the next rainfall, volcanic eruption, or earthquake. The causes of vulnerability include dynamic, place-based traits. So also must resilience-related endeavours embrace their widest contexts of dynamic human ecologies of catastrophe.

CHAPTER 9
Vulnerability reduction in development

Disasters: Monitors of development

Disasters are monitors of development. Disasters expose the shortcomings and strengths of preceding processes of change; that is, development or lack thereof. Whether these processes have been planned or whether they have been fortuitous – or whether they have reduced, augmented, eliminated, or created vulnerabilities – all this is exposed when hazards manifest. What development has done or has not done, what it has failed to achieve and what it has excluded or ignored, is exposed in the aftermath of disaster.

From IDNDR (1998), 'Lack of prevention is the debt of development, and disasters are the unpaid bills'. The 'relief machine' moves into what development has preferred not to include and perhaps hidden, deliberately or inadvertently. As a result, 'disaster imperialism' has created for itself the opportunity for response interventions, an aftermath created by defaulting development processes. Then, 'disaster capitalism' takes advantage of disaster to further marginalize people and places by taking over their lives and properties, making the same disaster-causing development mistakes as created the original disaster – and with clear intentionality to do so.

That some of these processes began long before 'development' was taken to be a moral imperative, but were initiated by colonial and postcolonial interests and priorities, does not change this reality. Much vulnerability creation and hence disaster risk creation has been continuing for centuries, whether by external colonialists invading or internal ones retaining power as elites of their own peoples.

These processes creating vulnerability are long term. Consequently, they require long-term processes to be ameliorated. Perpetuating short-term policies and interventions serves to attend to the 'victims' as the symptoms of the system. It also serves to perpetuate the causes and, as shown in Chapter 7, is unsustainable. The power of the relief machine and post-disaster industry grows on the inadequacies of development. These processes of disaster risk creation must be counteracted and reversed.

Vulnerability depends on conditions that are continuously changing over time and, therefore, the vulnerable condition itself also changes continuously. Vulnerability becomes an ecological concept, a dynamic process that is never static nor separate from other (development) actions undertaken. Changes in social conditions increase or decrease vulnerability, thereby altering disaster risk, even where the context of recurrent hazards remains constant. When hazards change to be not as bad as before, vulnerability and so disaster risk can still increase. Conversely, worsening hazards do not need to mean worsening disasters, if vulnerability is tackled.

Accepting these points and improving the identification of vulnerability means that the influences bringing about vulnerability's increase or decrease can be acknowledged and addressed. By adjusting and monitoring these influences in a development context, processes identified as vulnerability causes can be impeded, reversed, and stopped. The effects of hazards diminish, irrespective of changes to hazards themselves, meaning that some diminishing of disaster impacts will have been achieved.

Development can be moulded to these requirements. The objectives of development should involve reducing vulnerabilities, accommodating hazards, and avoiding disasters. The degree to which populations, their activities, and the places can reduce their vulnerability, accommodate hazards, and avoid disasters, is an expression of prevailing societal conditions – incorporating politics, economics, histories, cultures, customs, and much more. Examining prevailing conditions means embracing comprehensiveness, looking at the fullness of relationships, connections, and interlacing of people (individually and collectively) and environments (individual and collective elements). These groups are never separate, but influence and have always influenced each other.

This baseline is axiomatic to an 'ecological approach'. Ecology as a discipline analyses relationships and interactions between organisms and their environment. By analogy, disaster ecology – paralleling with risk ecology and vulnerability ecology – analyses relationships and interactions between organisms or society and disaster, notably disaster causes. Disaster ecology involves reactions and responses during and after a disaster, but must inevitably be founded in reactions and responses to the threat or idea of disaster. Attitudes, behaviour, and decisions would hopefully take an ecological approach to pivot to vulnerability reduction for heading off the threat or idea of disaster. Development contributes to and monitors such progress.

Disaster ecology is, in effect, the subset within wider 'human ecology' (Barrows, 1923) that deals with disasters (Aguirre et al., 1993; Burton et al., 1968; Hewitt, 1983). It is often forgotten in reinventing basic notions through contemporary, confusing phrasing such as 'socio-ecological systems', 'social-ecological systems', 'socio-environmental systems', 'social-environmental systems', and variations.

As per this ecological construct, hazardousness is typical and is a prevailing condition (Hewitt and Burton, 1971). Vulnerability is made to be so, leading to disaster. It does not have to be so, which would avoid disaster.

Small and local disasters exacerbate conditions of vulnerability which contribute to subsequent larger disasters. An ad hoc response to only larger disasters neither admits nor resolves the baseline problem of recurring small-scale, frequent disasters, often not recorded, monitored, or compiled (Marulanda et al., 2010). These less-reported, chronic disasters create further vulnerability, especially as the more frequent they are, the more 'normal', or rather normalized, they become. The vulnerability condition becomes 'normal', expected, and accepted; that is, normalized.

Reducing vulnerabilities to reduce disasters is well-known to have to move beyond 'protection', technology, construction, and one-way messaging for warnings and 'education'. Without neglecting those measures, they ought to be incorporated into including and involving people in their own decisions about their own lives, giving them the political power, control, and resources that they deserve and need to reduce their own vulnerabilities. This approach should cover everyone, from rich to poor, irrespective of cultural background or demographic traits, and whether free or incarcerated in different ways.

Vulnerability reduction enables human ecological adjustments to counter the causes, effects, and implications of disasters and development. It neither covers only nor emphasizes technological resistance to or protection from the events, processes, forces, and energies of the environment. Instead, it focuses on the wide-scale, long-term processes of development, with success in vulnerability reduction or failures through disasters monitoring the progress and approaches to development.

Governance

People and organizations dealing with and monitoring development and disasters for vulnerability reduction require, by definition, governance. Governance is the rules, regulations, norms, and systems indicating what to do, how to act, and how to monitor and enforce actions. Governance must involve applying the knowledge and evidence available, covering all forms: scientific across all disciplines and without discipline, traditional, professional (such as engineering, medicine, law, and social work), vernacular, and local, bringing together local and external forms and approaches.

This suggestion does not mean that comprehensive knowledge and full certainty is required in order to act. Conversely, comprehensive knowledge and full certainty are usually infeasible. Instead, applying knowledge and evidence means deciding and acting given uncertainties, within lack of knowledge and with awareness of unknowns. At times, it is infeasible to know the limits of knowledges or to know what is absent. Governance must account for these gaps and missing elements, offering as suitable a direction as possible, while documenting the limitations. Then, governance ought to be flexible and adaptable to pivot as new knowledge and evidence becomes available and as gaps are filled – or as new ones open up.

A focus on construction techniques, for example, may inadvertently exacerbate disasters by excluding those who cannot afford the techniques and forcing them to occupy other structures. One governance group can ardently seek to reduce vulnerability through development while another governance group – possibly within the same jurisdiction, government, or organization – can implement policies increasing vulnerability or pretending to divorce development and disasters. Purely technological approaches can exclude, because those who cannot partake in them become successively more marginalized, more deprived, and thus even more vulnerable.

Analysis and deeper understanding of the local level and contextualities will reveal the interplay between development and disasters, along with how much or how little external influences create and maintain vulnerability processes. Disaster impacts cannot be adequately assessed or understood without knowing and evidencing the conditions that prevailed before the disaster, since those conditions caused the disaster. Without tackling and governing these prevailing conditions, disasters must continue.

This task requires all knowledge forms contributing to all forms of governance. Laws, policies, rules, and regulations are typically formal and codified. Norms and expectations are typically informal and not necessarily fully codified. They all require different levels of monitoring, enforcement, flexibility to change, and openness to consultation. They all require full transparency.

Administering and monitoring these intersecting and ever-changing governance measures presents an immense challenge. Managing this mammoth task naturally leads to partition and delegation, which in turn produces silos, turf wars, disagreements, competitiveness, contradictions, and inadequate communication. Lack of connection impedes the identification of vulnerabilities, since action in one area can appear to solve a set of problems while creating problems elsewhere.

Heavy roofs tied securely to walls can keep a house together during high winds, as during a tropical cyclone. Without proper design across the entire house, heavy roofs can then crush occupants during an earthquake, as was witnessed during the 17 January 1995 Kobe, Japan earthquake (Menoni, 2001). Joined-up governance and designing for multiple hazards can overcome these presumed 'trade-offs'. Such creativity and action require financial investment.

Not everyone can afford financial investment, irrespective of the rewards reaped. Wider societal financial input and other forms of support, such as through knowledge and regulations, would ensure equitable vulnerability reduction, curtailing disaster risk creation for everyone. These endeavours – cutting across all sectors, departments, organizations, and governance levels – cannot be contained within or implemented by solely a 'disasters' or 'hazard' unit, office, or department. Siloing this work will merely lead to the separation and often disparaging of the tasks by others who do not have the 'disasters' mandate and so do not see it as being within their remit.

Instead, governance should be undertaken by a variety of 'desks', groups, and leaders, covering development programming and management functions. They would all incorporate vulnerability reduction, as part of development.

Otherwise, 'disaster sectors' or the 'disaster sector' become(s) entrenched and self-fulfilling. They feel obliged to devise or retain as many disaster-related tasks which they can keep for themselves, claiming this subject's territory and cajoling other sectors to cede to them the disaster remit. Disasters remain separated from development and from all those causative processes of vulner-ability for which countermeasures are development.

Countermeasures are cross-scalar, requiring connected governance from the hyperlocal through to the global. A pattern of development designed for vulnerability reduction requires an aggregation of numerous small-scale initiatives and interventions. Scaling up and aggregating does not provide all the answers, but provides input for assessing and responding to hazards as well as, more notably, vulnerabilities. This work would be coupled with scaling down and disaggregating from global, large-scale initiatives and interventions.

A municipality can remove houses from floodplains while supporting those homeowners for the move in order to create space for floods, irrespective of human-caused climate change, as completed for London, Ontario, Canada (Doberstein et al., 2019). A municipality can contribute yet not entirely control the global efforts needed to stop human-caused climate change and to monitor and respond to objects in outer space such as comets and asteroids that could hit the planet. Local governance can still address disasters in these circumstances: if development locally has reduced vulnerability, then by definition, disaster impacts have been reduced, even if a hazard is global.

One example of a hyperlocal approach is maintenance, tedious to many and frequently cut back to save money in the short term. The wall that collapses in a storm and kills people using it for shelter reflects not only the storm's strength, but also the wall's condition and the lack of other options for the people sheltering. Although the casualties can conveniently be ascribed to the storm, they may more accurately relate to lack of maintenance of the wall and the lack of other sheltering options. Funding improvements, monitoring, and maintaining small works become a matter of life and death within people's lack of options and the failure to consider storms which might or might not be changing. Not all these issues can be governed locally, by the people directly affected. Infrastructure maintenance sits within wider contexts of resource distribution. Hazards contribute to the need for maintenance, when they damage or weaken infrastructure. Lack of immediately observable concerns can preclude resources and prioritization of repair and maintenance.

Maintenance is not only a physical concept for infrastructure components, such as roofs, windows, doors, walls, and foundations. Maintenance is also required for wider systems. Examples come from agriculture, covering irrigation systems, food storage facilities, drainage networks, and communica-tions and transportation for acquiring and distributing agricultural products and services. Landscapes can be maintained and managed where governance of nature and the environment contributes to dealing with hazards. Examples are removing flammable vegetation from near properties, planting less flammable vegetation, using trees for wind breaks (hoping that the wind is never strong enough to topple or uproot them), stabilizing slopes to prevent slides, and using green spaces such as wetlands and parks to store precipitation runoff and to provide a buffer between water and infrastructure.

All these techniques are governed across multiple levels requiring co-ordination. One municipality might funnel water away from its infrastructure, augmenting the flow in a downstream municipality. An avalanche barrier should not deflect snow away from houses onto a well-travelled road.

Whether at the scale of the watershed, slope, or political jurisdiction, connected governance relates to vulnerability reduction for development. Development is part of the disaster ethic, of disaster governance, and of disaster risk governance. Without accepting this association, governance would be expected to create disaster risk and disasters. Disasters are, after all, the monitor as well as the destroyer of development.

Opportunities for reducing vulnerability

With governance measures and mechanisms in place, opportunities need to be created through and with development in order to reduce vulnerability. Options for dealing with hazards fall into four broad and interlinked categories leading to implications for reducing vulnerability.

First, choose not to worry about or focus on appropriate development. Instead, minimize governance for development and let people live how they want in the ways that they can. This approach is typically termed 'do nothing'. It is, as with every other option, the opposite, since it is an active choice to be laissez-faire; that is, opting not to govern or selecting minimalist governance is 'doing something' by choosing to 'do nothing' or to 'do little'. This apathetic approach must create disasters. Some who have political power and resources will use those opportunities to assist themselves, often at the expense of others. Inadequate development creating and maintaining vulnerability will be forced on some by others, leading to disasters.

Second, develop away from hazards, seeking to avoid hazards irrespective of vulnerabilities. This approach is not feasible, since any location has hazards. Moving upslope to avoid floods could increase contact with wind and slides. Shifting away from burnable vegetation could lead to landscapes with limited vegetation due to limited water, increasing contact with drought.

Efforts to modify hazards can themselves produce development augmenting vulnerability, as with Etkin's (1999) 'risk transference' (see also Chapter 4, 'Surviving many vulnerabilities'). Structural measures for floods (for instance, dams, levees, and dikes) separate people from water. People see the structures keeping them dry on a day-to-day basis, so they think that they are 'protected' from floods. They tend to implement development presuming that floods cannot happen, contributing to vulnerability. When floods do happen, as is inevitable, the damage is far greater due to this higher vulnerability. Risk has been transferred from the present into the future through efforts to separate society and hazards, hence it is risk transference.

Third, govern development with little attention paid to hazards, presuming that post-hazard actions can address disasters. By definition, disasters will occur; in fact, development is governed accepting that disasters will happen. Under this approach, post-disaster actions such as disaster response and humanitarian aid are designed to continue paying little attention to hazards. Then, they perpetuate vulnerability and more disasters. Dependency on external assistance is introduced or exacerbated, while external emergency resources disrupt local markets, prices, and self-support. Disaster aid reduces or warps local abilities for identifying, assessing, and acting on governance for development that reduces vulnerability, sustaining the mindset of not worrying about hazards until one appears.

Fourth, govern development to address hazards and vulnerabilities, thereby living with the hazards and risks (for example, UNISDR, 2004) in such a way that vulnerabilities are reduced. Disasters are reduced too. Lives, livelihoods, and lifestyles would be integrated with environmental threats and opportunities through development which actively identifies and counters disaster risk creation. Examples of disaster risk creation processes to overcome, stop, and prevent are:

- Discrimination, marginalization, oppression, and exploitation of people, their knowledges, their skills, and their abilities.
- Harm to the environment, including clearcutting, overfishing, pollution, and hunting species to extinction.
- Forced displacement of people and communities.
- Corruption, including self-supporting public expenditure, siphoning of public money, and failure to pay or support adequate taxes.
- Hoarding resources to deny others equity and equality.

While the key for development ought to be opportunities for vulnerability reduction, other opportunities emerge during recovery, rehabilitation, and reconstruction after a disaster. Recovery, rehabilitation, and reconstruction have metaphorical as well as physical meanings. They are concerned with policies and systems – that is, governance – as much as with the infrastructure that those policies and systems both require and make possible. They are social as well as physical processes. Recovery, rehabilitation, and reconstruction rebuild destroyed and damaged physical infrastructure and social systems. They should reduce vulnerability by modifying existing infrastructure and systems, even if undamaged, to avoid them succumbing to disaster in the future.

This approach brings people on board for development for vulnerability reduction. Too often, those not immediately affected by disaster disdain or express jealously that those affected by disaster are given food, water, shelter, and new opportunities. The perception can be that it is better to experience disaster in order to be better off afterwards, which can lead down a pathway of wanting or expecting vulnerability and disaster. By improving everyone's opportunities and by demonstrating the daily and millennial advantages of vulnerability reduction, development opportunities are created in which everyone wishes to be involved to help themselves and others.

Diffuse and bounded development programmes may fail to achieve the balance required between supporting those in most need without alienating those in less need at the moment. Account has to be taken of existing physical infrastructure and social systems to bring people on board, demonstrating improvements and opportunities for everyone.

Without co-ordinated and integrated policies and programmes – considering all people, all infrastructure, and all systems – separation, siloing, or sectoralism may induce or condone policies and decision-making leading to vulnerabilities. Whether it is dwellings or roads in more hazardous areas without taking appropriate measures; social divisions among groups; or disinterest in monitoring and enforcing evidence-informed regulations, development becomes a vulnerability creator.

Reducing vulnerability means working across knowledges and disciplines. Disciplines of engineering, planning, and architecture might dominate in design and in organizing development projects. In addition to their acknowledged pedigree of social concern, their predominance may reflect a formerly conventional and restricted view of development on behalf of project initiators and implementers. The ethos might be that disasters are mainly about damaged and destroyed physical infrastructure. Yet others must contribute to development for vulnerability reduction, including sociologists and lawyers. It is, of course, not restricted to only specialized disciplines or knowledges, rather incorporating all others dedicated toward avoiding disasters, no matter how broad their expertise.

Vulnerability is not a static condition. It is dynamic, evolutionary, and accretive. It is a process rather than a snapshot in space and time. Vulnerability reduction must be the same with development opportunities created for it.

From manufacturing disaster to preventive development

Disaster is manufactured by the creation and perpetuation of vulnerability. Disaster can also be a manufactured concept, constructed by others who introduce the notion to, and impose it on, people and places that previously lived with hazards (with various degrees of success) without providing a specific label for the experience. They accepted hazards as the norm and living with hazards as the 'normal'.

In the Cook Islands, missionary organizations introduced the concept and practice of externally mobilized relief after disasters (all material in this paragraph is from the London Missionary Society Archives). Differences of opinion emerged between headquarters in London and individuals in the Cook Islands. One severe tropical cyclone occurred in February 1841 and another later in the same year. A disaster relief consignment of clothes was sent from London for distribution to 'orphans and other cases of real distress'.

The Reverend Charles Pitman wrote in acknowledgement of the consignment in December 1841:

> ... but after all, dear Sir, generally speaking, the giving system is a bad one. There are many, as long as you will give, they will not work, plant, or strive to obtain what is necessary. If the people could get a sure market for what they could grow, I have no doubt that they would plant so as to obtain what was needful for their comforts, and what more is wanted?

The tropical cyclone of 1846 was also severe. This time, relief consignments of food in the form of rice and biscuits were despatched from London. Pitman politely protested again and at length against the 'almost useless expenditure' and the arrival of the food 16 months after the storm, and after abundant harvests in the meantime:

> Rice is an article of food to which the people here are not at all accustomed, and the want of utensils for cooking it, will be a great difficulty, as scarcely a person in our whole settlement possesses such a thing as a pot or pan to boil it in, their own food not requiring such articles for the purpose.

Pitman went on to express a strong preference for tools for reconstruction which he said would be 'invaluable'.

Tonga (see also Chapter 6, 'Vulnerability in Tonga') has long been said to have never been a colony. After being an independently self-governing kingdom, in 1900 it became a protectorate of the UK, and achieved full independence again in 1970. Others contest this narrative, pointing out significant colonialist governance (Tecun and Siu'ulua, 2023). Colonial reports were filed by the UK consul (the nearest UK High Commissioner being in Fiji) in which the concept and practice of disaster relief is, as found so far, first noted to appear in 1909, after a tropical cyclone struck the island of Niua Fo'ou and 'the Government of Tonga sent in relief but it was not required to any great extent' (Westgate, 1975). There was no further noted reference to (or need of?) relief until after the tropical cyclone of 1961, though there had been many severe hazards in the meantime. The eruption on Niua Fo'ou in 1946 is an example, sitting within Tonga's long history during which storms, earthquakes, volcanic eruptions, droughts, pathogens, tsunamis, and other hazards were endemic.

A key limitation of these analyses is thinking and writing in English based on records in English. Without having insights and descriptions from people of the Cook Islands and Tonga, who are fluent in the languages and who have a deep knowledge of each archipelago's history and cultures, it is hard to discern the exact meanings and interpretations of constructs such as 'disaster', 'vulnerability', and 'relief'. The concepts and practices might have existed and been enacted. Did people from one island assist people from another after a hazard? Are legends told of times of great difficulty or sudden change (an example being Lavigne et al., 2021) with the notion of 'disaster' or 'calamity' explicitly engrained? Or, as with the word 'hazard' in many languages, are all these ideas absent from local vocabularies across the millennia, leading to English misapprehensions of local stories – just as Lavigne et al. (2021) erroneously refer to a tsunami as a 'natural disaster'?

Were or are disaster and disaster response wholly external concepts? Were they introduced by external administrations from external sources using external words? Were they adopted locally for practical and pragmatic advantages, humanitarian and/or political, or did externals force their acceptance? The result could have been the introduction of a previously unknown dependency and the root of a new-found vulnerability. Or this dependency and vulnerability might have existed and been acknowledged, in different forms which have never been examined with and from local perspectives.

Similarly for preventive development – development that reduces vulnerabilities – what concepts, words, connotations, interpretations, and constructs exist across languages, cultures, and histories? Which local ones could be introduced into contemporary English and global modes to supplement, improve, and direct dominant approaches? Just as the 'cycle' should be retired due to its limitations and the far better alternatives (Chapter 7, 'Cyclical concepts'), what could be proffered by the cultures of those reading this book which would supplant or complement assumptions of design, development, disasters, and vulnerabilities, as presented in this book? And what could be proffered by the cultures of those who will never have an opportunity to read this book or, understandably, have no interest in reading it and engaging with the material? Instead, the material in this book ought to engage with their knowledges and understandings.

Desperate crisis-driven policy-making and decision-making is often in competition rather than with co-ordination across sectors and departments. It typically presumes a particular way of acting and enacting. It requires more interrelationship, integration, and co-operation drawing on wider perspectives. How to enact this approach without concomitant disadvantages remains a challenge. Could it be a well-informed, roaming minister or deputy from the Head of Government's or Head of State's office? Could it be regular meetings among representatives, named or not as a formal committee? Could it be appropriate individuals in each department or at each desk who proactively communicate? Or a combination? Plenty of options have been written about. Where are examples of long-term success?

This includes relief and development becoming less distinct, and the distinctions between them best avoided, to produce preventive development that avoids relief. Reactive relief obviated by proactive development could assist in achieving self-reliance in the long-term, drawing on and improving long-standing, well-meaning declarations to this effect (for instance, Madrid, 1995).

Without understanding vulnerability and the need for reducing it through development, policies may ensue for limiting development, in the mistaken belief that less will be lost when disasters occur. Such policies perpetuate disadvantage, dissatisfaction, inequity, and inequality, informing people that they do not deserve much now since they did not have much before. After the 26 January 2001 earthquake in Gujarat, India, equitable aid distribution appears to have been inhibited by caste and religious divides, with those who had privilege decrying the help given to people without privilege (Kumar, 2007).

By understanding vulnerability as a process of social interrelationships – incorporating political, cultural, historical, artistic, scientific, and economic dimensions among others – 'preventive development' takes its place within a spectrum of measures for a corresponding spectrum of conditions. The dramatic and obvious headlining effects of disasters are more appropriately understood as relatively superficial compared to the hidden, less overt, but longer-lasting underlying impacts. These hidden processes bring about more vulnerability.

By attending to root causes of vulnerability, everyday existence will be improved, disasters will have less impact or be absent, and post-disaster conditions will require less exogenous input. By definition, this should be the objective of development. Such development for vulnerability reduction depends upon institutional organization, co-ordination, and connection, overcoming the separation of sectors and activities. Disasters pervade and transcend all boundaries, physical and social. Consequently, so must solutions to disaster.

The following are examples of contributions to effective and identifiable reduction of vulnerability in development, repeated and detailed across many documents, declarations, projects, and programmes:

- Understanding the multi-sectoral and interrelated processes which create and perpetuate vulnerability.
- Documenting the requirements, identifying, articulating, and resolving the processes creating vulnerability.
- Accounting for disaster impacts in such a way that they are linked to development decisions and actions, so that disaster metrics demonstrate the impact of disasters upon development and, more meaningfully, the impact of development upon vulnerability.
- Co-ordinating otherwise separate and possibly conflicting activities by, for instance, vulnerability assessments being part of all development proposals, initiatives, monitoring, and evaluation.
- Determining the mechanisms and impacts of hazards and disasters in order to highlight vulnerabilities and to assist with equity and equality during disaster response.
- Reintegrating the perception and tackling of vulnerability within the processes that would otherwise lead to vulnerability accreting, further ensuring that responses to disasters address disaster causes and contexts.
- Assessing the shortcomings and strengths of established development patterns, priorities, and activities to rectify the shortcomings and to shore up the strengths.

- Using disasters as impetus toward identifying and fulfilling development needs, while recognizing and acting on the fundament that disasters are not and should never be a prerequisite for this undertaking.

For all the above, all scales are important. Local vulnerability reduction requires local programmes of local significance, just as larger-scale programmes can tackle larger-scale vulnerability and causes thereof. Workable practices should form links between prevailing pre-disaster contexts, post-disaster aftermaths, and continuing change and development for vulnerability reduction.

A balance of decentralization and centralization facilitates programmes to adapt to various local conditions and changing circumstances alongside other subnational, national, and supranational interests and approaches. Decentralization enhances opportunities for local participation in decisions and their implementation, which have a bearing upon their lives, livelihoods, and lifestyles. Centralization helps to ensure that local decisions do not cause problems elsewhere or clash with each other, undermining good intentions.

This work does not and should not begin with a disaster. Disaster-centric and disaster-specific endeavours miss the long-term disaster process of vulnerability accreting. While disaster-specific initiatives are meant to be designed to create improvements, and while disaster relief is often stated as being designed with development in mind, neither approach necessarily succeeds. They can be used to worsen development, with 'disaster capitalism' being notorious, just as other simultaneous activities can undermine vulnerability reduction (see also 'Disasters: Monitors of development', above). Post-disaster actions and development can cause disasters.

To avoid these situations, examples – far from being comprehensive – of projects and programmes to consider in tandem through a balance of centralization and decentralization are:

- Health clinics and centres, focusing on prevention, care, and wellbeing – including reproductive and sexual healthcare choices – while having diagnosis and treatment adequately staffed, equipped, and accessible to everyone.
- Education from early childhood through to tertiary and continuing professional development, adequately staffed, equipped, and accessible to everyone, with safe facilities.
- Water which is clean and available for all drinking, washing, and hygiene, as well as being sufficient for agriculture and industry.
- Food offering a variety of healthy, nutritious, and satisfying options, as local as possible, including supporting small-scale subsistence agriculture, aquaculture, and permaculture alongside options to scale up operations sustainably to support food-based livelihoods. Non-food cultivation should have similar characteristics, offering materials for clothes and structures, with examples being wool, cotton, and wood.

- Shelter and other infrastructure, seen as processes rather than as products (Turner, 1972), offering safe, comfortable, and healthy places for living, working, shopping, storing, and transporting, so that they are integral to home and community, not just functional.
- Energy including electricity produced as locally and pollution-free as possible, which would minimize hazard impacts on transmission systems and which would develop local expertise for monitoring and maintenance, assisting with repairs after a hazard and providing local livelihoods.
- Communications, ranging from community spaces for 'hanging out' and connecting through to remote and wireless options including reliable and affordable internet and phone coverage.
- Transportation which is safe, frequent, reliable, and accessible to everyone; minimizes pollution, including particulates, gases, liquids, noise, and light; and balances connections (such as bridges, tunnels, and causeways) with many places' preferences to be less connected. Faster and bigger transportation, from multi-lane highways to long-runway airports, is not necessarily better for or desired by everyone involved.
- Financing options and opportunities, such as ethical loans, savings, and insurance, that support livelihoods and ultimately provide pathways out of poverty and for poverty prevention.

Conversely, certain types of development are the antithesis to vulnerability reduction and should be avoided, with examples being:

- Causing or exacerbating destructive divisions on bases such as sex, sexuality, gender, culture, ethnicity, race, caste, and disability/ability.
- Growth-only approaches, presuming that expansion and more consumption are the way forward.
- Focusing on economic indicators, especially macroeconomic calculations such as gross domestic product (GDP) and growth rates of the economy.
- Efforts that do not seek ethical population stabilization as well as efforts that assume population numbers or population growth rates are the only or principal concerning factor for development.
- Forcible migration, displacement, or resettlement, especially without adequate compensation and support in new places.
- Forcible losses of traditional and vernacular resources, knowledges, and lifestyles without offering improved alternatives.

For all the above criticisms, numerous alternatives exist which have been shown to support development for vulnerability reduction. Some examples:

- Stopping female genital mutilation (FGM) by banning it and prosecuting offenders undermines traditional cultures and approaches, yet is fully in line with equity and development that reduces vulnerability.

- Rather than growth-based economies, other approaches could be steady state economies (Daly, 1973) and wellbeing economies (Dalziel et al., 2018).
- Measuring success through human outcomes, including health, wellbeing, educational attainment, equity, and equality, rather than through economic, monetary, or financial calculations.
- Ending taxation loopholes and offshore investment and savings options which permit the privileged to become even more privileged by helping them to evade paying their fair shares (Shaxson, 2011).

Development objectives have to be achieved simultaneously and in combination, not sequentially, one-off, piecemeal, or ad hoc. Numerous objectives by many labels start to align and converge, making it difficult to separate them: poverty reduction, equitable development, preventive development, sustainable development, sustainability, healthy livelihoods, and more jargon such as disaster risk reduction including climate change adaptation, not to mention pollution prevention and disaster risk management. The objectives of vulnerability reduction fit well with all of these and are significantly represented. Given the many labels, why should 'vulnerability' be used and why should 'vulnerability reduction' be a focus, rather than the other approaches?

One answer is that vulnerability reduction, poverty reduction, and sustainable development are largely synonymous, especially with similar actions, but they are not exactly the same. Climate change adaptation and disaster risk reduction or disaster risk management are not synonymous; the former with the acronym CCA offers nothing new to the latter of DRR and DRM. CCA sits as a subset within, and often distraction from, DRR and DRM. While vulnerability reduction and poverty reduction may sit within sustainable development, subject to definitions (for example, Ruggerio, 2021) as always, they may have differences and complementarities.

Processes of vulnerability accretion require identification and countering especially but not only within contexts of poverty. People with political power, control, and resources still choose to build houses in floodplains without flood resistance measures and to travel to avalanche-prone locations without learning about avalanches. While this might be their choices and their lives, so they deal with the consequences, it still remains a process of vulnerability. Plus, their choices can impose vulnerability on others, such as hotel workers serving them in avalanche-prone locations. Where the hotel jobs pay well and are secure, poverty reduction and vulnerability reduction are not necessarily the same.

Fairness is an aspect of vulnerability reduction revealing strong links between vulnerability and poverty. These situations do not mean that only poverty accrues vulnerability or that vulnerability linearly leads to poverty.

They are intertwined, again supporting 'human ecology' producing 'disaster ecology' (Chapter 6, 'A multi-hazard history of Antigua' and 'Disasters:

Monitors of development', above). It is not sufficient for development to call itself 'sustainable', 'preventive', or 'equitable', simply because it has incorporated some attention to a potential for or actuality of hazards. Development of, for, by, and with people and places, in each of its parts and constituents as well as combined and scaling up, achieves sustainability. Development to achieve sustainability should permanently reduce vulnerability, along with poverty, inequity, and inequality.

Socially sustainable development inclusive of everyone, particularly the poorest and most marginalized, will further remove dependency. Dependency, often emerging from poverty and marginalization, is a significant cause of vulnerability. Local consultation, initiative, and participation avoids negative impacts from hazardousness while improving everyday lives, livelihoods, and lifestyles, immediately and far into the future, provided this action is:

- Informed, by and for everyone.
- Multi-sectoral, so connecting sectors, disciplines, knowledges, wisdoms, expertises, and abilities.
- Positive; for instance, following the title of this book's first edition, 'development in disaster-prone places' rather than, too often, 'development reduction creating disaster-prone places'!
- Not waiting for a disaster in order to begin.

Tested frameworks exist for implementation, such as FPIC (fair, prior, informed consent; Tamang, 2005), to emulate and adjust according to specific needs and contexts.

These programmes and projects are to be initiated not upon global aggregates of impact and loss, nor solely upon country information received via governments or the media, nor focusing on disasters with the largest metrics, headlines, or numbers of clicks. Proportional impact and proportional vulnerability (Chapter 2, 'Local-to-global vulnerabilities') need to inform decisions too, to account for localized and everyday experiences. Proportional vulnerabilities and proportional impacts reflect the comparative scale of disasters. The greatest scale of impact can be upon the smallest number of people, the smallest places, and the smallest jurisdictions (Chapter 2, 'Islands and vulnerability'). Absolute impact might be small in the national or global scheme, while locally affecting everything to a high degree (Chapter 6):

- Areas of highest population or infrastructure density or of highest population or infrastructure numbers are not always the areas of highest losses or of worst damage.
- Less dramatic, less superficially impressive, and less accessible loss and damage does not necessarily mean less loss and damage.
- Rural populations in aggregate may be larger than those in nearby urban areas; the rural–urban divide is ambiguous, artificial, and arbitrary anyway, especially when considering peri-urban and suburban 'in-between' areas.

- Calculable and tangible losses can have far less impact than intangible and incalculable losses, such as heritage, sense of home, culture, sentimental value, and irreplaceable items or data.

Assumptions about the size or scale of a vulnerability situation and about the extent of a disaster or disastrous condition can yield the opposite conclusion to what people and places experience.

Avoiding the manufacturing of disaster and supporting development means communication, collaboration, and choices. Who can do all these and how to do them varies substantially. Often those making decisions about vulnerability and development are not those suffering the consequences from those decisions.

Conclusion

Lessons for vulnerability reduction in development include:

- Resolving vulnerability while contextualizing hazards and hazardousness. That is, considering vulnerabilityness as much as hazardousness.
- Incorporating the hazard–vulnerability interplay into development.
- Examining actions in the aftermath of one disaster as the context of the next in order to avoid (re-)creating disaster.
- Desisting from one-off, piecemeal, and ad hoc approaches to single disasters as (isolated) events, instead seeking connections and processes.
- Ensuring that technology and technological approaches are accepted, not in isolation, but as part of society and social programmes serving people and places. Different technical levels are appropriate to different societal conditions, contexts, and circumstances.
- Integrating, not separating, nature/environment, people/society, and places/locations, so that all are accounted for together when using development for vulnerability reduction and addressing hazardousness.

Vulnerability reduction in development means more than survival; it is about thriving, for lives, livelihoods, and lifestyles. Supporting people and places over the longer term to thrive in their homes, their households, their localities, and beyond to their regions and countries, with global opportunities too. Self-reliance and self-help are the focus, provided that others – present now or into the future – are not harmed and that governance structures do not devolve all responsibility to the individual, family, or household. Social processes such as health, education, food, water, energy, communications, and transportation are among the sectors that help people to thrive through collective efforts. Keywords/buzzwords incorporate equity, equality, and sustainability, referring to the inseparability of environmental/natural, social/human, and place-based/locational.

Dependency on external goodwill or whims is to be reduced and removed, letting people thrive in their own ways without causing difficulties for others now or in the future. The focus for development and vulnerability reduction is people and places, society living with each other enfolded with nature. All scales are considered and connected.

Emphasizing disaster magnitude, global comparisons of vulnerability, and 'rapid onset' or 'quick onset' hazards such as tornadoes and earthquakes obscure these prospects. Expression of disaster sizes and highlighting larger-scale disasters or the most obvious impacts reflect a privileged comparative view which sidelines people's daily experiences and the reality of smaller scales; that is, the local disasters with catastrophic local impacts. Slow-onset hazards and creeping disasters (Glantz, 1994, 1999; Staupe-Delgado, 2023; Staupe-Delgado and Rubin, 2022) at any scale are significant contributors to development problems, undermining efforts in vulnerability reduction.

Vulnerability is essentially a local condition, experienced by people in their places, although frequently caused and influenced by large-scale, external creators and drivers. Understanding vulnerability invariably ensues out of local, everyday, lived experience and analysis. Though vulnerability pervades globally, generalized and generic 'globalization' is a mere part of the picture. The tagline 'all vulnerability is local' holds, without meaning that it is disembodied from wider scales.

In addition to being connected across space scales, vulnerability is connected across time scales. Vulnerability is processual, happening over time so that it builds up and is maintained over the long term. Since disasters come from vulnerability, disasters too are slow-onset and processual, happening over the long term, and realistically and locally related to vulnerability conditions; that is, the vulnerability process interacting with the development process.

To reduce vulnerability, development must account for this localization and process of vulnerability.

CHAPTER 10
Conclusion
Vulnerability futures

From this book's discussion on prevailing conditions of vulnerability for development and disasters, two predominant conclusions emerge.

The first and paramount conclusion is that, as already known and accepted, 'natural disasters' rarely exist, because disasters come from vulnerabilities and not from natural hazards. Because the vulnerability process is complex, all disasters are 'complex' (and complicated, wicked, super-wicked, and other such descriptors).

Disasters reflect a grounded realism of interactions among vulnerability creation, vulnerability perpetuation, and poor development, all together being disaster risk creation: vulnerability futures and future vulnerabilities. That disasters are not natural shows how responses to disasters and their causes have been simple, simplistic, selective, and partial, still resulting from the overriding objectives of convenient and insidious institutional, organizational, ideological, or political standpoints. And so responses to disasters and their causes continue to feed into future vulnerabilities and hence future disasters.

The second conclusion is that, again as already known and accepted, redressing the causes of disasters is – could be and should be – within the remit, capacity, ability, capability, resources, skills, knowledges, and wisdoms of humanity. Societies can and should create their own futures with reduced vulnerabilities. Development can and should ameliorate and avoid disasters. Vulnerability reduction can and should mean that hazards do not manifest as disasters.

From meanings and experiences of vulnerabilities, through to efforts to survive and thrive via vulnerability reduction, from recognizing specific and general disaster risk creators and drivers, through to detailing specific and general ways to counter disaster risk creation, the development patterns are clear. A pattern of vulnerability leads to disaster. A pattern for development can lead away from disaster, but instead often converges with vulnerability creation. The pattern of vulnerability futures can be decided for or against preventive development and fewer disasters.

Disasters are a monitor of development. As expressed in many ways over past decades (for instance, IDNDR, 1998) and hopefully continuing through future decades, disasters are the unpaid bills and debt collection of poor development and abject failures in prevention. It might seem cheaper to accrue debt or to not pay bills now. The eventual and inevitable costs far exceed what the initial payments could ever have been.

It is not despairingly impossible. We can and do invest, with many successes of disasters avoided (https://disastersavoided.com) and significant paybacks from them. Development and disasters, through vulnerability reduction irrespective of natural hazards, does lead to better development and prevented disasters. For some people in some places, life, livelihood, and lifestyle are being supported and improved, so they can choose their own vulnerability futures and future vulnerabilities.

More tangibly, positive change across development and disasters is exemplified by:

- *Improving and expanding inclusivity.* People who previously were not admitted to exist, and who would have been killed as non-human when identified, are now more or less fully accepted in some places. Discrimination against them is outlawed and the law is, at times, monitored and enforced.
- *Rebalancing power.* Democracies and freedoms exist in many places, at least at some level, as many empires have been dismantled and many colonies have taken independence, self-governance, and self-government. Neither author of this book expects to be arrested, tortured, or executed for authoring this book, which is a major advance from bygone eras.
- *Adjusting understandings.* Despite this book being in English using a narrow and narrow-minded applied science structure and style, many different forms of expressions are accepted and respected for conveying and using diverse knowledges and modes of expression. Knowledges and modes of expression are becoming wisdoms to reap the rewards of humanity's vast repertoire of ways of observing, interpreting, analysing, and communicating.
- *Linking across scales.* Knowledges, wisdoms, and understandings increasingly encompass cross-scale connections. For time, it means knowing the present as it is, while recognizing the present as a process based in the past and as a definer of the future. Time connects from faster than nanoseconds to beyond the universe's age. Space covers from more than the universe's volume to the components of subatomic particles. For the scale of planet Earth, space melds needs and actions from individual to global. Governance scales cover worldwide through to individualism.
- *Being realistic.* Complexity, nonlinearity, a lack of endpoints, and absence of one-size-fits-all are the norms, not the exceptions. The world is hard, harsh, and complicated. Boxes and silos, including those of disasters and disaster risk reduction, are arbitrary and artificial – as are those of development, vulnerability, hazards, and risks. While many continue to prefer and act otherwise, these points are more and more presented as axioms and truisms.
- *Bettering focuses on people and places.* Previously viewed as inconsequential externalities, much more attention and respect are being accorded to

quality of life, livelihoods, and lifestyles; mental health and wellbeing; fairness, reasonableness, and respect; being fully involved and informed; and intangible, non-monetary, non-financial, and non-economic impacts and outcomes. They all display vagueness and ambiguities. This is the complex world. This is reality.

*   *Bringing kindness, compassion, and caring*, far beyond what empathy and sympathy could ever provide. Hate, hostility, ostracization, and boundaries are common, even (especially?) within the small world of development and disaster researchers publishing academic works in English. Much can be resolved by communicating openly, humbly, considerately, and humanely. Why not do so?

Counterexamples to these points abound. It can be three steps forward and two steps back or two steps forward and five steps back. Viewed over centuries and millennia, humanity is far better off in all the above points and in many more.

Nevertheless, ending on a positive note would be too quixotic; far too much of a 'false positive' note, bubbling over with 'hopium', the baseline element of hope. Disasters continue. They are made to be prevalent. People and places remain vulnerable. They are made to be more vulnerable.

To demonstrate the tunnel vision of presentism, in the week prior to this chapter first being revised from the first edition, over 135 people perished in an earthquake in Japan; Morocco and Panama struggled with drought; and thousands of properties were flooded with cold, dirty water across the UK. By the time this chapter was finalized for submission to the publisher, those disasters had been forgotten by most people not directly affected. Instead, headlines had blared out many further disasters, raising eyebrows and eliciting commiseration continents away for a few hours or a few days. Because, as per the previous paragraph, disasters continue apace, people and places remain vulnerable, and ending on a fully positive note would be going too far with the evidence. Irrespective of the positive changes, we have a long way yet to go.

Not-so-positive change abounds. Increased dominance of complicated, misleading jargon supports debunked ideas over baseline common sense. Misinformation, disinformation, degradation of insight, and fakeness supplant actuality. Long-term knowledge and wisdom are lost due to loss of long-term interest in long-term knowledge and wisdom. Action fails to draw on prior lessons, repeating errors and claiming that it is all new and was previously unknown. We talk, write, and publish sentences and speeches/manuscripts as long as they will get by reviewers and editors, confusing our audiences with the illusion of erudite sayings which apparently translate into effective action. When no one else will publish our words, we microblog, snap, and message pithy aphorisms confusing our audiences with the illusion of erudite sayings which apparently translate into effective action. We descend into enmity, refusing reconciliation with our peers when we agree on more than 99 per cent, preferring to let some poorly worded remarks or minor disparities create impenetrable barriers. We obscure, neglect, and forget the basics, fearful of communicating it as it really is. A tiny, powerful minority wilfully creates vulnerability and so disasters, wishing to do so due to the short-term benefits they accrue at the expense of the long-term for the powerless majority – and for themselves.

All people and all places experience natural hazards, unnatural hazards, and their combination. All people and all places are disaster-prone. All people and all places require development for and by themselves so that they become less disaster-prone, creating their own futures without disaster risk creation. All people and all places should have development options and opportunities to implement vulnerability reduction processes for overcoming vulnerability processes.

References

Adams, J. (1999) *Risk*, UCL Press, London.

Aguirre, B.E., Saenz, R., Edmiston, J., Yang, N., Agramonte, E. and Stuart, D.L. (1993) 'The human ecology of tornadoes', *Demography* 30(4): 623–33. https://doi.org/10.2307/2061810

Angenheister, G. (1921) 'A study of Pacific earthquakes', *New Zealand journal of science and technology* 4: 209–231.

Arkell, W.J. (1965) 'The effects of storms on Chesil Beach in November 1954', *Proceedings of the Dorset natural history and archaeological society* 76: 141–5.

Auchinleck, G.G. (1956) *The rainfall of Antigua and Barbuda*, compiled from available records, The Antigua Sugar Association, St. John's.

Audet, F. (2015) 'From disaster relief to development assistance: Why simple solutions don't work', *Contemporary international history* 70(1): 110–8. https://doi.org/10.1177/0020702014562595

Aven, T. (2015) *Risk analysis*, Wiley, Chichester.

Azim, M.I. and Kluvers, R. (2019) 'Resisting corruption in Grameen Bank', *Journal of business ethics* 156: 591–604. https://doi.org/10.1007/s10551-017-3613-4

Baines, G. and McLean, R.F. (1976a) 'Re-surveys of 1972 hurricane rampart of Funafuti Atoll, Ellice Islands', *Search* 7(1–2): 36–7.

Baines, G. and McLean, R. (1976b) 'Sequential studies of hurricane deposit evolution at Funafuti Atoll', *Marine geology* 21(1): M1–8. https://doi.org/10.1016/0025-3227(76)90097-9

Baird, A., O'Keefe, P.O., Westgate, K., and Wisner, B. (1975) *Towards an explanation and reduction of disaster proneness*, occasional paper No 11, Disaster Research Unit, University of Bradford, Bradford.

Baldacchino, G. (2005) 'Editorial: islands – objects of representation', *Geografiska annaler: series B, human geography* 87(4): 247–51. https://doi.org/10.1111/j.0435-3684.2005.00196.x

Baldacchino, G. (ed.) (2018) *The international handbook of island studies: a world of islands*, Routledge, Abingdon. https://doi.org/10.4324/9781315556642

Ball, D. (1973) *Funafuti, Ellice Islands, physical development plan*, Building Research Establishment, Garston, Watford.

Ball, N. (1975) 'The myth of the natural disaster', *The ecologist* 5(10): 368–9.

Bankoff, G. and Hilhorst, D. (eds.) (2022) *Why vulnerability still matters: the politics of disaster risk creation*, Routledge, Abingdon.

Barrows, H.H. (1923) 'Geography as human ecology', *Annals of the Association of American Geographers* 13(1): 1–14.

Beck, U. (2013) *World at risk*, Wiley, Chichester.

Beckerman, W. (1966) *International comparisons of real incomes development centre*, Organisation for Economic Co-operation and Development, Paris.

Bettey, J.H. (1970) *The island and royal manor of Portland: Some aspects of its history with particular reference to the period 1750–1851*, The Court Leet of the Island and Royal Manor of Portland in association with University of Bristol, Department of Extra-Mural Studies, Portland and Bristol.

Brindze, R. (1973) *Hurricanes: monster storms from the sea*, Atheneum, New York.

Burton, I., Kates, R.W. and White, G.F. (1968) *Human ecology of extreme geophysical events*, Natural hazard research working paper 1, Department of Geography, University of Toronto, Toronto, ON.

Campbell, J.R. (1984) *Dealing with disaster: hurricane response in Fiji*, East–West Center and Government of Fiji, Honolulu and Suva.

Campbell, M.D. (1977) *Summary report on 1977 assignment in Tonga*, Director of External Aid, Ministry of Foreign Affairs, Wellington.

Canterbury Earthquakes Royal Commission – Te Komihana Rūwhenua o Waitaha (2012) *Final report: Volume 6. Canterbury Television Building (CTV)*, Canterbury Earthquakes Royal Commission – Te Komihana Rūwhenua o Waitaha, Wellington.

Carr, A.P. (1969) 'Size grading along a pebble beach Chesil Beach, England', *Journal of sedimentary petrology* 39(1): 297–311. https://doi.org/10.1306/74D71C3A-2B21-11D7-8648000102C1865D

Carr, A.P. (1978) 'The long Chesil shingle', *Geographical magazine* 50(10): 677–80.

Carr, A.P. and Blackley, M.W.L. (1974) 'Ideas on the origin and development of Chesil Beach, Dorset', *Proceedings of the Dorset Natural History and Archaeological Society* 95: 9–17.

Carr, A. and Gleason, R. (1972) 'Chesil Beach, Dorset and the cartographic evidence of Sir John Coode', *Proceedings of the Dorset Natural History and Archaeological Society* 93: 125–31.

Central Hurricane Relief Committee (1978) *Report of a visit to the Ha'apai Group 4–11 January 1978 regarding Hurricane Anne, 14 January*, Central Hurricane Relief Committee, Nuku'alofa.

Chambers, R. (2002) *Participatory workshops: A sourcebook of 21 sets of ideas and activities*, Routledge, Abingdon.

Chiswell Residents' Action Group (1979a) *An analytical report concerning the flooding problems of Chiswell, Portland*, Chiswell Residents' Action Group, Chiswell.

Chiswell Residents' Action Group (1979b) *Letter to the President of the European Commission 11 April 1979*, Chiswell Residents' Action Group, Chiswell.

Chiswell Residents' Action Group (1979c) *CRAG bulletin nos. one and two March 1979 and 23 April 1979*, Chiswell Residents' Action Group, Chiswell.

Collens, A.E. (1927) *Leeward Islands hurricane warnings and amended hurricane code*, St. John's.

Collens, A.E. (1928) *Leeward Islands; report of the committee appointed to assess hurricane damage of September 11–12, 1928*, St. John's.

Colonial Office (1886–1938; 1947–1954) *Report on the blue book (Leeward Islands)*, Her Majesty's Stationery Office (HMSO), London.

Copans, J. (ed.) (1975) *Sécheresses et famines du Sahel*, F. Maspero, Paris.

Cuny, F.C. (1983) *Disasters and development*, Oxford University Press, Oxford.

Daly, H.E. (ed.) (1973) *Toward a steady-state economy*, W.H. Freeman, San Francisco.

Dalziel, P., Saunders, C. and Saunders, J. (2018) *Wellbeing economics: the capabilities approach to prosperity*, Palgrave Macmillan, Cham https://doi.org/10.1007/978-3-319-93194-4

Davey, R.I. (1980) 'Attempts to prevent flooding at Chiswell, Portland', *Disasters* 4(4): 380–2. https://doi.org/10.1111/j.1467-7717.1980.tb00130.x

Davis, I. (1978) *Shelter after disaster*, Oxford Polytechnic Press, Oxford.

Davis, I., Ressler, E.M. and Westgate, K. (1980) *Human settlements and disasters: a series of five slide lectures*, Commonwealth Association of Architects, London.

Department of Census and Statistics (1978) *Statistical pocket book of the Democratic Socialist Republic of Sri Lanka*, Department of Census and Statistics, Colombo.

Department of the Colonies reports on the past and present state of Her Majesty's colonial possessions, for the years 1845–1848, 1849–1850, 1850–1851, 1852–1853, 1854–1855, 1856–1857, 1858–1859, 1860–1861, 1862–1863, 1864–1865, –1887.

Descloitres, R., Descloitres, C. and Reverdy, J.C. (1973) 'Urban organisation and social structure in Algeria', in I.W. Zarman (ed.), *Man, state and society in the contemporary Maghrib*, pp. 424–38, Praeger, London.

Devereux, S. (1994) *Theories of Famine*, Harvester Wheatsheaf, Hertfordshire.

Dobbie, C.H. and Partners (1979) *Preliminary report on Flooding at Portland, report to the Wessex Water Authority*, Dobbie and Partners, Southampton.

Doberstein, B., Fitzgibbons, J. and Mitchell, C. (2019) 'Protect, accommodate, retreat or avoid (PARA): Canadian community options for flood disaster risk reduction and flood resilience', *Natural hazards* 98: 31–50. https://doi.org/10.1007/s11069-018-3529-z

Dorset County Council (1964) *Report on Chiswell area, Portland, (with suggestions for improvement and policy with regard to development and redevelopment)*, South Area Planning Office, Dorset.

Dorset Daily Echo, 22 December 1942.

Dorset Evening Echo, 22 June 1972, 4 April 1977, 12 December 1978, 13 December 1978, 14 December 1978, 15 December 1978, 16 December 1978, 13 February 1979, 14 February 1979, 15 February 1979, 2 March 1979, 19 March 1979, 1 April 1979.

ECLA (1974) *Report on the damage caused in Antigua and Barbuda by the earthquake of 8 October 1974 and its repercussions (prepared by Silbourne St. A. Clark). ECLA/POS 74/15*, ECLA (United Nations Economic Commission for Latin America, Office for the Caribbean), Port of Spain.

ECLAC (1985) *Damage caused by the Mexican earthquake and its repercussions upon the country's economy*, ECLAC (United Nations Economic Commission for Latin America and the Caribbean), Santiago.

ESCAP (1979) *Damage caused by tropical cyclones, floods and droughts in individual countries or areas in the ESCAP region 1978 Sri Lanka*, ESCAP (United Nations Economic and Social Commission for Asia and the Pacific), Bangkok.

Etkin, D. (1999) 'Risk transference and related trends: driving forces towards more mega-disasters', *Environmental hazards* 1(2): 69–75. https://doi.org/10.1016/S1464-2867(00)00002-4

FEMA (2017) *Pre-disaster recovery planning guide for local governments*, FEMA (Federal Emergency Management Agency), Washington, DC.

Fordham, M. (1998) 'Making women visible in disasters: problematising the private domain', *Disasters* 22(2): 126–43. https://doi.org/10.1111/1467-7717.00081

Fottrell, E., Azad, K., Kuddus, A., Younes, L., Shaha, S., Nahar, T., Aumon, B.H., Hossen, M., Beard, J., Hossain, T., Pulkki-Brannstrom, A.-M., Skordis-Worrall, J., Prost, A., Costello, A. and Houweling, T.A.J. (2013) 'The effect of increased coverage of participatory women's groups on neonatal mortality in Bangladesh: a cluster randomized trial', *JAMA pediatrics* 167(9): 816–25. https://doi.org/10.1001/jamapediatrics.2013.2534

Gaillard, J.C. (2022) *The invention of disaster: power and knowledge in discourses on hazard and vulnerability*, Routledge, Abingdon. https://doi.org/10.4324/9781315752167

Gaillard, J.C., Cadag, J.R.D. and Rampengan, M.M.F. (2019) 'People's capacities in facing hazards and disasters: an overview', *Natural hazards* 95: 863–76. https://doi.org/10.1007/s11069-018-3519-1

Garcia, C. and Fearnley, C.J. (2016) 'Evaluating critical links in early warning systems for natural hazards', *Environmental hazards* 11(2): 123–37. https://doi.org/10.1080/17477891.2011.609877

Garriott, E.B. (1900) *West Indian hurricanes*, US Department of Agriculture, Washington, DC.

Glantz, M.H. (ed.) (1976) *The politics of natural disaster: the case of the Sahel drought*, Praeger, New York.

Glantz, M.H. (1994) 'Creeping environmental problems', *The world & I* June: 218–25.

Glantz, M.H. (ed.) (1999) *Creeping environmental problems and sustainable development in the Aral Sea basin*, Cambridge University Press, Cambridge. https://doi.org/10.1017/CBO9780511535970

Glantz, M.H. and Jamieson, D. (2000) 'Societal response to Hurricane Mitch and intra-versus intergenerational equity issues: whose norms should apply?', *Risk analysis* 20(6) 869–82. https://doi.org/10.1111/0272-4332.206080

Golec, J.A. (1980) *Aftermath of disaster: The Teton dam break*, PhD dissertation, Disaster Research Centre, Ohio State University, Columbus.

Government of Sri Lanka (1978) *Parliamentary debates (Hansard) official report (uncorrected) vol 3(1) no 7 Thursday 7 December*, Colombo.

Haas, J.E., Kates, R.W. and Bowden, M.J. (eds.) (1977) *Reconstruction following disaster*, The MIT Press, Cambridge.

Hall, N. (1996) 'Coping with typhoons in the Philippines: builders and farmers tell their story', *BASIN News* No 12 August, Building Advisory Service and Information Network, St Gallen.

Handmer, J. (2003) 'We are all vulnerable', *The Australian journal of emergency management* 18(3): 55–60.

Hartmann, B. and Boyce, J.K. (1983) *A quiet violence: view from Bangladesh village*, Zed Books, London.

Heilprin, A. (1903) *Mont Pelée and the tragedy of Martinique* J. B. Lippincott, Philadelphia, PA.

Herman, E.S. and Chomsky, N. (2002) *Manufacturing consent: the political economy of the mass media*, 2nd edn, Pantheon Books, New York.

Hewitt, K. (ed.) (1983) *Interpretations of calamity: from the viewpoint of human ecology*, Allen & Unwin, London. https://doi.org/10.4324/9780429329579

Hewitt, K. (1997) *Regions of risk: a geographical introduction to disasters*, Addison Wesley Longman, Essex.

Hewitt, K. and Burton, I. (1971) *The hazardousness of a place: a regional ecology of damaging events*, University of Toronto Press, Toronto, ON.

Hills, A. (1998) 'Seduced by recovery: the consequences of misunderstanding disaster', *Journal of contingencies and crisis management* 6(3): 162–70. https://doi.org/10.1111/1468-5973.00085

Horn, Z. (2021) 'Are we heading for disaster? The problem with resilience in disaster management and recovery', *Australian journal of emergency management* 36(2): 11–2.

Hossain, H., Dodge, C.P. and Abed, F.H. (eds.) (1992) *From crisis to development: coping with disasters in Bangladesh*, University Press, Dhaka.

IDNDR (1998) 'Experts tell committee meeting of the IDNDR that El Niño is in its dying stage', Press release IHA/98/07, 15 June 1998, UN OCHA (United Nations Office for the Coordination of Humanitarian Affairs), Geneva. https://www.unocha.org/publications/report/world/experts-tell-committee-meeting-idndr-el-ni%C3%B1o-its-dying-stage

IPCC (2021–2022) *Sixth assessment report*, IPCC (Intergovernmental Panel on Climate Change), Geneva.

Islam, S. (ed.) (1992) *History of Bangladesh 1704-1971: political history*, Asiatic Society of Bangladesh, Dhaka.

Island Vulnerability (2024) *Small states conference on sea level rise, 14–18 November 1989, Malé, the Maldives*, MDV/SLR. https://www.islandvulnerability.org/slr1989.html

Jeffery, S.E. (1981) *The creation of vulnerable populations*, Centre for Development Studies, University of Bath, Bath.

Jeffery, S.E. (1982) 'The creation of vulnerability to natural disaster: case studies from the Dominican Republic', *Disasters* 6(1): 38–43. https://doi.org/10.1111/j.1467-7717.1982.tb00742.x

Johnston, I. (2015) 'Disaster management and climate change adaptation: a remote island perspective', *Disaster prevention and management* 23(2): 123–37. https://doi.org/10.1108/DPM-06-2013-0096

Karababa, F.S. and Guthrie, P.M. (2007) 'Vulnerability reduction through local seismic culture', *IEEE technology and society magazine* 26: 30–41. https://doi.org/10.1109/ISTAS.2006.4375887

Kates, R.W. (1970) *Natural hazard in human ecological perspective: hypotheses and models*, Natural hazard research working paper 14, Natural Hazards Center, Boulder, CO.

Kavaliku, S.L. (1974) Letter to the New Zealand High Commissioner (MW.12/6/2) 26 November, Nuku'alofa.

Kelly's Directory (1939) *Kelly's directory of Dorsetshire*, Kelly's Directories, London.

Kench, P.S., Ford, M.R. and Owen, S.D. (2018) 'Patterns of island change and persistence offer alternate adaptation pathways for atoll nations', *Nature Communications* 9: article 605. https://doi.org/10.1038/s41467-018-02954-1

Kerr, I.S. (1976) *Tropical storms and hurricanes in the South West Pacific: November 1939 to April 1969*, NZ Meteorological Service Miscellaneous Publication 148, Wellington.

Kincaid, J. (1988) *A small place*, Virago Press, London.

Kingdom of Tonga (1976) *Third development plan 1975–1980: policy and objectives, programme and strategies for social and economic progress*, Central Planning Office, Nuku'alofa.

Klöck, C. and Fink, M. (eds.) (2019) *Dealing with climate change on small islands: towards effective and sustainable adaptation*, Göttingen University Press, Göttingen.

Kreimer, A. and Munasinghe, M. (1991) 'The environment and disaster management', *Land use policy* 8(4): 269–81. https://doi.org/10.1016/0264-8377(91)90017-D

Kumar, M. (2007) 'A journey into the bleeding city: following the footprints of the rubble of riot and violence of earthquake in Gujarat, India', *Psychology and developing societies*, 19(1): 1–36. https://www.doi.org/10.1177/097133360701900101

Lavigne, F., Morin, J., Wassmer, P. Weller, O., Kula, T., Maea, A.V., Kelfoun, K., Mokadem, F., Paris, R., Malawani, M.N., Faral, A., Benbakkar, M., Saulnier-Copard, S., Vidal, C.M., Tu'I'afitu, T., Kitekei'aho, F. Trautmann, M. and Gomez, C. (2021) 'Bridging legends and science: field evidence of a large tsunami that affected the Kingdom of Tonga in the 15th century', *Frontiers in earth sciences* 9, article 748755. https://doi.org/10.3389/feart.2021.748755

Lewis, J. (1978) *Mitigation and preparedness for natural disasters in the Kingdom of Tonga*, Report to the Ministry of Overseas Development, London.

Lewis, J. (1979a) 'The vulnerable state: an alternative view', in L.H. Stephens and S.J. Green (eds.), *Disaster assistance: appraisal, reform and new approaches*, pp. 104–129, New York University Press, New York.

Lewis, J. (1979b) 'Volcano in Tonga', *Journal of administration overseas* XVIII(2): 116–21.

Lewis, J. (1979c) *Vulnerability to a natural hazard: geomorphic, technological and social change at Chiswell, Dorset*, Natural hazard research working paper 37, Natural Hazards Center, Boulder, CO.

Lewis, J. (1981a) 'Some perspectives on natural disaster vulnerability in Tonga', *Pacific viewpoint* 22(2): 145–62. https://doi.org/10.1111/apv.222005

Lewis, J. (1981b) 'The Sri Lanka cyclone 1978: socio-economic analysis of housing destruction', *Marga* 6/2 pp 1–33. (Also published as 'Cyclone destruction in Sri Lanka: Some socio-economic analysis', *Disaster management* 2/3. New Delhi).

Lewis, J. (1982) *The economic and social effects of natural disasters on the least developed and developing island countries: with special reference to Antigua and Barbuda; Republic of Cape Verde; Comoros Federal Islamic Republic (and Mayotte); Republic of Maldives; Western Samoa, a report for UNCTAD VI; Belgrade 1983*. Consultant UNDRO/UNCTAD, Marshfield.

Lewis, J. (1983a) Change, and vulnerability to natural hazard Chiswell, Dorset, *The environmentalist* 3: 277–87. https://doi.org/10.1007/BF02316390

Lewis, J. (1983b) *The long-term implications of Hurricane Isaac (March 1982) Mission Report*, United Nations Centre for Human Settlements (Habitat), Nairobi.

Lewis, J. (1984a) 'A multi-hazard history in Antigua', *Disasters* 8(3): 190–7. https://doi.org/10.1111/j.1467-7717.1984.tb00874.x

Lewis, J. (1984b) 'Environmental interpretations of natural disaster mitigation: the crucial need', *The environmentalist* 4: 177–80. https://doi.org/10.1007/BF02334667

Lewis, J. (1984c) 'Vulnerability to a cyclone: damage distribution in Sri Lanka', *Ekistics: the problems and science of human settlements* 51(308): 421–31.

Lewis, J. (1988) *Sea level rise: the implications of sea-level rise for island and low-lying countries*, Commonwealth Expert Group on Climatic Change and Sea-Level Rise, Commonwealth Secretariat, London.

Lewis, J. and Kelman, I. (2010) 'Places, people and perpetuity: community capacities in ecologies of catastrophe', *ACME: an international e-journal for critical geographies* 9(2): 191–220. https://doi.org/10.14288/acme.v9i2.866

Luffman, J. (1789) *A brief account of the island of Antigua, together with the customs and manners of its inhabitants, as well white as black: as also an accurate statement of the food, cloathing, labor, and punishment, of slaves. In letters to a friend. Written in the years 1786, 1787, 1788*, printed for T. Cadell, in the Strand, London.

Maceda, E.A., Gaillard, J.C., Stasiak, E., Le Masson, V. and Le Berre, I. (2009) 'Experimental use of participatory 3-dimensional models in island community-based disaster risk management', *Shima* 3(1): 72–84.

Madrid (1995) *The Madrid Declaration: Declaration of the Humanitarian Summit Meeting held in Madrid; signed by the Administrator USAID; Executive Directors of UNICEF & WFP; European Commissioner for Humanitarian Aid; United Nations Under-Secretary General responsible for Humanitarian Affairs; United Nations High Commissioner for Refugees; and the Presidents of the Liaison Committee of Development NGOs to the European Union, Médecins Sans Frontières, International Committee of the Red Cross, and Interaction (American Council for Voluntary International Action)*. Madrid.

Maguire, B. and Hagan, P. (2007) 'Disasters and communities: understanding social resilience', *Australian journal of emergency management*, 22: 16–20.

Manyena, S.B. (2006) 'The concept of resilience revisited', *Disasters* 30(4): 433–50. https://doi.org/10.1111/j.0361-3666.2006.00331.x

Maragos, J.E., Baines, G.B.K. and Beveridge, P.J. (1973) 'Tropical Cyclone Bebe creates a new land formation on Funafuti Atoll', *Science* 181: 1161–4. https://doi.org/10.1126/science.181.4105.1161

Marulanda, M.C., Cardona, O.D. and Barbat, A.H (2010) 'Revealing the socioeconomic impact of small disasters in Colombia using the DesInventar database', *Disasters* 34(2): 552–70. https://doi.org/10.1111/j.1467-7717.2009.01143.x

Maskrey, A. (1989) *Disaster mitigation: a community-based approach, development guidelines, no 3*, Oxfam, Oxford.

Mathews, J.J. (1957) *Reporting the wars*, University of Minnesota Press, Minneapolis.

McCall, G. (1994) 'Nissology: a proposal for consideration', *Journal of the Pacific society* 17(2–3): 93–106.

McLean, R.F., Bayliss-Smith, T.P., Brookfield, M. and Campbell, J.R. (1977) *The hurricane hazard: natural disaster and small populations*, Population and environment project in the eastern islands of Fiji Islands, reports no 1, Australian National University, Canberra.

McLuhan, M. (1964) *Understanding media: the extensions of man*, McGraw-Hill, New York.

Menoni, S. (2001) 'Chains of damages and failures in a metropolitan environment: some observations on the Kobe earthquake in 1995', *Journal of hazardous materials* 86(1–3): 101–19. https://doi.org/10.1016/S0304-3894(01)00257-6

Mitchell, J.K., Devine, N. and Jagger, K. (1989) 'A contextual model of natural hazard', *Geographical review* 79(4): 391–409. https://doi.org/10.2307/215114

Morning Chronicle. 30 December 1824.

Morris, S. (n/d) Files on the history of Chiswell, Dorset

Morris, S. (1979) *Resume on the history of flooding at Chiswell since 1824*, Mimeo, Dorset.

Nixon, R. (2011) *Slow violence and the environmentalism of the poor*, Harvard University Press, Cambridge, MA.

Norton, J. and Chantry, G. (2008) 'More to lose: the case for prevention, loans for strengthening, and "safe housing" insurance: the case of central Vietnam', in L. Bosher (ed.), *Hazards and the built environment: attaining built-in resilience*, pp. 61–73, Taylor and Francis, Abingdon.

Nunn, P.D. (1988) *Future sea-level rise in the Pacific*, SSED (School of Social and Economic Development) working paper no. 12, University of the South Pacific, Suva.

Nunn, P.D., Hunter-Anderson, R., Carson, M.T., Thomas, F., Ulm, S. and Rowland, M.J. (2007) 'Times of plenty, times of less: last-millennium societal disruption in the Pacific basin', *Human ecology* 35, 385–401. https://doi.org/10.1007/s10745-006-9090-5

Observer. 19 March 1979.

OECD (2010) *The United Kingdom: Development Assistance Committee (DAC) Peer Review*, OECD (Organisation for Economic Co-operation and Development), Paris.

OFDA/AID (1978) *Sri Lanka – cyclone situation report 1, 27 November; cyclone situation report 2, 28 November; cyclone situation report 3, 12 December*, Department of State, Washington, DC.

O'Keefe, P., Westgate, K. and Wisner, B. (1976) 'Taking the naturalness out of natural disasters', *Nature* 260: 566–7. https://doi.org/10.1038/260566a0

Oliver-Smith, A. (1979) 'Post disaster consensus and conflict in a traditional society: the 1970 avalanche of Yungay, Peru', *Mass emergencies* 4: 43–5.

Olson, R.S. and Gawronski, V.T. (2003) 'Disasters as critical junctures? Managua, Nicaragua 1972 and Mexico City 1985', *International journal of mass emergencies and disasters* 21(1): 5–35. https://doi.org/10.1177/028072700302100101

Olson, R.A. and Olson, R.S. (1977) 'The Guatemala earthquake of 4 February 1976: social science observations and research suggestions', *Mass emergencies* 2: 69–81.

ONRS (1980) *Dossiers documentaires no 14*, Centre de recherches en architecture et urbanisme, Organisation national de la recherche scientifique, Paris.

Ordnance Survey (1930) Isle of Portland 6"–1 mile Dorset Sheet LVIII SE, Ordnance Survey, Southampton.

Paton, D. and Johnston, D. (2001) 'Disasters and communities: vulnerability, resilience and preparedness', *Disaster prevention and management* 10: 270–7. https://doi.org/10.1108/EUM0000000005930

Paton, D. and Johnston, D. (eds.) (2006) *Disaster resilience: an integrated approach*, Charles C Thomas, Springfield, IL.

Patterson, B.R. (1977) *Geological aspects of the Tonga earthquake: 23 June 1977*, Engineering Geology Section EG 297, New Zealand Geological Survey, DSIR (Department of Scientific and Industrial Research), Lower Hutt.

Petal, M. (2009) 'Education in disaster risk reduction', in R. Shaw and R.R. Krishnamurthy (eds.), *Disaster management: global challenges and local solutions*, pp. 285–304, Universities Press, Hyderabad.

Peters, L.E.R. (2021) 'Beyond disaster vulnerabilities: an empirical investigation of the causal pathways linking conflict to disaster risks', *International journal of disaster risk reduction* 55: article 102092. https://doi.org/10.1016/j.ijdrr.2021.102092

Peters, L.E.R. (2022) 'Disasters as ambivalent multipliers: influencing the pathways from disaster to conflict risk and peace potential through disaster risk reduction', *Journal of peacebuilding and development* 17(2): 151–72. https://doi.org/10.1177/15423166221081516

Portland Borough Council (1962) *Derelict buildings, demolition orders minute no. 799*, Portland Borough Council, Portland.

Portland Flooding Sub-Committee (1979) *Minutes of meeting 6 April (including report of the borough engineer prepared by Morris, S.)*, Weymouth and Portland Borough Council, Weymouth.

Pozsgai-Alvarez, J. (2020) 'The abuse of entrusted power for private gain: meaning, nature and theoretical evolution', *Crime, law and social change*, 74: 433–55.

Prince, S.H. (1920) *Catastrophe and social change*, PhD dissertation, Columbia University, New York.

Quarantelli, E.L. (1976) *Social aspects of disasters and their relevance to pre-disaster planning*, preliminary paper #30, Disaster Research Center, University of Delaware, Newark, NJ.

Quarantelli, E.L. (1985) 'An assessment of conflicting views on mental health: the consequences of traumatic events', in C.R. Figley (ed.), *Trauma and its wake*, pp. 173–215, Brunner/Mazel, New York.

Quarantelli, E.L. (1986) 'Planning and management for the prevention and mitigation of natural disasters, especially in a metropolitan context: initial questions and issues which need to be addressed', *Planning for crisis relief international seminar*; (UNCRD) United Nations Centre for Regional Development, Nagoya.

RADIX (2024) *Power, prestige and forgotten values: A disaster studies manifesto / Priorities, values, and relationships: A disaster studies accord* [website]. https://www.radixonline.org/manifesto-accord

Rahman, A. (1991) 'Development responses to natural disaster', in P. Wignaraja, A. Hussain, H. Sethi and G. Wignaraja (eds.), *Participatory development: learning from South Asia*, United Nations University Press/Oxford University Press, Tokyo/Karachi.

Rahman, M.M., Tasnim, F., Uddin, A., Chayan, M.S.I., Arif, M.S.I., Asikunnaby and Hossain, M.T. (2023) 'Assessing vulnerability in ethnic Munda community: a study on a cyclone-prone area of Bangladesh', *International journal of disaster risk reduction* 95: article 103884. https://doi.org/10.1016/j.ijdrr.2023.103884

Rawson, R.W. (1868) *Report on the Bahamas hurricane of October 1866, with a description of the city of Nassau*, N.P. Nassau Guardian, Nassau.

Rayhan, M.I. (2010) 'Assessing poverty, risk and vulnerability: a study on flooded households in rural Bangladesh', *Journal of flood risk management* 3(1): 18–24. https://doi.org/10.1111/j.1753-318X.2009.01051.x

Reagan, A.B. (1921) 'The "flu" among the Navajos', *Transactions of the Kansas Academy of Science* 30: 131–8. https://doi.org/10.2307/3624053

Reardon, G. (1992) 'Wind effects on the Tongan "hurricane house"', in Y. Aysan and I. Davis (eds.), *Disasters and the small dwelling: perspectives for the UN IDNDR*, pp. 175–82, James & James, London.

Reid, J. (2018) 'The cliché of resilience: governing indigeneity in the Arctic', *Arena journal* 51/52: 10–7.

Rogers, G. (ed.) (1986) *The fire has jumped: Eyewitness accounts of the eruption and evacuation of Niuafo'ou*, Tonga Institute of Pacific Studies, University of the South Pacific, Suva.

Rousseau, J.-J. (1756) 'Rousseau à François-Marie Arouet de Voltaire (Lettre 424, le 18 aôut 1756)', in R.A. Leigh (ed.) (1967) *Correspondance complète de Jean Jacques Rousseau, Tome IV 1756–1757*, pp. 37–50, Institut et musée Voltaire, Geneva.

Ruberu, T.S. (1976) *Sociological implications of malaria and malaria control programme in Sri Lanka*, Office of the Superintendent, Anti-Malaria Campaign Colombo.

Ruggerio, C.A. (2021) 'Sustainability and sustainable development: A review of principles and definitions', *Science of the total environment* 786: article 147481. https://doi.org/10.1016/j.scitotenv.2021.147481

Rutherford, I.N. (ed.) (1977) *Friendly islands: a history of Tonga*, Oxford University Press, Melbourne.

Salas-Zapata, W.A. and Ortiz-Muñoz, S.M. (2019) 'Analysis of meanings of the concept of sustainability', *Sustainable development* 27: 153–61. https://doi.org/10.1002/sd.1885

Scanlon, J. and Frizzell, A. (1979) 'Old theories don't apply: implications of communications in crises', *Disasters* 3(3): 315–9. https://doi.org/10.1111/j.1467-7717.1979.tb00157.x

Selwyn, P. (1980) 'Smallness and islandness', *World development* 8(12): 945–51. https://doi.org/10.1016/0305-750X(80)90086-8

Sen, A. (1981) *Poverty and famines: an essay on entitlement and deprivation*, Clarendon Press, Oxford.

Shaxson, N. (2011) *Treasure islands: tax havens and the men who stole the world*, Bodley Head, London.

Snarr, D.N. and Brown, E.L. (1979) 'Permanent post-disaster housing in Honduras: aspects of vulnerability to future disasters', *Disasters* 3(3): 287–92. https://doi.org/10.1111/j.1467-7717.1979.tb00154.x

Sollis, P. (1994) 'The relief-development continuum: some notes on rethinking assistance for civilian victims of conflict', *Journal of international affairs* 47(2): 451–47.

Sri Lanka Post Office (1978) *Telephone directory 1978 part 1 provincial exchanges (revised up to 31 December 1977)*, Postmaster General and Director of Telecommunications, Colombo.

Staupe-Delgado, R. (2023) *Disasters and life in anticipation of slow calamity: perspectives from the Colombian Andes*, Routledge, Abingdon. https://doi.org/10.4324/9780429288135

Staupe-Delgado, R. and Rubin, O. (2022) 'Challenges associated with creeping disasters in disaster risk science and practice: considering disaster onset dynamics', *International journal of disaster risk science* 13: 1–11. https://doi.org/10.1007/s13753-022-00391-9

Stevenson, R.L. (1892) *A footnote to history: eight years of trouble in Samoa*, Cassell, London.

Stolarski, J., Kitahara, M.V., Miller, D.J., Cairns, S.D., Mazur, M. and Meibom, A. (2011) 'The ancient evolutionary origins of *Scleractinia* revealed by azooxanthellate corals', *BMC evolutionary biology* 11: article 316. https://doi.org/10.1186/1471-2148-11-316

Streets, D.G. and Glantz, M.H. (2000) 'Exploring the concept of climate surprise', *Global environmental change* 10(2): 97–107. https://doi.org/10.1016/S0959-3780(00)00015-7

Sutton, K. (1969) 'Algeria's population growth, 1954–66', *Geography* 54(3): 332–6.

Sutton, K. (1978) 'The progress of Algeria's agrarian reform and its settlement implications', *Maghreb review* 3(5–6): 10–6.

Sutton, K. and Lawless, R.I. (1978) 'Population regrouping in Algeria: traumatic change and the rural settlement pattern', *Transactions of the Institute of British Geographers* 3(3): 331–50. https://doi.org/10.2307/622160

Tamang, P. (2005) 'An overview of the principle of free, prior and informed consent and indigenous peoples in international and domestic law and practices', *Australian indigenous law reporter* 9(2): 111–6.

Tappis, H. and Doocy, S. (2017) 'The effectiveness and value for money of cash-based humanitarian assistance: a systematic review', *Journal of development effectiveness* 10(1): 121–44. https://doi.org/10.1080/19439342.2017.1363804

Tecun, A. and Siu'ulua, S.A. (2023) 'Tongan coloniality: contesting the "never colonized" narrative', *Postcolonial studies* 27(2): 165–182. https://doi.org/10.1080/13688790.2022.2162353

Terry, F. (2002) *Condemned to repeat? The paradox of humanitarian action*, Cornell University Press, Cornell, NY.

Tibby, J., Lane, M.B. and Gell, P.A. (2007) 'Local knowledge and environmental management: a cautionary tale from Lake Ainsworth, New South Wales, Australia', *Environmental conservation* 34: 334–41. https://doi.org/10.1017/S037689290700433X

Timmerman, P. (1981) *Vulnerability, resilience and the collapse of society: a review of models and possible climatic applications*, environmental monograph no. 1, Institute for Environmental Studies, University of Toronto, Toronto, ON.

Tobin, G.A. (1995) 'The levee love affair: a stormy relationship', *Water resources bulletin* 31(3): 359–67. https://doi.org/10.1111/j.1752-1688.1995.tb04025.x

Tobin, G.A. (1999) 'Sustainability and community resilience: the Holy Grail of hazards planning?' *Environmental hazards* 1(1): 13–25. https://doi.org/10.1016/S1464-2867(99)00002-9

Tomblin, J.F. and Aspinall, W.P. (1975) 'Reconnaissance report of the Antigua, West Indies, earthquake of 8th October 1974', *Bulletin of the seismological society of America* 65(6): 1553–73. https://doi.org/10.1785/BSSA0650061553

Torry, W.I. (1979) 'Hazards, hazes and holes: a critique of the environment as hazard and general reflections on disaster research', *Canadian geographer* 23(4): pp. 368–83. https://doi.org/10.1111/j.1541-0064.1979.tb00672.x

Transparency International (2023) What is corruption? [website] Transparency International, London. https://www.transparency.org/en/what-is-corruption

Turner, J.F.C. (1972) 'Housing as a verb', in J.F.C. Turner and R. Fichter (eds.), *Freedom to build: dweller control of the housing process*, pp. 148–75, Macmillan Company, New York.

Turton, D. (1992) 'Warfare, vulnerability and survival: a case from Southwestern Ethiopia', *Disasters* 15(3): 254–64. https://doi.org/10.1111/j.1467-7717.1991.tb00459.x

UNCTAD (1983) *The incidence of natural disasters in island developing countries*, TD/ B/961, UNCTAD (United Nations Conference on Trade and Development), Geneva.

UNDP (2004) *Reducing disaster risk: a challenge for development*, UNDP (United Nations Development Programme), New York.

UNDRO (1979) *Report of the UN Disaster Relief Coordinator on the cyclone in Sri Lanka 23/24 November 1978, case report no 006*, UNDRO (Office of the United Nations Disaster Relief Coordinator), Geneva.

UNISDR (2004) *Living with risk*, UNISDR (United Nations International Strategy for Disaster Reduction), Geneva.

United Nations (1977) *Statistical year book 1977 (1976 provisional figures)*, United Nations, New York.

USAID (c. 1973) *Case report: Gilbert & Ellice Islands-Fiji-Tonga-hurricanes Fall/1972-Spring/1973*, USAID (US Agency for International Development), Washington, DC.

Visvalingam, T., Black, R.H. and Bruce-Chwatt, L.H. (1972) *Report on the assessment of the malaria eradication programme in Ceylon*, Government of Ceylon/WHO, New Delhi.

Walshe, R., Adamson, G.C.D. and Kelman, I. (2020) 'Helices of disaster memory: how forgetting and remembering influence tropical cyclone response in Mauritius', *International journal of disaster risk reduction* 50: article 101901. https://doi.org/10.1016/j.ijdrr.2020.101901

Watts, F. (1906) *Report on the sugar industry in Antigua and St Kitts-Nevis, 1881 to 1905*, Colonial Reports, Her Majesty's Stationery Office (HMSO), London.

Watts, M.J. (1983) *Silent violence: food, famine and peasantry in northern Nigeria*, University of California Press, Berkeley.

WCED (World Commission on Environment and Development) (1987) *Our common future*, Oxford University Press, Oxford.

Western Gazette. 30 June 1972, 9 March 1973, 13 February 1976, 23 February 1979, 1942.

Westgate, K.N (1975) *A disaster history of Tonga 1909–1963*, Disaster Research Unit, University of Bradford, Bradford.

Weymouth and Portland Borough Council (1979a) *Official notice and reports minutes of meeting 15 March*, Weymouth and Portland Borough Council, Weymouth.

Weymouth and Portland Borough Council (1979b) *Official notice and reports for 15 March policy and resources committee*, Weymouth and Portland Borough Council, Weymouth.

Weymouth Local History Museum (c. 1805) *The common of Chesilton*, John Williams Upham, Watercolour (ref. no. PE 17) ('John Penn' series no. XVII), Weymouth Local History Museum, Weymouth.

Wilde, G.J.S. (2014) *Target risk*, PDE Publications, Toronto, ON.

Wilhite, D.A. and Glantz, M.H. (1985) 'Understanding the drought phenomenon: the role of definitions', *Water international* 10(3): 111–20. https://doi.org/10.1080/02508068508686328

Winchester, P. (1992) *Power, choice and vulnerability*, James & James, London.

Wisner, B., Blaikie, P., Cannon, T. and Davis, I. (2004) *At risk: natural hazards, people's vulnerability and disasters*, 2nd edn., Routledge, Abingdon.

Woodcock (1843) *A narrative of the late awful and calamitous earthquake in the West India islands of Antigua, Montserrat, Nevis, St Christopher, Guadaloupe [sic], &c. &c. on 8 February, 1843: Eye-Witness*, Colonial Office, London.

World Bank (1976) *World Tables 1976 Social indicators table 6, holding and consumption*, Johns Hopkins University Press, Baltimore, MD.

Index